ARTS IN THEIR VIEW

A study of youth participation in the arts

John Harland
Kay Kinder
Kate Hartley

Published in March 1995
by the National Foundation for Educational Research,
The Mere, Upton Park, Slough, Berkshire SL1 2DQ

Contents

Acknowledgements

We would like to begin by acknowledging the crucial contributions made by the four organisations which co-funded the study: the Arts Council of England (formerly the Arts Council of Great Britain), the Baring Founding, the Calouste Gulbenkian Foundation and the National Foundation for Educational Research (NFER). Without their support for the initial proposal, the project would never have got off the ground. Our particular thanks are extended to Judy Bradley of the NFER, David Carrington of the Baring Foundation, Simon Richey of the Calouste Gulbenkian Foundation, and Maggie Semple of the Arts Council of England for their very valuable advice and guidance throughout the project.

We would also like to thank the following fieldworkers who helped us carry out the interviews upon which the research is based: Laila Ahmed, Mena Ahmed, John Bateman, Juliet Burley, Rachel Christophers, Roger Coleman, Christopher Dixon, Clare Metcalf, James Robson, Karlene Rushford, Kay Sambell, Sheila Sudworth, James Tooley, Luke Wootten and Mary Wootten.

For supporting the analysis of the data, we are particularly grateful to the statisticians, Cres Fernandes, Neil Rubra and Lesley Kendall, and to Anne Wilkin for all her assistance with the qualitative case studies. We are also grateful to Katie Froud for her helpful comments on earlier drafts of the report and to Ralph Tabberer, Enver Carim, Mary Hargreaves and Tim Wright for their contributions to the design and publication of the book. Our thanks are also extended to Sue Medd and Joan Campbell for their excellent secretarial work.

Last, but certainly not least, we are indebted to the 704 young people who gave up their time to be interviewed. We hope the report that follows is an accurate account of the extremely diverse testimonies they provided.

PART ONE

THE RESEARCH AND ITS CONTEXT

1. Issues and Concerns in the Policy Context

This chapter explains both the background to and rationale of the research project. It suggests a number of current policy issues and arenas of arts provision for which the report may have particular relevance.

One of these is the major area of arts education at primary and secondary school. Though it is stressed that the data refer to pre-National Curriculum arts provision, the young people's accounts of their school arts experiences (see Chapter 8) clearly raise questions about the status of arts in schools, the organisational context for their delivery and the future of arts provision in education as LEA infrastructures diminish. These overarching issues are briefly discussed.

Beyond the school context, the report is felt to have relevance for the whole area of funding young people's own arts and cultural initiatives, and the chapter covers the debate about appropriate targeting, with particular reference to the seminal work of Paul Willis. Finally, 'youth arts' provision, arising from the traditions of theatre, youth work and community arts, is highlighted as an area for which the study may offer useful data, and the chapter concludes by looking at the work of key contributors as well as summarising some general issues and concerns.

Introduction This book reports the findings of a research project which set out to portray young people's views on the arts and their involvement in them. Central to the study's approach has been the commitment to garner the accounts of young people who do or do not engage in the arts rather than, for example, collect the perspectives of agencies active in the provision of the arts and cultural commodities. The initial idea for such a project was conceived at the time of the 1990 street riots in the Meadowell Estate in Tyneside. As part of the post-mortem analyses and discussions (e.g. Byrne, 1993) which followed in the aftermath of this and similar disturbances, it seemed natural to give consideration to the quality of young people's opportunities in such communities for psychological, as well as material, reward. Given the limited prospects of finding satisfying employment in many inner-city areas, it seemed appropriate, for instance, to raise questions about the contribution that the arts or outlets for informal cultural creative energies could make, by way of widening access to activities which may offer greater scope for self-fulfilment and expression. In order to explore such questions, the need for some basic information immediately emerged: how many young people currently participate in the arts? In what art forms do they participate? How do rates and patterns of involvement vary according to different types of young people? What influences lead some to engage in the arts, while others reject them? What are the effects of arts participation and what are young people's perceived needs for support in the arts?

Surprisingly, apart from the illuminating but small-scale ethnographic research of Paul Willis (1990) and the small quantity of statistical data in the General Household Surveys (GB: Office of Population Censuses and Surveys, 1994), very little research especially that with a national perspective, was available to answer such questions. Moreover, it appeared that youth participation in sport attracted more attention and funding (e.g. the University of Aberdeen's survey of the place and effect of sport in the leisure and lifestyles of young people in Hendry *et al.*, 1989; Allied Dunbar, 1992; Rowley, 1992; Sports Council, 1994). Hence, this project was initiated largely as a response to this important lacuna in policy-related research into youth and the arts and in a period of continuing controversy about young people and their behaviour. For instance, the results have been analysed at a time when there has been talk about '*waging a battle*' on the so-called '*yob culture*' (e.g. Prime Minister, John Major's speech to the Social Market Foundation on 9th September 1994). Against this background, it is hoped that the findings of the research, based, as they are on young people's own testimonies about the arts, have important messages for policy-makers seeking to make genuine responses to the problems and challenges commonly associated with disaffected and underprivileged young people.

In this way, the prime motive for proposing the research was to provide empirical evidence on the patterns of youth participation in the arts, in order that the study may inform future policy and practice. At no stage, however, was the study designed to conclude with the making of firm recommendations about policy and practice, since that reflects neither our expertise nor our brief. The professionals involved on a daily basis in the planning and provision of the arts and cultural activities, along with young people themselves, are clearly the best equipped and most informed people to assess any implications the research findings may have for the formation of policy and practice. In recognition of this, we believe our function is to relay and portray the experiences and accounts of young people, to interrogate the evidence for signs and patterns of (less obvious) realities and trends, and to interpret the data in such a way that occasional questions are raised for the reader, the policy-maker and the practitioner.

One of the problems inherent in the task of reviewing the policy context and literature on young people's participation in the arts is that the subject under study straddles several different policy domains. It incorporates, for example, the separate policy arenas of the school curriculum, the organisation and management of schools, the local authority infrastructure and provision, the youth service and other voluntary clubs for young people, the various agencies encompassed within the sphere of 'youth arts', arts provision within further and higher education institutions, as well as the national Arts Councils and Regional Arts Boards (RABs). Clearly, a detailed historical account of each of these arenas lies beyond the scope and resources of the research and the researchers conducting it. As an alternative strategy, we begin by highlighting a number of key issues and concerns which reflect the policy context and which are pertinent to the themes investigated in the research.

Some Key Terms

Before reviewing these themes, it is worth pausing to clarify how such terms as 'the arts', 'participation', 'youth arts' and 'youth' are used in the report. A very broad interpretation of 'the arts' was offered to respondents in the interviews and is applied in the presentation and discussion of the results. The term 'the arts' includes, but is not restricted to, such 'high arts' as opera, theatre, dance, painting, sculpture, literature, film, music, as well as the informal 'common cultural' activities such as scratching and dubbing, graffiti, style and fashion as depicted by Willis (1990). It also allows for contemporary, as well as traditional, approaches within each art form (e.g. hip-hop and rock bands as well as classical music and jazz). Furthermore, it includes artistic and cultural variations both within and beyond the Western European tradition. Indeed, respondents were encouraged in the interviews to interpret the term in whatever way they wished (e.g. in assessing the extent to which television or football was an art). Likewise, the parameters of the term were broadened further by asking interviewees about their participation in activities which they deemed to be 'imaginative or creative'.

Although the term, 'participation', like the research itself, is principally concerned with 'producer' and 'active creator' roles in the arts, it was considered broad enough to encompass 'receiver', 'consumer' and 'audience' roles as well. Hence, some questions on the latter roles were included in the interview (see Chapter 6). It is also acknowledged that, following the observations of Gardner (1973), Serafine (1979) and Willis (1990), the processes of 'production/making' and 'receiving/consuming' can be interrelated with one another.

Following Chamberlain (1991) and Feldberg (1991), 'youth arts' is taken to denote the provision of opportunities for young people to make art and to engage with creative work made for them by others (see the discussion later in this chapter). As such, its use here incorporates both 'production' and 'consumption' roles. The term, 'youth arts' is generally used to refer to the broad area of arts policy-making and provision for young people outside of and beyond formal education. With strands of involvement in the theatre, community arts and the youth service, 'youth arts' is an important sphere of provision, in recognition of which most RABs have designated responsibility for it to at least one officer. In the early 1990s several RABs highlighted 'youth arts' as a priority area. The 'youth arts' field is serviced by a number of national bodies (e.g. Artswork, British Youth Council, National Association of Youth Theatres, National Youth Agency and Youth Clubs UK). It is also the focus of a specialist press (e.g. '95 per cent', 'Young People Now' and 'Over the Edge') and interesting case studies of 'youth arts' projects are to be found in Whitfield (1991) and Rust and Allen (1992).

Any definition of 'youth' or 'young people' is bound to be arbitrary, but in operational terms, the research took 'youth' to mean people between the ages of 14 and 24. It is readily conceded, however, that people over the age of 24 may well be deemed 'young' and 'youthful' (especially since all the authors fall within this category). It must also be stressed that because all interviewees were asked for recollections of their arts experiences when younger, the scope of the inquiry was extended below the age of 14 to incorporate accounts of childhood engagements in the arts, particularly those in primary school and the early years of the secondary phase. It is important to remember that these recollections are derived from young people whose primary school experiences pre-date the introduction of the National Curriculum.

With these definitions in mind, we can move on to the task of identifying a number of salient policy issues and concerns relating to the broad area of young people's experiences in the arts. Given its statutory status and importance for all young people, it seems appropriate to start with the place of the arts in the school curriculum.

Arts in the Curriculum

1. **Concerns remain that, in spite of the entitlement established for all children, the arts in the National Curriculum are underrated compared with other areas of the curriculum and under pressure from priorities which allegedly stem from a dominant but narrow ideological commitment to work-oriented instrumentalism.**

Concerns about the marginalisation of the arts in schools, and the curriculum in particular, pervade much of the recent literature on arts education. Studying pre-National Curriculum practice in one city's primary schools, Alexander (1991), for example, observed that arts education *'frequently lacked seriousness, integrity and challenge'*. Similarly, writing about provision in a northern LEA's (local education authority's) special and mainstream primary and secondary schools in the mid-1980s, Sellors and Hull (1989) concluded that:

1. *Art and craft was frequently used as a servicing agency and was without planned progression.*

2. *Dance and drama provision was either very limited or even absent.*

3. *Music was often performance-based with little opportunity for practical music making.*

4. *Verbal arts provision was included in every class programme, but for some children there was very little which could be considered imaginative and/or expressive.*

5. *Few schools had an arts policy.*

6. *Many teachers lacked confidence and skill in teaching the arts.* (p. 32)

At a national level, the influential report from the Calouste Gulbenkian Foundation (1982; second edition in 1989) offered a similar assessment. While stressing that in some primary and secondary schools the arts were flourishing, too often the provision was inadequate and at risk. With reference to the primary sector, the report stated:

> *We share the view of HMI [GB: DES, 1978] that work in the arts in many primary schools is disappointing. In some cases children do very little work in the arts. This may be because some teachers ... do not put a high priority on creative work. In some schools, where there is arts provision, children are working too far within their own capabilities – those in the top of the primary school still doing work of which they are capable much earlier. Sometimes this is because teachers' expectations of them are too low and the work lacks direction. At other times, it is because the work is over-directed and gives children little room to exercise their creative powers ... There is often, for example in the visual arts, a repetitious series of exercises or filling-in of collage outlines supplied by the teacher.* (p. 49)

The report was no more sanguine about the state of the arts in secondary schools:

> *There are ... problems in staffing and facilities resulting from cuts in public spending and falling rolls ... worsening pupil-teacher ratios, longer hours for teachers and a reduction in the range of subject options. There is also evidence that examination courses tend to be protected at the expense of non-examination courses and of courses for 'less able' children ... All levels and areas of education are being affected by cuts in book-stocks, equipment and specialist materials. In these circumstances we can expect the gap to widen between those areas where parents can be generous to education and can afford to give schools substantial help, and those where families are less well-off. The arts have never been lavishly provided for in schools as a whole.* (p. 61)

The only art form to be given 'core' subject status in the National Curriculum was literature as part of English. Art and music were designated foundation subjects and initially were intended to be compulsory for all pupils between the ages of 5 and 16. Drama was said to be part of English and dance was subsumed under physical education. These proposals did not allay early fears and concerns about the vulnerability of arts education in the school curriculum. Swanwick (1988), for example, commenting on the implications of the National Curriculum for the arts, suggested that '*the marginalisation of the arts has shifted little in 84 years*' and that the aims and early documentation of the National Curriculum lack vision of the contribution the arts could make to the individual, community and the curriculum (e.g. the National Curriculum accentuates the '*life of work*' rather than the '*work of life*'). Stubbs (1990) argued that the arts should cast off their image as '*Cinderella subjects*' and be afforded parity of status with core subjects, otherwise balance in the curriculum was compromised. McGraw (1987), in urging greater awareness outside of the teaching profession of the struggle that the performing arts '*face in being recognised as a valid educational cog in the National Curriculum machine*' expressed fears that the developments made in subjects like drama over the past 25 years were in danger of being swept away by the National Curriculum.

According to Robinson (1991a, 1991b), the government's decision to drop art and music from the list of compulsory subjects at key stage 4 was highly regrettable and counter-productive, not least because it sent unhelpful messages to '*governing bodies, struggling to balance the books, about the government's perception of the arts in the curriculum*'.

The Dearing review rejected the re-instatement of compulsory art and music at key stage 4. Although the consultation process included the option of re-installing all ten National Curriculum subjects through to the age of 16, the case for excluding or re-introducing art and music was not discussed in the Final Report (Dearing, 1994). However, the review recommended that more of what is taught at all key stages should be left to the school's discretion. In theory, at least, this could give teachers the opportunity to introduce more arts activities into the curriculum. Finally, it is noteworthy that under the alternative curriculum framework proposed by the National Commission on Education (1993), it appears that the arts would fare no better. For instance, at key stage 2, while citizenship and a modern foreign language would form part of a compulsory core, the expressive arts, including art and music, would be optional. In all, many arts educators and teachers remain concerned about the status of the arts in the curriculum.

Discrete or Integrated Arts?

2. **A long-standing issue in arts education – and one that has been intensified by the introduction of the National Curriculum – is whether the arts should continue to be taught through discrete subjects or integrated in some way under a unitary concept.**

The introduction of the National Curriculum increased awareness of the pressures on an overcrowded timetable. It also created opportunities to re-think curriculum frameworks, areas of knowledge and skills, and subject constellations. These two factors gave an added sense of urgency to the argument about whether particular art forms should continue to be seen as discrete areas of study or whether there were concepts and processes underlying each art form which had sufficient in common with one another for 'the arts' to be conceived, organised and perhaps even taught, as a unitary discipline. Conferences and seminars debated the issue (Hargreaves, 1989; Croall, 1991) and in 1991 a flurry of articles on the subject appeared in *The Times Educational Supplement*. (Similar controversies occurred in other areas of the curriculum, most notably technology.)

Proponents of the unitary or integrated approach pointed to the similarity of aesthetic processes and purposes underpinning the individual art forms (Abbs, 1988). Robinson in various publications (Calouste Gulbenkian Foundation, 1982; 1989; and the National Curriculum Council, 1990) argued that the arts should be seen as a generic area of the curriculum and that in planning and organising the curriculum, schools should begin by thinking of the arts collectively rather than of separate subjects. He stressed that this does not mean that the arts should always be taught through 'combined' or 'integrated' courses, nor that generalist arts teachers should replace specialist teachers (Robinson, 1991b). On the contrary, '*a principal reason for planning for the arts collectively in schools is to allow for more sophisticated forms of differentiation in arts teaching*' (ibid). Taking a similar stance, Stubbs (1990), supported an eclectic use of different course structures (e.g. single-art form, multi-disciplinary, mixed-media, and modular framework courses), and concluded that '*the future of music education is ... firmly within a balanced arts curriculum that is managed as a single curriculum area*'.

The defence of the separate single art form provision has been argued on theoretical and strategic grounds. According to the latter, subject identities are considered to be worth preserving, particularly at a time when the adoption of a unitary model could be seized upon as a way of reducing the time currently available for art and music. Not surprisingly, a large proportion of art and music specialists make up the largest lobby opposing the move towards a generic area and supporting the *status quo*. For example, Taylor (1986), a music specialist, warned that a unitary approach could lead to one art form being subsumed and pressed into the service of another. He contended that the role of the teacher should be to extend understanding of each art form rather than to encourage superficial comparisons between them.

This point of view received philosophical support from Best (1991), who rejected as educationally damaging the notion that there is such an entity as a general capacity for 'artistic' appreciation which can be nurtured by any and all art forms. The National Society for Education in Art and Design, the subject association for art and design teachers, adopted a similar position and questioned the rationale for an integrated approach. Its general secretary maintained that:

> *references to combined arts provide timetablers and government ministers with the obvious temptation to solve problems of the over-*

pressed National Curriculum by cutting the time allocation and other resources for the arts – especially if they are encouraged to believe they are dealing with a single subject. (Steers, 1990)

In England and Wales, the proponents of the 'separatist' viewpoint have successfully resisted moves towards a combined approach and the Dearing review has come down firmly against proposals to integrate art and music.

Support for Arts Provision in Schools

3. **There are widespread concerns over the uncertainty surrounding the future of arts provision in schools as a result of structural changes to the education system, principally changes in the management and funding of schools, changes in LEA services, and changes arising out of the 1993 Education Act.**

Recent structural reforms to the education system and their implications for arts provision in schools have been well documented in two reports published by the Arts Council of Great Britain – the Arts Council of England since April 1994 (Rogers, 1993a and 1993b). The first contained the results of a national survey of the state of LEA advisory and inspection services. The second reported on the deliberations of three regional seminars and a national convention, which considered the theme, 'The Arts in Education: Where Now?' These two reports contain much that is germane to our present focus on issues and concerns in the policy context for youth participation in the arts.

The survey found that over the last four years LEA services were in a state of great change and significant contraction. While all subject areas were experiencing upheaval and cut-backs, it was the arts which were most severely affected. As a consequence of the privatisation of LEA support structures, in all but a handful of authorities, long-standing services such as curriculum support and advice, instrumental music and artists-in-schools projects were having to take their chance in the 'free market'.

The survey produced telling evidence on the virtual demise of the 'traditional' LEA advisory service. In arts subjects, almost half the advisers' posts and almost three-quarters of advisory teachers posts had gone. Only a quarter of LEAs were left with full-time advisers or inspectors for all the four main arts subjects. Fewer than half of the LEAs were continuing to fund schemes which put artists and performers into schools. Additionally, a survey of LEA instrumental music services found that the percentage of centrally funded services had dropped from 92 per cent to 37 per cent in the five year period prior to the survey, and that only 13 per cent of those responding to the survey were confident of retaining central funding in the foreseeable future (Sharp, 1991). Another survey (Coopers and Lybrand and MORI, 1994) found that there was a growing reliance on the private funding of instrumental music tuition from parental fees, though it also concluded that '*there is no evidence to suggest a decline in the number of pupils receiving instrumental tuition and some evidence to indicate an increase in the quality ...*'.

However, the Arts Council reports (Rogers, 1993a and b) maintained that as sources (e.g. TVEI) for putting artists into schools evaporated, advisers noted that there was now less variety in what was provided and it was more irregular and infrequent. The report summarised the main reasons for this decline in LEA provision and drew attention to the following factors:

♦ the impact of local management of schools (LMS);

♦ the privatisation of many LEA services. Many LEAs now rely on a range of contracts and service level agreements to supply schools with specific services;

♦ the requirements of the National Curriculum – most LEAs have been required to concentrate on core subjects rather than non-compulsory areas of the curriculum;

♦ the growth of the grant-maintained schools sector;

♦ the development of OFSTED inspections, which have taken over most of the inspection duties of LEAs so levels of staffing have already been reduced;

♦ the reduction of LEA powers, stemming mainly from the Education Reform Act 1988, the Education (Schools) Act 1992, and the new Education Act 1993; and

♦ for some authorities, the prospect of the emergence of smaller-scale councils under the current review of local government boundaries could mean that the existing variation in provision between authorities could be repeated among smaller councils.

The two reports showed that LEAs were responding to the new demands and contexts in a variety of ways. While many advisers expressed scepticism about the effectiveness of running support services in a privatised market, others were more sanguine about the future. One senior officer in an LEA commented '*my LEA never did provide much anyway. It's a question of getting rid of the dependency culture within schools*'.

As a response to these changes, the reports described the emergence of new structures, agencies and networks. These included:

♦ local authority departments other than education (e.g. leisure services) offering support and projects to schools;

♦ independent agencies operating on a commercial basis, often comprising former LEA advisers and inspectors;

♦ the growth of networks based on art forms;

♦ greater involvement by the Arts Council and RABs in brokering and funding education work; and

♦ partnerships between local authorities, RABs, businesses, trusts and performing companies (e.g. the creation of a new agency into which schools, colleges, arts practitioner agencies, local authorities and RABs pool financial and human resources to establish a service which the participants can buy into as required).

Although the immediate future and effectiveness of these new developments and agencies are highly unpredictable, one point of considerable certainty stands out from the two reports: the locus of control over the amount and quality of arts provision in schools now resides very much with schools (as well as national government). It is now the responsibility of schools, particularly school managers and governors, to decide how much to spend on the arts and where to buy the support and services they need. As hinted at by the Coopers and Lybrand and MORI (1994) study of instrumental music provision, some schools, especially those that can marshal private funding and parental support, may find that the changes brought about through LMS, devolved budgets and the privatisation of central services precipitate an improvement in the quality of arts provision and support available to teachers and pupils. For other schools, particularly those without recourse to parental and private subsidies, the amount and quality of services to support arts education may deteriorate. Consequently, many observers fear that, without the central equalising role previously adopted by many local authorities, recent structural reforms will result in a widening of the gap in arts provision for schools.

Alternative Perspectives on the 'Arts' and Young People

4. **Looking beyond the confines of formal education, there is the key issue of whether or not the everyday activities of young people are so full of richness and vitality that more 'arm's-length' funding should be targeted at fostering informal cultural projects, especially the creative consumptions of commercial and media products.**

A radical perspective on young people's cultural activities, along with an alternative set of ideas for future youth policy and provision, is advanced in the influential work of Paul Willis (1990). Willis argues that the term the 'arts' is restrictive and has become over-associated with its '*institutional manifestations*', which protect traditional arts and often destroy the vitality of living and relevant cultural forms. In its place he uses the '*wider and more generous*' concept 'culture' to promote the notion that young people are already engaged in everyday creativity which is not recognised as such. Willis claims that young people, although often strangers to the traditional arts, are regularly involved in imaginative, expressive and decorative activities, which are deemed to contain a richness and vibrancy frequently in the form of creative responses to the consumption of commercial and mass-media artefacts (e.g. pop music records, fashion). The main themes of the argument are summed up as follows:

> *By now we hope to have established in the reader's mind two linked and dominant cultural tendencies: (i) the unexpected life and promise of everyday ground aesthetics in the ordinary life activities of young people; (ii) articulated, surprisingly for some, for the most part through the popular cultural products and media of the mainly commercial market.* (p. 55)

Armed with this perspective, Willis endeavours to shift the terms of the policy debate rather than offer firm blue-print recommendations for the future. For him, policies should be formed on the recognition that much of what the 'arts establishment' is attempting to encourage 'is already there', especially in young people's creative consumptions of commercial and media culture. It is argued that these informal cultural processes or 'grounded aesthetics' should be fostered, with subsidies and other redistributive strategies targeted at making cultural commodities (e.g. recordings, videos, reproduction equipment) cheaper for young people, particularly for the unemployed and low-income groups. Additionally, Willis is sceptical of the capacity of large-scale 'establishment' institutions to fulfil this role and maintains *that new policy initiatives need to find quite new, much more indirect, less structured, more democratic, means for their execution'* (p. 56). Thus, 'de-institutionalised' institutions are advocated, in which informality, privacy, personal choice, openness, psychological ownership and maximum scope of feasible power for young people are placed at a premium. Greater availability of the 'high arts' is urged through experiments in shifting the conditions of access in order to allow new, often non-elite groups, to 'colonise' them. The inclusion of young people in the decision-making processes governing cultural and media institutions is recommended. Instead of narrow vocationalism, Willis also suggests that educational courses and youth training programmes should provide more opportunities in informal cultural initiatives and activities, including an expansion of training projects to assist young people develop musical techniques and skills. In addition to channelling changes and resources through reformed institutions, he also proposes that more 'arm's-length' funding could be targeted directly at communities of young people who organise themselves and make demands for control of activities and the use of resources. The latter approach is evident in the Arts Council's recent 'Making a Difference' initiative, which aims to support innovative 16-26 year olds who are creating new styles and images through less traditional routes. With the financial assistance of the Calouste Gulbenkian Foundation, the initiative encourages grant applications from self-managed groups which have received little previous funding. Awards are selected by a committee which includes young people.

Without doubt, the proposals advanced by Willis raise fundamental questions about the future direction of youth policy in general, and the arts in particular (e.g. what forms of art or informal cultural creativity should be validated and promoted through funding? Should such funding be channelled through institutions and providers or made available to young people themselves?). However, the plausibility of many of the policy challenges floated by Willis are grounded on some essential assumptions which are far from established empirically. While it is undoubtedly the case, for example, that some young people function as 'creative consumers' or as producers of 'grounded aesthetics', there are important questions to be asked about the prevalence of such activities among young people. Are the everyday activities of young people as full of imaginative or creative richness and vitality as Willis would have us believe? It is hoped that the research reported here can provide another source of information to address such questions and the policy implications which arise from them.

The proposal that more funding should be directed at supporting young people's own informal cultural activities accords with many of the central priorities espoused by the youth arts movement. It is to this area of provision that we turn for a final set of important issues and concerns relating to young people's participation in the arts.

Youth Arts Issues

5. **The broad array of agencies and activities subsumed under the umbrella term 'youth arts' engage several salient issues and challenges relating to the provision of opportunities for young people to participate in the arts outside and beyond formal education.**

Focusing primarily on arts participation outside of formal education, youth arts, according to Feldberg (1991), grew out of three traditions: theatre, community arts and the youth service. In the absence of a national co-ordinating body to synchronise policy and developments in this area, reformist elements within the youth service have taken the lead in arguing for a more coherent approach to youth arts policy-making (e.g. Youth Clubs UK, 1992; Chamberlain, 1991; Randell and Myhill, 1989).

Chamberlain (1991) offers a participatory definition of youth arts, which is deliberately broad in order to incorporate the kinds of things that young people are expressing through such forms as street dance, graffiti, fanzines, bhargra and rap:

> The term 'youth arts' refers to the opportunities for young people to make art and so experience the processes involved.   (p. 9)

While accepting the importance of actual involvement in 'making' and 'doing', Feldberg (1991) argues that 'the possibility for young people to engage with work made for them by others is an equally strong and vital aspect of youth arts' (p. 4). She describes how the development of theatre in youth work through the late 1970s and early 1980s became an important strand in the emergence of youth arts provision. She stresses that there is little appropriate training for actors working in this area and that funding for it has often fallen between two stools: the youth service and the RABs.

Arts workers and artists working with young people through a community arts tradition are identified as a second strand. To distinguish this source of provision from youth arts work which is rooted in the youth service and youth work principles, Feldberg uses the term 'youth-oriented arts work'. It also includes the arts animateurs posts funded by RABs and local authority grants which directly engage young people with specific skills or interests. Again, the case for training for professional artists, community arts workers, animateurs and workshop leaders is strongly advanced. She concludes that '*all this work needs coherence and direction, proper training, support, management and funding*' (p. 9).

According to Feldberg, the third important contributor to youth arts provision is the youth service. During the 1980s, many youth workers attempted to move the service away from its preoccupations with sports, and largely male clientele, towards the values of participation, empowerment and decision-making recommended by the Thompson Report. In 1982 the Thompson Report stressed that:

> the fundamental purpose of the youth service is to provide programmes of personal development comprising, in shorthand terms, social and personal education.

Chamberlain (1991) uses survey evidence to argue that the youth service is failing to work through the arts sufficiently to meet the needs of many young people. According to Feldberg, '*arts work in the youth service really took off in the mid-eighties*', but Chamberlain observes limits to these developments and his book contains a useful identification of some of the key barriers to youth arts finding a higher profile in the youth service. These include adult attitudes which undervalue youth arts, a lack of confidence among youth workers to lead and organise arts activities, and an underestimation of young people's needs in this area, resulting in a lack of resources allocated to them. Chamberlain recommends that local arts policies need to be developed and initiated through partnerships with the RABs and other agencies. The current focus in devising a common curriculum for the youth service presents a clear opportunity to establish the arts in youth club activities, providing sufficient attention is paid to young people's own cultural preferences, tastes and styles.

Various policy documents and publications on youth arts give rise to a number of key issues and concerns which may be informed by the research reported here. To conclude this brief review of the policy context, these issues and concerns are summarised below.

♦ Several writers suggest young people's involvement in the arts may be influenced by social class, education, ethnicity, urban or rural residency, gender and disability. If this is so, what are the implications for equal opportunity and access to arts participation?

♦ A recurring theme in many articles on youth arts is what kinds of art activities or informal cultural projects should be funded. What are young people's needs?

♦ Implicit in much of the debate is an issue over the way the funding should be channelled: should it go to the providers or directly to young people themselves?

♦ There are several references to the pressing need for young people to have more training opportunities in the arts.

♦ Finally, other writers have asked whether the relationship between youth arts and formal education institutions is as effective as it could be.

Summary In this opening chapter, five important themes or contexts been identified as key areas of policy discussion to which this research may contribute. Two of these focused on school curriculum issues; one pointed to recent changes in the management and organisational structures of educational institutions; and a further two themes raised questions about the provision of arts activities for young people outside of formal education, much of which is encapsulated within the broad policy domain of what has become known as 'youth arts'. Before describing the results of the research (see Chapters 3-10) and summarising their implications for these five themes (see Chapter 14), the following chapter outlines the main aims and research methods adopted by the study.

2. The Research Project

This chapter offers an overview of the aims of the study, its chronology and the research methods used. It describes how, in 1993, data for the study were collected through an interviewing programme which involved young people between the ages of 14 and 24 in five regions of England. It also outlines how the sample of 700 young people was devised and then accessed. The subsequent weighting of the sample for statistical analysis is explained and broad demographic details (e.g. age, social class, ethnicity) of the interviewees are provided.

Aims of the Study

The study was proposed and designed with the expressed intention of providing empirical evidence which could inform future planning and policy-making relating to young people's engagement with the arts. In view of the paucity of funded research in this area and the uncertain policy context outlined in the previous chapter, the overall aim of the study was to provide a national picture of young people's participation in the arts – both within and outside formal education. Essentially, this involved investigating firstly, the nature, type and degree of involvement in the arts and, secondly, the reasons and factors which influence varying levels of participation and non-participation. More particularly, four specific objectives were selected for the study:

(i)   to portray different patterns and experiences of youth involvement in the arts and examine these in relation to the independent variables and demographic characteristics of young people (e.g. how are young people's engagements in the arts affected by gender, ethnicity and social class?);

(ii)   to study and illuminate successful and sustained engagement in the arts and evaluate factors which are perceived to inhibit and facilitate it (e.g. are there identifiable trends as to how, why and when young people are most likely to take up or sustain – and conversely avoid or drop – arts involvement?);

(iii)   to depict and analyse young people's attitudes to youth arts participation (e.g. what are young people's own definitions and interpretations of the 'arts'? What do they perceive to be the value and outcomes of involvement in the arts?); and

(iv)   to highlight any perceived needs and opportunities in the arts which remain unfulfilled (e.g. what kinds of wished for involvement in the arts remain or remained un-met?).

Research Methods

The research method selected for the study consisted of a large-scale interviewing programme, involving a sample of approximately 700 young people between the ages of 14 and 24. Interviewing was selected as the most appropriate data collection method because of its capacity to capture the views and experiences of young people from all walks of life and backgrounds. It was felt (very strongly) that the more usual survey technique of postal questionnaires carried assumptions about literacy, culture and access to certain kinds of young people, which would seriously restrict the type and range of viewpoints garnered. In comparison to the postal questionnaire, the interview also allowed the researchers to follow up initial responses with specific probes, which were particularly relevant to the individual interviewee.

During March and April 1993, draft interview schedules were developed and piloted through exploratory interviews with different types of young people. A copy of the final interview schedule is reproduced as Appendix I. A fieldforce of 16 interviewers was recruited and trained. The use of interviewers with local knowledge was especially helpful in obtaining access to, and gaining the trust of, young people in specific urban and rural settings (e.g. particularly communities with high proportions of members of ethnic minority groups).

Between May and December 1993, 704 young people between the ages of 14 and 24 were interviewed in five regions of England: London (141), Oxfordshire (140), Tyneside/Northumberland (142), North Yorkshire (140) and West Yorkshire/ Leeds/Bradford (141). The duration of the interview lasted from anything between 25 minutes to an hour and 20 minutes, but the estimated average length could be put at 35-40 minutes. Recordings of a sub-sample of interviews were retained for qualitative analysis. The piloting of the draft schedules, in conjunction with discussions with experts and sponsors in the youth arts field, proved beneficial in that no major difficulties in using the schedule were reported. Although the schedule was found to have the necessary versatility to be suitable for uniform administration to a wide cross-section of young people, several members of the fieldwork team noted how the interviewing process revealed the individuality of the interviewees and remarked on the danger of making stereotypical generalisations about respondents.

While the overall structure of the schedule proved to be satisfactory, concerns were expressed about the sequencing of individual items and the order in which examples of art forms were listed in some items. For example, the focus on 'imaginative or creative' activities in Items 18 and 19 may have influenced some responses to Item 20, which asked respondents to define what the term 'the arts' meant to them. Similarly, putting 'music' first as an example in Item 21(a) on the importance of the 'high arts' may have affected the direction of some responses. Some interviewees seemed to find the repetition of the same item for different phases of their life (e.g. leisure interests currently and when at primary and secondary schools) a little frustrating and puzzling. Most significantly, many interviewees had difficulty in articulating the nature of any effects of the arts upon them. In spite of these problems, the schedule worked well on the vast majority of occasions and it engendered a very large set of qualitative and quantitative data. It was particularly effective in framing questions about arts participation in a variety of ways.

Accessing the Sample

One of the major methodological challenges posed by this project arose out of the absence of a single institutional frame from which a random sample of young people could be drawn, apart from 14-16 year olds in compulsory schooling. Hence, identifying, selecting and gaining access to a broadly representative sample presented a considerable problem. Attempts to access potential interviewees through census returns were prohibitively expensive and access to samples used by existing cohort studies, which were not researching arts experience, was not forthcoming. Consequently the research adopted what was deemed to be the most practical yet methodologically acceptable alternative: a system of quota sampling with the random opportunity accessing of individual respondents. Accordingly, for each of the five selected regions, a quota sampling sheet was constructed on the basis of five key independent variables: gender, age, urban/rural residency, ethnicity and current status (e.g. at school, college, full-time employment, unemployment). In addition, to reflect broad social class trends in the population as a whole, interviewers were instructed to aim for a 55:45 ratio of interviewees from middle class (i.e. professional, technical and skilled non-manual) and working class (i.e. skilled manual, partly skilled and unskilled) backgrounds. Similarly, interviewers were also required to include young people with physical disabilities in their sub-samples.

The five selected regions, which included areas covered by four Regional Arts Boards (RABs), were chosen to provide a range of different geographical settings and communities (e.g. inner cities, industrial, suburban, isolated rural, ethnic minorities) while, simultaneously, allowing the fieldwork to be conducted in a cost-effective manner. Within each of these regions, teams of interviewers identified and approached potential interviewees through a variety of routes and avenues. These included random samples in schools, colleges, universities, employing organisations, training providers, and youth clubs; the use of 'snowballing' techniques by means of which targeted types of individuals were contacted through informal networks and friendship groups; and chance meetings on street corners, public transport or in public houses. In order not to skew the sample towards any particular type of young person or leisure-time activity, fieldworkers were advised to take no more than four respondents from any one source, though schools, where up to six could be drawn, were an exception to these guidelines.

The Achieved Unweighted Sample

In the main, the teams of interviewers succeeded in achieving the quotas set for each region. A balance of males and females was achieved (50 per cent of each). With regard to age, the quotas were designed to place more emphasis on the under-20 year olds relative to the 21-24 year old phase, which was treated as an age band rather than four discrete year groups. Overall, apart from a slight dip for 20 year olds, the intended distribution of ages was obtained (see Table 2.1). Because of the disproportionately low number of 21-24 year olds in the sample, when considering the results of the research, it is always worth taking into account disaggregation of the frequencies by age in order to assess the effects of the biases in achieved age distribution.

Table 2.1   Age of interviewees

Ages	N	Age bands	N	%
14	91			
15	91	14-16	266	38
16	84			
17	85			
18	72	17-20	302	43
19	81			
20	64			
21-24	136	21-24	136	19
TOTALS	(704)		(704)	100

The proportion of interviewees living in rural areas (i.e. in settlements with a population of less than 10,000) was 27 per cent, and these were spread across four of the five regions. Similarly, with regard to current status, a satisfactory spread of young people in different occupational and educational circumstances was achieved (see Table 2.2).

Table 2.2   Current status of interviewees

Status	%
School (Years 9-11)	33
Full-time post-16 education	23
Training Schemes	6
Employment (full- and part-time)	28
Unemployment	8
Missing Cases	2
TOTAL	(704)

Distribution according to ethnicity is shown in Table 2.3. It should be stressed that the size of the non-white sub-sample was deliberately increased and is, therefore, disproportionately large relative to the population as a whole. An overall target of 150 respondents from the ethnic minorities was set; the achieved total was 144 (i.e. 21 per cent of the total sample). The number of interviews with ethnic minority respondents was increased to allow for greater validity and reliability in the frequencies for this group. As a general rule, when considering ethnicity, the report offers comparisons between white Europeans and the ethnic minorities (i.e. the sub-sample made up of the three groups: Afro-Caribbean, Asian and other). On particular occasions where key differences emerge within the ethnic minority sub-sample, variations between the Afro-Caribbean and Asian groups are displayed.

Table 2.3   Ethnic group membership of interviewees

Ethnic Group	**%**
Black/Afro-Caribbean	8
Indian/Pakistani/Bangladeshi (Asian)	9
Other	4
White European	77
Missing Cases	2
TOTAL	(704)

The interviewees' descriptions of their parents' occupations were coded according to the 'Standard Occupational Classification' (GB: Office of Population Censuses and Surveys, 1990), which permitted the allocation of respondents to a further classification of social class based on occupation. The social class categories comprised:

I   Professional, etc. occupations
II   Managerial and technical occupations
III   Skilled occupations
        (N) non-manual
        (M) manual
IV   Partly skilled occupations
V   Unskilled occupations

Taking the higher or sole social class indicator of interviewee's parents, the sample produced an approximate 65:35 ratio of middle class (Social Class I, II and IIIN) to working class respondents (Social Class IIIM, IV and V); 55:45 was the target. In the main, this slight imbalance was caused by the difficulties interviewers faced in ascertaining the respondent's parents' higher or sole social class indicator prior to arranging an interview with the young person. Finally, the sample also included 64 (9 per cent) young people who saw themselves as having a physical disability.

The Weighting of Results

It can be seen from the above that the achieved (unweighted) sample contained three disproportionate distributions relative to the population as a whole:

(i)   an over-representation of respondents from ethnic minorities;

(ii)   an under-representation of respondents from working class backgrounds, especially those with parents in Social Class IV and V; and

(iii) an under-representation of 21-24 year olds, with a corresponding over-representation of 17-20 year olds and, especially, 14-16 year olds.

To correct for the over-representation of non-white interviewees and the under-representation of young people from a working class background, the results presented throughout the report are based on weighted results. In order to avoid the excessive use of weighting, the disproportionate age distribution has not been corrected through a weighting procedure. Instead, all key results for the overall sample have been disaggregated by age so the effect of the imbalance can be gauged and assessed in considering the significance of the findings.

Unless stated to the contrary, all the tables in the main data presentation chapters of the report are based on the combined weighting adjustments for ethnicity and social class. Since small numbers of respondents did not provide codable information on parental occupations and ethnic membership, the weighting of the data was derived from 681 young people. In general, the total respondents in any table will sum to this number, except where some of the respondents did not answer the question(s) under consideration.

Before turning to present the research's findings, it is necessary to offer some background details on the key characteristics of the young people included in the weighted sample.

Firstly, Table 2.4 shows the distribution of the weighted sample among different current status positions, disaggregated by gender and type of geographical location in which the interviewee resided (i.e. urban or rural). It may be helpful to think of the sample in three blocks. Just over a third (36 per cent) of this sample were school students in Years 9-11, while just under a third (31 per cent) were in employment. Half of the remaining third were students in full-time post-16 education (including advanced and non-advanced courses), while the rest were divided equally between those on training schemes and those in unemployment.

Interestingly, a much higher proportion of female respondents had employed status: 38 per cent compared with 24 per cent of males. In contrast, male respondents had higher proportions in unemployment, post-16 education and on training schemes. Both sexes had the same percentage at school. In contrast to their urban counterparts, rural interviewees were less likely to be in employment and more likely to be in post-16 education or on training schemes.

Table 2.4   Current status by gender and urban/rural residency

Status	Total sample %	Gender Male %	Female %	Residency Urban %	Rural %
At school (Years 9-11)	36	36	36	37	33
Full-time post-16 education	15	17	13	13	20
Training scheme	9	11	7	6	15
In employment	31	24	38	34	24
Unemployed	9	12	6	10	8
TOTALS	(667)	(329)	(338)	(482)	(185)

These figures are based on the weighted results.

Table 2.5, which shows current status percentages broken down by age, reveals that the 17-20 year old group had the greatest diversity of current positions. Whereas the vast majority (94 per cent) of under-17 year olds were still at school (in Years 9-11) and most (67 per cent) of the 21-24 year old group were in employment, the 17-20 year old group were more thinly spread across the categories, with 43 per cent in employment and 28 per cent in full-time post-16 education. This group also had the highest percentage on training schemes.

Table 2.5   Current status by age

Status	Total sample %	Age Under-17 %	17-20 %	21-24 %
At school (Years 9-11)	36	94	0	0
F/T post-16 education	15	4	28	9
Training scheme	9	1	16	7
In employment	31	0	43	67
Unemployed	9	1	13	17
TOTALS	(669)	(255)	(285)	(129)

These figures are based on the weighted results.

Table 2.6 disaggregates the results for the current status of respondents in the weighted sample by social class and ethnicity. With regard to the latter, the data suggest that interviewees from the ethnic minorities were marginally more likely to be unemployed and less likely to be in employment or training than those of white European origin. With regard to social class, it should be noted that interviewees from Social Class IV and V were over-represented in the school (Years 9-11) group. Consistent with this bias, interviewees from Social Class IV and V backgrounds were similarly over-represented in the under-17 year old age band. Respondents in Social Class I and II had a significantly higher percentage participating in full-time post-16 education and lower percentage entering training schemes. The category with the highest employment proportion was the skilled group (Social Class III), with the partly and unskilled group (IV and V) displaying the highest share in unemployment.

Further analyses revealed that each of the three broad social class groups (displayed in Table 2.6) had roughly the same proportions of male and female respondents. As could be expected, higher proportions of white Europeans were located within Social Class I, II and III, while a larger share of the ethnic minorities were found in Social Class IV and V (e.g. 16 per cent of white Europeans compared to 10 per cent of ethnic minorities had professional and managerial backgrounds – Social Class I and II; 30 per cent of white Europeans compared to 43 per cent of ethnic minorities were in Social Class IV and V). Again predictably, relative to the partly and unskilled group (IV and V), interviewees in Social Class I, II and III were slightly more likely to live in rural areas (e.g. 35 per cent of urban respondents were from Social Class IV and V compared to 24 per cent of rural respondents).

Table 2.6   Current status by social class and ethnicity

| Status | Total sample % | Social Class (N = 668) | | | Ethnicity (N = 675) | |
		I and II %	III (N and M) %	IV and V %	White European %	Ethnic Minorities %
At school (Years 9-11)	36	33	30	47	35	39
Full-time post-16 education	15	34	14	9	15	15
Training scheme	9	2	9	11	9	6
In employment	31	24	39	21	32	28
Unemployed	9	7	8	12	9	12
TOTALS	(668)	(103)	(352)	(213)	(608)	(67)

These figures are based on the weighted results.

Other analyses showed that the three age groups were fairly evenly distributed between urban and rural areas, male and female respondents, and white Europeans and ethnic minorities.

A total of 437 interviewees who had completed Year 11 of compulsory schooling gave details of their 16+ examination passes (i.e. CSE Grade 1s, GCE passes and GCSE grades of C or above). Of this group, 27 per cent reported that they had not obtained any 16+ examination passes; 17 per cent indicated that they had acquired passes in one to three subjects; 21 per cent reported that they had achieved four to six passes; and 35 per cent indicated that they had been awarded seven or more passes. These data have been used throughout the report to allow key results to be disaggregated by a further independent variable of 16+ educational attainment. When considering breakdowns by educational attainment, it should be remembered that only those respondents who had completed Year 11 have been included in these analyses and that the data are based on respondents' self-reports of their examination passes.

To conclude, the weighted sample produced distributions for key biographical variables which were broadly consistent with those which could be expected in the population as a whole. There were, however, two exceptions to this trend. Firstly, the 21-24 year old group was under-represented and, secondly, Social Class IV and V contained a disproportionately high share of under-17 year olds in school (Years 9-11). Due allowance for these imbalances needs to be made when interpreting the findings.

The research yielded a substantial amount of both quantitative and qualitative data. Wherever possible, these two types of evidence have been analysed together and juxtaposed in the writing of the report. (Chapter 12 is an exception in that it deals exclusively with qualitative data.) In endeavouring to draw on both quantitative and qualitative methods, it is recognised that the research may be judged to have been over-ambitious in aiming for a mix of these two separate traditions. It clearly runs the risk of falling between two stools or, as they say in Yorkshire, it is in danger of being 'neither watercress, nor lettuce'. We hope that this is not the case and that the final analysis goes some way to overcome the limitations associated with relying solely on any one methodological tradition. Every effort has been made to achieve statistical accuracy in the data, while at the same time remaining responsive to the nuances expressed in the individual accounts of interviewees. In doing so, the analysis has wrestled with the age-old problem of seeking to acknowledge the sheer individuality of interviewees, and the significance of unique insights which an individual often generates, while simultaneously attempting to uncover general trends and frequencies. In this way, it is hoped that the research provides a wider frame in which the testimonies and experiences of individual respondents can be interpreted and appreciated.

A coding frame for the large quantity of open-ended items in the interview schedule was developed and used to interpret the completed schedules. One of the pivotal open-ended questions analysed in this way asked young people to identify their current leisure interests. The responses to this item are described and discussed in the next chapter.

PART TWO

PRESENTATION OF THE FINDINGS

3. Current Leisure Interests

This chapter presents findings arising from an open question which was intended to capture the young people's own nominations of their main leisure interests (prior to any probe or specific focus upon the extent of arts involvement). Both detailed and also broad categories of leisure-time activities are given. It was found that, of the five broad categories which were created (social; sport; media - arts audience; arts participation and miscellaneous), only about a quarter of the sample participated in at least one art form. Participation was most frequently mentioned in connection with music and the visual arts.

The chapter also examines detail differences in leisure-time pursuits (including arts) which were associated with variables such as gender, location, social class, ethnicity, age and educational attainment. Media-arts audience emerged as the leading leisure category for females, while sport was the highest ranking leisure activity for males.

Introduction

In the first five chapters of the report, evidence on young people's participation in, and attitudes to, the arts in 1993 is presented and interpreted. While subsequent chapters focus more squarely on young people's experiences in the arts at particular phases in their lives (e.g. Chapter 8 is concerned with interviewees' perceptions of the arts in schools), Chapters 3 to 7 provide a broad overview of what constituted the 'current' degree of arts involvement as portrayed by all the young people interviewed in the study. Moreover, the inquiry is not limited to the narrow focus of 'arts' participation: as emphasised in this present chapter and the following one, the research has gone to considerable lengths to sketch and gauge the extent of 'arts' involvement against the wider backdrop of young people's general leisure pursuits and day-time commitments.

Overall Leisure Interests

After the opening biographical items, the first substantive question in the interview schedule (see Item 17 in Appendix 1) enquired, '*what do you count as your main interests or most enjoyable activities at the weekends or in the evenings?*'. The question aimed to provide an overview of the main leisure-time activities, interests or hobbies of young people. Asked prior to items explicitly mentioning the 'arts', the question afforded a genuine indication of those activities that were uppermost in their minds and lives instead of predicating their thinking by tuning them into a bias towards artistic, creative or imaginative pursuits.

This approach to the sequencing of questions was considered to have two main advantages. Firstly, any respondents' references to the 'arts' in response to this question would have high validity, since the responses were volunteered rather than prompted by the interviewer. Because of this, participation rates in the arts were likely to be lower than subsequent questions which specifically referred to involvement in the 'arts'. Secondly, it allowed interviewees to cite 'artistic' activities without the need for an interviewer definition of the 'arts' and similar terms. Additionally, the question made it possible to place young people's involvement in artistic enterprises in the context of the wide range of activities engaged in by young people. Most importantly, this facilitated some gauging of the importance of 'artistic' activities relative to other types of pursuits, cultural expression and behaviour. This contextualisation of leisure-time interests applies when looking at the results for the sample as a whole, as well as those for individual interviewees (e.g. it can give an indication of the breadth and direction of an individual's interests, their motivation and energy, and their available spare time from work or educational commitments).

It was obvious that interviewees varied enormously in the relative importance they attached to leisure-time activities. For some, spare-time pursuits were not imbued with great personal significance or meaning. Instead, for many of these respondents, work or educational courses were seen as the salient sources of psychological reward. For others, including some who were not fortunate enough to have fulfilling jobs, leisure-time activities constituted the essential arena of their lives, in some cases contributing greatly to a person's self-identity and sense of worth. As one 17 year old female stated of her artistic leisure-time activities:

> *They are an important part of our lives. When you work hard you need something to live for, because work provides you with a means for a living, but you need something to live for.*

The statistical results derived from interviewees' responses to this question are displayed in Table 3.1. This table shows the frequencies with which detailed categories of leisure-time activities (e.g. 'swimming/diving' and 'pubs/drinking') were mentioned. Some caution should be taken in making comparisons between detailed categories, as some classifications used for coding the responses are more specific than others (e.g. those playing the piano and the flute would be coded once under 'playing a musical instrument', while those playing 'football' and 'rugby' would be coded twice – once for each sport). In addition, the detailed categories have been grouped under five broad categories – (i) Social, (ii) Sport, (iii) Media - Arts: Audience, (iv) Arts: Participation and (v) Miscellaneous. It should be noted that while the percentages for the detailed categories represent the proportions of the sample (i.e. 681) who mentioned the category (e.g. 2 per cent mentioned 'golf'), care should be taken in summing the percentages for the detailed categories since most interviewees cited more than one detailed category both **within** and across the broader ones. Consequently, two additional statistics have been calculated for the broad categories. Firstly, the table sets out the percentages of respondents who mentioned at least one detailed category within each broad grouping. Secondly, Table 3.1 also contains the average (mean) number of responses given by respondents in each of the broad categories (i.e. the sum of the responses in each broad category divided by the number of respondents mentioning at least one activity in the relevant broad category). It can be seen, for example, that the broad categories of 'sports' and 'media-arts: audience' recorded the highest mean number of responses (0.9 for each).

Table 3.1   Current leisure interests

Activity	%
Social	
Socialising with friends	35
Pubs, drinking	17
Going to clubs, discos, raves, parties	10
Dating, sexual relationships	5
% of respondents mentioning at least one social activity (Mean N = 0.7)	**53**
Sports	
Sports (general)	8
Watching live sport	3
Watching, listening to sport on media	1
Running, jogging, athletics	4
Cycling, mountain bikes	7
Swimming, diving	12
Tennis, badminton, squash	7
Football	15
Cricket	2
Rugby, hockey	5
Golf	2
Fishing, angling, shooting	4
Ice-skating, basketball, bowling	4
Snooker, pool, table-tennis	4
Keep fit, aerobics, gymnastics	5
Boxing, judo, martial arts	3
Mountaineering, orienteering, camping	4
Horse riding	1
Water sports, rowing, surfing	2
Other sports	1
% of respondents mentioning at least one sport activity (Mean N = 0.9)	**55**

Activity	%
Media-arts: audience	
Watching TV, videos	25
Cinema	15
Listening to recorded music, radio music	13
Music (general)	5
Concerts, live music	2
Theatre	5
Art galleries, museums	1
Reading	22
% of respondents mentioning at least one media-arts: audience activity (Mean N = 0.9)	**57**
Arts: participation	
Playing musical instrument	6
Music-making, writing songs	4
Singing	2
Dancing (general)	2
Ballet, tap, modern, jazz	1
Ballroom, country dancing	1
Drama, acting, theatre involvement	3
Painting, drawing	6
Photography	1
Writing stories, poems, plays	1
Sewing, fashion, textiles	2
Sculpture, making	1
Other arts	1
% of respondents mentioning at least one arts: participation activity (Mean N = 0.3)	**23**
Miscellaneous	
Walking, messing around in street, town, woods	7
Travelling, days out with family, friends	5
Youth club	3
Scouts, Guides, Cubs, Young Farmers	4
Shopping	3
Eating out	1
Computers	8
Working: part-time, overtime	8
Indoor games, model-making	1
Gardening	1
Cooking	2
Educational courses	1
Cars and motorbikes	5
Other general, miscellaneous activities	5
% of respondents mentioning at least one miscellaneous activity (Mean N = 0.5)	**43**
TOTAL	(681)

Interviewees could give more than one response, so percentages will not sum to 100 per cent.
These figures are based on the weighted results (see Chapter 2).
Only 1 per cent (6 respondents) mentioned no main leisure interest.

A striking finding displayed by Table 3.1 is that only 23 per cent of the sample – a little fewer than one in four – participated in at least one art form. In other words, 77 per cent did not mention participation in any form of artistic leisure activity. The broad categories with the highest percentages doing at least one constituent activity were 'media-arts: audience' (57 per cent), 'sport' (55 per cent) and 'social' (53 per cent). The relatively high position of 'media-arts: audience' is bolstered by the fact that this broad category included watching TV and videos (a quarter of all interviewees mentioned this), reading (22 per cent) and cinema (15 per cent). In the main, all three areas of activity were considered by most interviewees to be undertaken with little or no explicit 'artistic' intention or outcome.

An important finding to emerge from the table is that over half of the young people interviewed in the study participated in at least one sport in their leisure time. In contrast, active involvement in the arts was very much a minority undertaking, with young people taking part in them at half the rate of sports participation. Put another way, on average respondents mentioned only 0.3 'arts: participation' categories compared to 0.9 for 'sport' and the same for 'media-arts: audience' categories. The differences are substantial. However, while the statistics underline the fact that youth participation in the arts is a minority leisure interest, it is worth registering at this point that the qualitative evidence frequently testified to the importance attached to the arts by individual members of this minority. A comment from a 20 year old unemployed female was typical of this group:

> The arts are very important to me. They form the basis of my leisure-time activities.

and another from a 17 year old male on a training scheme:

> The arts can mean whatever you like doing. Anything a bit creative or creative by someone else is quite important. Art is what I do when I'm not at work.

Turning to the detailed categories in Table 3.1, the most common leisure-time activity by a considerable margin was socialising with friends, with 35 per cent of the sample mentioning it. Watching TV and videos (25 per cent) and reading (22 per cent) were the next most popular. Meeting friends on the street or going to pubs, clubs, discos, raves or parties were the main areas for social contact mentioned by young people, over and above the general activity of socialising with friends.

The main contributors to the 'sports' broad category were participants in football (15 per cent) and swimming and diving (12 per cent). The remainder was made up of smaller percentages from various branches of sport, though cycling and tennis, badminton and squash figured highly. It was noteworthy that only 2 per cent referred to the allegedly national sport of cricket.

The total for the 'miscellaneous' broad category was made up of various small percentages, the largest of which were activities with computers

(8 per cent) and working (8 per cent). Only 3 per cent mentioned going to a youth club as a main or most enjoyable leisure-time interest, while 4 per cent cited other clubs such as the Girl Guides or Young Farmers clubs.

Reference has already been made to the three most prevalent activities within the 'media-arts: audience' category: watching TV/videos (25 per cent), reading (22 per cent) and cinema (15 per cent). A fourth activity which attracted a high number of mentions was listening to music. Listening to recorded and radio music was by far the most frequent of these.

For the 'arts: participation' category, playing a musical instrument and painting and drawing were the most commonly cited activities, each mentioned by 6 per cent of the interviewees. With three detailed categories, music-related activities were found to be one of the most popular participatory art forms for young people – at least as far as their leisure-time pursuits were concerned. Additional analyses revealed that 71 respondents (10 per cent) mentioned at least one musical activity, while 52 respondents (8 per cent) cited at least one of the visual arts.

Along with the fact that the adoption of spectator roles *vis-à-vis* the media and the arts is often easier, less demanding and more accessible than actually taking part (this factor seems to have had less effect on reducing sports participation), interviewees often considered participation in the arts to be something only for the talented. Again, this was less the case in sport, where young people seemed happier to play games and so on, purely for fun and for the need to be physical, whether or not they saw themselves as gifted in the sport concerned. A 17 year old female in full-time education exemplified this perception of a 'talent barrier' to arts participation:

> *I enjoy them* [i.e. listening to/watching the arts] *if they are there and if I want to go and see them. You have to be pretty talented to do something like that, so I enjoy watching people. I'm slightly envious.*

This comment echoes a frequent and recurring theme in many of the interviewees' attitudes to arts participation: namely 'I'd like to, but I'm no good at it'. A 23 year old female in part-time employment implied that the 'talent barrier' problem was related to an over-emphasis on performance:

> *It's a shame that the arts are connected to performance rather than experiencing it for the sake of it. Creative activities should be integrated into everyday life.*

Another interviewee commented:

> *Don't take* [the arts] *too seriously. They should be enjoyed.*

Allied to the observation that the perceived lack of ability discourages young people to participate in the arts was the equally inhibiting attitude that the arts were for 'snobs' and 'not for my class'. A 19 year old male in full-time education expressed this view as:

From my experience, the arts seemed to have been for the upper class of people - hard for people with my background to break through.

Similarly, an employed 21 year old female remarked:

[Creative arts] *should be valued in everybody. There is too much snobbery. Personal expression should be encouraged in everyone.*

These points will surface again when consideration is given to how leisure-time activities are affected by social class backgrounds. First, the findings on leisure-time pursuits are compared for interviewees who lived in urban or rural settings.

Leisure Interests in Urban and Rural Areas

The opportunities for, and constraints upon young people's leisure interests are likely to be influenced by the nature of the urban or rural environments in which they live. It could be expected, for example, that young people in rural areas would be more involved in physical outdoor pursuits, while their counterparts in urban areas would be more inclined to avail themselves of the increased facilities for shopping, entertainment, leisure and sport. Looking at the responses to the question on leisure-time interests, some interesting variations according to urban or rural locations emerge. The most significant of these differences in the detailed leisure-time categories are reproduced in Table 3.2 below.

Table 3.2   Selected leisure interests by urban and rural areas

Activity	Total sample %	Urban Respondents %	Rural Respondents %
Cycling, mountain bikes	7	5	14
Swimming, diving	12	11	16
Tennis, badminton, squash	7	5	12
Rugby, hockey	5	2	11
Fishing, angling, shooting	4	2	9
Watching TV, videos	25	28	16
Cinema	15	16	11
Listening to recorded music	13	15	8
Reading	22	24	16
Painting, drawing	6	5	10
Computers	8	9	4
Cars and motorbikes	5	3	9
TOTALS	(681)	(492)	(189)

Interviewees could give more than one response, so percentages will not sum to 100 per cent. These figures are based on the weighted results (see Chapter 2).

While the participation rates for such sports as cycling, swimming, tennis, squash, rugby, hockey, fishing and shooting were higher in rural areas, 'media-arts: audience' activities like reading, going to the cinema, listening to music, and, most markedly, watching television and videos were more prevalent in urban areas. Computers also showed a noticeable difference in favour of urban respondents, whereas cars and motorbikes revealed a similar difference but in the reverse direction. The only appreciable difference for 'arts: participation' activities arose in connection with painting and drawing which involved a higher proportion of rural interviewees.

Detailed categories not listed in Table 3.2 produced no reliable differences either way. In some cases, this was quite surprising since it could have been expected that the greater availability of such amenities as theatres, art galleries, museums, and live concerts would have attracted a higher share of urban than rural young people. The fact that they did not may suggest that the proximity and accessibility of such facilities are not the overriding factors associated with young people's attendance at them, but caution needs to be applied here, since so few respondents – urban or rural – mentioned these, it would be impossible to detect reliable differences without a much larger sample.

Shopping, travelling and days out with family or friends, cooking, boxing, judo and martial arts, water sports and ice-skating, basketball and bowling were all activities mentioned more frequently by urban interviewees, though the small numbers involved, especially within the rural sub-sample, give grounds for caution.

In Table 3.3 below, the results for the broad categories of current interests are broken down for urban and rural respondents.

Table 3.3   Current leisure interests in broad categories by urban and rural areas

	% of respondents who mentioned one or more in each activity group			Mean number of responses	
Status	Total sample %	Urban %	Rural %	Urban	Rural
Social	53	53	55	0.7	0.7
Sport	55	50	67	0.8	1.2
Media-arts: audience	57	61	46	1.0	0.6
Arts: participation	23	21	29	0.3	0.4
Miscellaneous	43	45	39	0.6	0.5
TOTALS	(681)	(492)	(189)	(492)	(189)

Interviewees could give more than one response, so percentages will not sum to 100 per cent.
These figures are based on the weighted results (see Chapter 2).

The table clearly shows that rural young people had a higher participation rate in 'sport' and 'arts:participation', while their counterparts in urban areas had higher rates of involvement in 'media-arts: audience' and 'miscellaneous activities'. Quite striking is the finding that 'sport' was the most frequently mentioned leisure-time pursuit for interviewees in rural areas, while 'media-arts: audience' was the most frequently mentioned leisure-time interest of urban respondents.

Leisure Interests and Gender

Traditionally, many leisure-time pursuits have been strongly associated with deeply ingrained stereotypical patterns and divisions. Data from this research confirm the continuing existence of such patterns and point to less obvious variations according to gender. The most significant differences along gender lines are set out in Table 3.4 (i.e. items with a difference of 5 per cent or more have been included, though it should be noted that some activities with less than a 5 per cent difference were not engaged in by any members of one gender – e.g. cricket).

Table 3.4   Selected leisure interests by gender

Activity	Total sample %	Gender Male %	Female %
Socialising with friends	35	24	46
Sports (general)	8	10	5
Swimming, diving	12	3	21
Football	15	29	2
Fishing, angling, shooting	4	8	0
Snooker, table-tennis, pool	4	8	1
Keep fit, aerobics, gymnastics	5	1	10
Cinema	15	10	20
Theatre	5	2	8
Reading	22	12	31
Music-making, writing songs	4	6	1
Shopping	3	1	6
Computers	8	14	2
Cars and motorbikes	5	8	2
TOTALS	(681)	(338)	(343)

Interviewees could give more than one response, so percentages will not sum to 100 per cent. These figures are based on the weighted results (see Chapter 2).

Substantiating conventional expectations, activities with a strong female orientation included shopping, keeping fit, aerobics and gymnastics, whereas those with a male bias focused on computers, cars, motorbikes, football, fishing, angling, shooting, snooker, table-tennis and pool. Perhaps also to be expected, but with less significance in the differences were sewing, fashion, textiles and cooking for females, and drinking in pubs, boxing, judo and the martial arts for males.

One result which was not entirely to be expected emerged in relation to socialising with friends: only 24 per cent of males mentioned it compared to 46 per cent of females. Of course, the data do not permit an examination to gauge whether females actually spent more time socialising with friends than males or were simply more willing than males to register it as a legitimate and enjoyable leisure-time interest and activity. The figures also show that females have a greater participation rate in swimming and diving, whereas music-making and writing songs showed a higher rate of male involvement. Going to the cinema and theatre were noticeably female-oriented and the participation rate of males in reading was remarkably low in contrast to females. Painting and drawing also revealed a slight bias towards females. An overview of these different orientations can be gained by looking at the results for the broad categories disaggregated by gender (see Table 3.5).

Table 3.5   Current leisure interests in broad categories by gender

| | % of respondents who mentioned one or more in each activity group | | | Mean number of responses | |
| | Total sample | Male | Female | Male | Female |
Status	%	%	%		
Social	53	48	59	0.6	0.8
Sport	55	63	47	1.1	0.8
Media-arts: audience	57	49	64	0.7	1.1
Arts: participation	23	19	27	0.2	0.4
Miscellaneous	43	44	42	0.6	0.5
TOTALS	(681)	(338)	(343)	(338)	(343)

Interviewees could give more than one response, so percentages will not sum to 100 per cent.
These figures are based on the weighted results (see Chapter 2).

Summarising the variations highlighted by the table, female respondents indicated higher involvement rates in 'media-arts: audience', 'social' activities and 'arts: participation', whereas male respondents reported greater participation in 'sport'. Hence, for females, 'media-arts: audience' emerged as the leading broad leisure-time category, while 'sport' was the main category for males. A major finding relating to participation in the arts is that while the overall rate of active artistic involvement was found to be just under one in four (23 per cent), the rate for males fell to just under one in five (19 per cent). This compares to a rate of participation in sport among males of over three in every five (63 per cent).

Finally, it may be significant that females tended to mention more leisure-time interests than males. By dividing the total number of responses for each gender by the total number of respondents for each gender, the (mean) average number of responses per respondent can be calculated. As a result of these calculations, females had an average overall response rate of 3.5 compared to males of 3.2 (though the problem of defining categories is worth recalling and the difference is fairly small).

Leisure Interests and Social Class

The social class of young people seems likely to influence their leisure-time pursuits in several important ways: through inculcation into different values, norms and attitudes with regard to appropriate behaviour and cultural activities; through exposure to parents with varying levels of formal education; and through differing amounts of opportunities determined by variations in available material resources and time. Consistent with these expectations, analyses of leisure interests (in detailed categories) disaggregated by social class revealed some interesting variations, particularly in 'social' and 'media-arts: audience' activities, and, to a lesser extent in 'arts: participation' (see Table 3.6).

Table 3.6   Selected leisure interests by social class

Activity	Total sample %	I and II %	III (N and M) %	IV and V %
			Social Class	
Socialising with friends	35	31	45	21
Pubs, drinking	17	10	19	16
Clubs, discos, etc.	10	7	13	7
Tennis, badminton, squash	7	13	8	1
Football	15	8	17	16
Watching TV, videos	25	18	21	34
Cinema	15	19	16	11
Listening to recorded music	13	19	12	13
Reading	22	30	21	19
Playing musical instrument	6	15	7	1
Painting, drawing	6	8	3	11
Youth club	3	1	2	7
Travelling, days out with family, friends	5	2	2	11
Computers	8	6	6	11
Cars and motorbikes	5	2	4	7
TOTALS	(681)	(105)	(359)	(217)

Interviewees could give more than one response, so percentages will not sum to 100 per cent. The figures are based on the weighted results (see Chapter 2).

Social activities were particularly important to interviewees with parents in skilled occupations (Social Class III N and M). Within this group, 45 per cent mentioned socialising with friends as a key leisure-time interest, whereas only 31 per cent of respondents in Social Class I and II and, still less, 21 per cent of those in Social Class IV or V did so. Similarly, the skilled group registered the highest proportion referring to pubs and drinking, and clubs, discos, raves and parties as leisure pursuits. It is difficult to explain this emphasis in the responses of young people in the skilled group classification.

Within sporting categories, tennis, badminton and squash emerged as largely middle class activities (e.g. only 1 per cent of the partly and unskilled group mentioned them), while football perpetuated its traditional image as a working class sport. Other differences perhaps worth noting were that keeping fit, aerobics, gymnastics, horse riding, fishing, angling and shooting were more popular with middle class respondents.

For 'media-arts: audience' categories, watching TV and videos assumed greater importance for working class respondents: mentioned by a third (34 per cent) of those in Social Class IV and V, it amounted to their most frequently mentioned form of leisure activity. Cinema attendance displayed a reversed (though less pronounced) trend towards middle class interviewees. Indeed, apart from visiting art galleries and museums and music (general), both of which produced insignificant differences, all the other 'media-arts: audience' categories were more popular with the Social Class I and II group. This was particularly the case for reading, though attendance at concerts, live music and theatres also showed a declining interest through the three Social Class classifications. Comments from interviewees suggested that social attitudes (e.g. *'theatres are for arty snobs'*) and lack of money (e.g. *'theatres are too expensive for many people'*) were crucial factors in inhibiting attendance at artistic and cultural events.

Within the 'miscellaneous' broad category, there were four leisure activities which were comparatively less popular with middle class respondents and high in popularity for working class ones: attending youth clubs, travelling and days out with family or friends, computers and cars and motorbikes. The youth club finding is especially interesting and may have important implications for efforts to promote the arts through the youth service.

Participation in the arts also included some interesting differences. Particularly striking is the variation in popularity of playing a music instrument from the Social Class I and II group at 15 per cent, through the skilled group at 7 per cent to those in Social Class IV and V at 1 per cent. More puzzling are the frequencies for painting and drawing among the three groups: 8 per cent for the professional class, followed by a dip to 3 per cent for the skilled group, followed by a rise to 11 per cent for the partly and unskilled group. As later sections will show, this distinctive 'U'-shaped relationship re-surfaces in subsequent analyses of social class and the visual arts.

The results for the broad leisure-time categories broken down by social class are set out in Table 3.7. It is interesting to note that interviewees in the Social Class IV and V mentioned fewer interests (3.2 per respondent) than interviewees in the two other groups (3.4). Essentially, the broad category figures confirm the trends indicated by the detailed categories. 'Social' activities were more likely to be mentioned by interviewees in the skilled group (Social Class III N and M), for whom they formed the most frequently cited leisure pursuit.

Table 3.7   Current leisure interests in broad categories by social class

| Activity Group | Total sample % | % of respondents who mentioned one or more in each activity group Social Class | | | Mean number of responses Social Class | | |
		I and II %	III (N and M) %	IV and V %	I and II %	III (N and M) %	IV and V %
Social	53	41	63	44	0.5	0.8	0.5
Sports	55	57	59	46	1.0	1.0	0.8
Media-arts: audience	57	66	54	56	1.0	0.8	0.9
Arts: participation	23	34	21	22	0.5	0.2	0.3
Miscellaneous	43	37	39	55	0.4	0.5	0.7
TOTALS	(681)	(105)	(359)	(217)	(105)	(359)	(217)

Interviewees could give more than one response, so percentages will not sum to 100 per cent.
These figures are based on the weighted results (see Chapter 2).

Although individual sporting activities varied for the three groups, the overall involvement rate in 'sport' was similar for the professional and skilled classes, though slightly lower for the partly and unskilled class. The latter class gave more responses in the 'miscellaneous' category: the four activities which largely account for this were identified above. The most popular category for interviewees in Social Class I and II was 'media-arts: audience', mentioned by a higher proportion of this group than either of the other two. Most significantly, the professional group also recorded a much higher participation rate in the arts. Consequently, whereas the overall rate of arts participation for the total sample was less than one in four (23 per cent recorded one or more arts pursuits), the corresponding rate for the Social Class I and II group increased to one in three (34 per cent). Thus, as well as a bias towards females, youth participation in the arts also evinced clear signs of a strong association with middle class young people.

Leisure Interests and Ethnicity

Ethnicity could influence young people's leisure-time pursuits through its indirect association with social class and urban contexts, as well as directly through differences in cultural traditions and creative contexts handed down from one generation to the next. From Table 3.8, it can be seen that, although there are differences across the full range of detailed categories, there are pronounced variations within the 'media-arts: audience' category. As well as showing the frequencies of leisure-time interests for white Europeans (Column 1) and ethnic minorities (Column 2), Table 3.8 also breaks down the latter into frequencies for Afro-Caribbean (Column 3) and Asian (Column 4) sub-groups, though the small numbers for these should be noted and treated with caution. (For an explanation of why the totals for these two sub-groups are considerably smaller than the actual number of Afro-Caribbeans and Asians interviewed – 55 and 60 respectively – see Chapter 2.) Hence, although the figures appear small, they are in fact based on a larger consistency of interviewees.

Table 3.8   Selected leisure interests by ethnicity

Activity	Total sample %	White European (Col. 1) %	Ethnic Minorities (Col. 2) %	Breakdown for the two main groups in Col. 2 Afro-Caribbean (Col. 3) %	Asian (Col. 4) %
Pub, drinking	17	18	3	1	5
Clubs, discos, raves, parties	10	10	14	16	9
Rugby, hockey	5	5	0	0	0
Fishing, angling, shooting	4	5	0	0	0
Boxing, judo, martial arts	3	3	9	14	6
Watching TV, videos	25	23	42	25	52
Cinema	15	14	21	10	30
Listening to recorded, radio music	13	14	7	3	10
Theatre	5	5	0	0	0
Reading	22	21	27	16	42
Playing musical instrument	6	7	4	8	0
Painting, drawing	6	7	2	0	3
Cooking	2	1	7	7	5
Cars and motorbikes	5	6	0	0	0
TOTALS	(675)	(608)	(67)	(31)	(26)

Interviewees could give more than one response, so percentages will not sum to 100 per cent.
These figures are based on the weighted results (see Chapter 2).

With regard to social activities, the tendency for the white European group to spend leisure time going to pubs and drinking was not matched in the reported behaviour of the ethnic minorities group. Instead, this group – especially the Afro-Caribbean sub-sample – were more likely to be active in attending clubs, discos, raves and parties.

Of the sports, rugby, hockey, fishing, angling and shooting were mentioned only by interviewees in the white European group. On the other hand, there was a greater proportion of the ethnic minorities involved in boxing, judo and the martial arts.

The differences within the 'media-arts: audience' category were marked. Members of the ethnic minorities group were almost twice as likely as their white European counterparts to mention watching TV and videos as a leisure-time activity. This difference was largely attributable to the popularity of TV and videos among Asian ethnic minorities; the corresponding rate for Afro-Caribbeans was only very slightly above that of the white European group. Likewise, with cinema: Asian respondents displayed a very high rate of attendance at cinemas compared to white Europeans and Afro-Caribbean interviewees, who in fact had lower proportions going to the cinema than white Europeans. In contrast to the trend with visual media, white Europeans were twice as likely as ethnic minorities to cite listening to recorded and radio music as a leisure-time activity. Most strikingly, theatre-going was reported to be an entirely white European pursuit for young people. The higher share of ethnic minorities referring to reading was due to the significant number of Asian interviewees mentioning the reading of the Koran and other religious books as a key activity in their leisure time; once again, among the Afro-Caribbean minority, reading scored lower than it did for the white European group.

Similarly, for the 'arts: participation' category, there was as much variation within the ethnic minorities group than between it and the white European group. Playing a musical instrument, for example, showed only a slight bias towards white Europeans, yet within the ethnic minorities it was revealed as an activity, along with other musical items, which had a strong orientation towards Afro-Caribbean interviewees. Alternatively, painting and drawing, in which the ethnic minorities had a lower participation rate than white Europeans, was more likely to be undertaken by Asian rather than Afro-Caribbean young people. Similarly, Asians had a higher rate of involvement in sewing, fashion and textiles.

Turning to the 'miscellaneous' category, a higher share of the ethnic minorities (in this case, both Afro-Caribbeans and Asians) than white Europeans cited cooking as a leisure-time activity. The reverse was the case for cars and motorbikes.

The above findings point towards a greater proportion of the ethnic minorities being involved in 'media-arts: audience' than white Europeans, though the converse is the case for 'arts: participation'. These trends are confirmed in Table 3.9, which shows the ethnic breakdown of current leisure interests in the broad categories.

Table 3.9   Current leisure interests in broad categories by ethnicity

	% of respondents who mentioned one or more in each activity group			Mean number of responses	
Status	**Total sample %**	**White European %**	**Ethnic minorities %**	**White European**	**Ethnic minorities**
Social	53	54	49	0.7	0.5
Sport	55	55	54	1.0	0.8
Media-arts: audience	57	56	66	0.9	1.0
Arts: participation	23	24	13	0.3	0.2
Miscellaneous	43	44	44	0.6	0.5
TOTALS	(674)	(608)	(67)	(608)	(67)

Interviewees could give more than one response, so percentages will not sum to 100 per cent.
These figures are based on the weighted results (see Chapter 2).

Firstly, it may be noted that white European interviewees gave more responses – 3.4 per respondent compared to 3.0 for ethnic minority interviewees. The table shows that the really significant differences surface in connection with 'media-arts: audience' and 'arts: participation'. 'Social', 'sport' and 'miscellaneous' broad categories were similar between the two main groups, as well as within the ethnic minorities group, though the Afro-Caribbean minority indicated a higher participation rate in 'sport' (e.g. athletics, boxing and basketball) compared to Asians.

Relative to white Europeans and Afro-Caribbeans, the Asian ethnic minority registered greater interest in 'media-arts: audience' activities and this accounts for the higher percentages for ethnic minorities as a whole. The specific elements of the media which appealed to Asian interviewees have been outlined above and endorse the findings of research into black and Asian attitudes to the arts in Birmingham (Harris Research Centre, 1993). Most strikingly, the 'arts: participation' rate for the ethnic minorities was remarkably low. Whereas almost one in four (24 per cent) of white European interviewees participated in at least one artistic activity, only one in eight of the ethnic minorities (13 per cent) did so. This comparatively low level of involvement was equally applicable to Afro-Caribbeans and Asians, though, as indicated earlier, differences were apparent in the nature of the activities engaged in by small numbers within each sub-group. These results, supported by the general impressions gained from the interviews as a whole, suggest that, whereas Afro-Caribbean young people were more likely to display distinctive ethnic cultural traits, as well as mainstream integrated cultural patterns, the Asian sub-sample was more culturally divergent and ethno-centric in its depiction of prevailing leisure pursuits.

Leisure Interests and Age

A fundamental but indirect influence of age on young people's leisure interests is mediated through its close relationship with another key independent variable, current status or position. For instance, most under-17 year olds are likely to be at school, while the majority of 17-20 year olds are likely to be in full-time further or higher education, on youth training schemes or in jobs requiring few or no formal qualifications. As discussed in the next section on current status, all these aspects can affect the time, money, encouragement and opportunities available to support or restrict young people's involvement in leisure-time pursuits. Moreover, there are also the direct effects of age: changes in interests, attitudes and lifestyles as the young person matures, as well as changes in the interests, attitudes, cults and fashion of young people from one generation to the next. Leisure activities could also be expected to shift in line with the transitions young people make as they progress from school or college to a working or adult life.

Table 3.10 below shows the breakdown according to age, which appears to have a widespread effect on many activities. Items not included in the table produced few or no significant differences between the three age bands. When interpreting variations between the age bands, differences are likely to, but do not automatically, indicate an increasing or declining level of interest in an activity as young people grow older – instead, they may reflect sudden shifts in cultural trends and fashions of different age bands. Consequently, some caution needs to be applied in drawing inferences from the results.

Firstly, it is clear that key social activities were rated more important leisure activities by the older groups: socialising with friends and going to pubs and drinking were mentioned by progressively increasing proportions in the three age bands. Clubs, discos, raves and parties were most popular with 17-20 year olds.

Several sports (e.g. sports in general, football, rugby, hockey, running, jogging and athletics) attract high percentages among the under-17s then decline progressively through the two other age bands. Since none of these sports have been the focus of very transitory 'fads', this probably indicates that participation in these sports decreases as young people grow older. Conversely, sporting activities that were comparatively more popular with the upper end of the age range studied included keep fit, aerobics and gymnastics, orienteering and camping. For some reason, fishing, angling and shooting appears to be a hobby particularly attractive to 17-20 year olds. Judo, boxing and the martial arts seemed to be especially popular with the over-21 year olds.

Within the 'media-arts: audience' category, watching TV and videos emerged as a major part of the lives of under-17 year olds: almost a third of them deemed it important enough to register it as one of their main leisure-time pursuits. This proportion fell for the 17-20 group and still further for the over-21 year olds. Without longitudinal cohort studies, it is difficult to say whether these figures point to a contemporary boom in TV and video viewing which will remain high as the under-17s mature or to a popularity among school-aged young people which will decline with age. Displaying a reverse trend, going to the cinema appears to increase with age; so does theatre attendance, but from a lower base-line. The qualitative evidence suggested that the over-21 year olds were more able to afford theatre tickets and had matured in their attitudes in that they were less likely to consider it 'not the thing to do' or 'snobbish'. For example, a 23 year old male in full-time employment enthused:

> [I] *want to see more and more* [plays] *... five years ago I would have said it was a lot of 'arty farty' nonsense!*

Reading also increased with age.

Table 3.10 Selected leisure interests by age

Activity	Total sample %	Under-17 %	Age 17-20 %	21-24 %
Socialising with friends	35	29	38	42
Pub, drinking	17	4	21	32
Clubs, discos, raves, parties	10	5	16	7
Sports (general)	8	10	8	2
Running, jogging, athletics	4	6	3	0
Football	15	20	15	6
Rugby, hockey	5	7	4	0
Fishing, angling, shooting	4	2	8	0
Keep fit, aerobics, gymnastics	5	1	7	8
Mountaineering, orienteering	4	3	2	11
Watching TV, videos	25	32	22	16
Cinema	15	8	15	27
Listening to recorded, radio music	13	13	16	10
Theatre	5	3	4	11
Reading	22	19	22	26
Playing a musical instrument	6	9	6	3
Music-making, writing songs	4	5	1	6
Youth club	3	5	1	5
Scouts, guides, cubs	4	5	2	7
Travelling, days out with family, friends	5	8	2	5
Computers	8	13	5	4
Cars and motorbikes	5	5	7	1
TOTALS	(681)	(261)	(288)	(132)

Interviewees could give more than one response, so percentages will not sum to 100 per cent.
The figures are based on the weighted results (see Chapter 2).

Of 'arts: participation' activities, playing a musical instrument decreased as age increased perhaps indicating a decline in interest as young people move outside the sphere of influence and encouragement of formal education and parents. To a lesser extent, participation in dancing and singing also appeared to fall off as age increased. Interestingly, music-making and writing songs showed signs of an upturn in interest among the 21-24 year old group, especially, when compared with a notable lack of interest in these activities among 17-20 year olds.

Within the 'miscellaneous' category, it is interesting to note that involvement in various types of clubs (e.g. youth clubs, scouts, young farmers, church clubs etc.) is lowest for the 17-20 year old group. The over-21 year old group seemed to find a renewed interest in joining clubs and societies, with many of those mentioning clubs assisting in the running and organisation of them. Activities which appeared to decrease with age included shopping, cars, motorbikes and computers (though the latter may reflect greater access to computers among younger generations). Interests associated with an increase as young people got older included cooking and eating out.

Table 3.11 presents the results for the broad categories broken down by age. These results confirm that the under-17 year old group was least likely to see social interaction as a key leisure-time pursuit. In contrast, it was among the most frequently mentioned activities for the two older groups. Interestingly, the level of sporting activities registered by the school-aged group appears to have been sustained by 17-20 year old group, only to decline for the oldest group. However, it is conspicuous that the participation rate for sport among the over-21 year old group was still almost twice the rate of their participation in the arts. The arts participation rate was especially low for the 17-20 year old group, who were markedly less engaged in the arts than the school-aged group. The apparent increased level of involvement by the over-21 year old group is an interesting finding and one that is clearly important to trawl subsequent resultss for a possible explanation. Involvement in 'media-arts: audience' activities showed a steady increase with age (largely accounted for by results in cinema, theatre and reading, offsetting a decline in watching TV and videos as a key leisure interest).

Table 3.11   Current leisure interests in broad categories by age

Activity Group	Total sample %	% of respondents who mentioned one or more in each activity group			Mean number of responses		
		Under-17 %	17-20 %	21-24 %	Under-17	17-20	21-24
Social	53	37	65	61	0.4	0.8	0.9
Sports	55	56	58	45	1.0	1.0	0.7
Media-arts: audience	57	54	57	62	0.8	0.9	1.0
Arts: participation	23	28	18	24	0.4	0.2	0.3
Miscellaneous	43	55	33	44	0.7	0.4	0.5
TOTALS	(681)	(261)	(288)	(132)	(261)	(288)	(132)

Interviewees could give more than one response, so percentages will not sum to 100 per cent.
These figures are based on the weighted results (see Chapter 2).

Leisure Interests and Current Status

The current position or status of the interviewees may have an influence on their use of leisure time in a number of ways. Firstly, areas of study or work can often overflow into a person's spare time and affect the activities they pursue in it. Additionally, colleges and universities provide numerous opportunities and openings to develop a wide range of leisure-time activities. Current position will also greatly affect the amount of money a young person has at his or her disposal to spend in the evenings or at the weekend. More indirectly, current position will mediate an influence through its close association with age (e.g. it will reflect changes due to various aspects of maturation). Similarly, current position is also closely connected with the influence of social class and educational attainment (e.g. few young people with relatively high numbers of GCSE passes enter training schemes).

Hence, either directly or indirectly through its association with variables already discussed, current status appeared to be related to differences in the patterns of young people's leisure interests. The main variations in leisure pursuits according to current status are set out in Table 3.12.

Table 3.12 Selected leisure interests by current status

Activity	Total sample %	At school Years 9-11 %	16+ FT education %	Training %	Employment %	Unemployed %
Socialising with friends	35	28	35	42	42	39
Pubs, drinking	17	3	24	12	29	19
Clubs, discos, raves, parties	10	5	13	17	13	10
Sports (general)	8	9	6	16	4	5
Cycling, mountain bikes	7	8	16	6	6	2
Swimming, diving	12	13	8	16	10	14
Football	15	22	13	25	9	9
Rugby, hockey	5	8	8	4	1	0
Fishing, angling, shooting	4	2	9	4	4	6
Ice-skating, basketball, bowling	4	3	2	5	1	9
Snooker, pool, table-tennis	4	5	1	9	2	8
Keep fit, aerobics, gymnastics	5	1	4	14	9	1
Watching TV, videos	25	33	12	28	19	35
Cinema	15	8	23	4	22	13
Theatre	5	3	8	0	8	1
Reading	22	19	33	13	23	16
Playing a musical instrument	6	9	15	0	3	0
Writing stories, plays, poems	1	1	1	0	0	6
Sculpture, making	1	0	0	0	0	6
Youth club	3	4	1	6	0	15
Computers	8	14	3	2	3	13
Cooking	2	2	1	0	5	0
TOTALS	(667)	(239)	(101)	(58)	(208)	(61)

Interviewees could give more than one response, so percentages will not sum to 100 per cent.
The figures are based on the weighted results (see Chapter 2).

Consistent with the disaggregated results for age, students at school produced the lowest percentage mentioning socialising with friends as a main leisure interest. Relative to their peers in training and employment, students in post-16 full-time education also had a slightly lower percentage for this activity, perhaps reflecting the likelihood of them being surrounded by friends throughout the day and a greater range of available alternative leisure interests and facilities. Obviously, school students had the lowest proportion going to pubs and drinking, but those on training schemes also had a relatively low participation rate in this category. As an alternative activity, this group recorded the highest percentage alluding to clubs, discos, raves and parties.

Several sporting categories were especially popular with interviewees on training schemes. Sports in general, swimming, diving, football, ice-skating, basketball, bowling, snooker, pool, table-tennis, keep fit, aerobics and gymnastics all gained the highest percentage involvement from trainees. Cycling and mountain bikes, fishing, angling and shooting were common pursuits among those in post-16 full-time education. Football was the most popular sport among school-aged students.

Within the 'media-arts: audience' category, school students, trainees and the unemployed had high proportions mentioning watching TV and videos as a key leisure-time activity. Conversely, cinema, which was less frequently cited by these three groups, was most popular with the other two groups: post-16 students and the employed. Likewise, these two groups were the main attenders of theatres, which attracted few or no trainees or the unemployed. Such findings closely mirror the social class results, which indicated that theatre-going was a very middle class pursuit. In a similar vein, reading as a leisure activity was most popular with post-16 students, and least popular with trainees and the unemployed.

Of the 'arts: participation' activities, playing a musical instrument revealed a bias towards post-16 students, and to a lesser extent, school students. There were no cases of trainees or the unemployed referring to it as a leisure-time pursuit. Music-making, writing songs and singing produced similar trends, though the former was less popular with post-16 students and relatively more appealing to school students. Drama, acting and theatre involvement achieved its highest participation rate (6 per cent) among post-16 students, most probably indicating the availability of drama and theatre groups in institutions of higher education. Interestingly, the main participants in writing stories, plays and poems and sculpture and making were to be found among the unemployed group, with minimal or non-existent involvement from other groups.

With regard to 'miscellaneous' activities, while a significant proportion of unemployed respondents mentioned youth club attendance, few or none of the post-16 students or the employed group did so. Computers were mentioned more frequently by school students and the unemployed, increased amounts of spare time perhaps being an important factor. Cars and motorbikes were most popular with trainees and school students. References to cooking were highest among the employed group.

The above trends are summarised in Table 3.13, which presents the breakdown of leisure interests in broad categories by current status. It may be noted that the highest number of interests mentioned was volunteered by the post-16 student group (3.5 per respondent) and the lowest (3.2 per respondent) came from the unemployed group, though the difference is not great.

Table 3.13   Current leisure interests in broad categories by current status

	% of respondents who mentioned one or more in each activity group					
	Total sample	At School	16+ FT Educ.	Training	Employed	Unemployed
Activity Group	%	%	%	%	%	%
Social	53	35	57	65	66	64
Sport	55	57	54	78	48	47
Media-arts: audience	57	55	58	51	62	48
Arts: participation	23	29	34	13	16	19
Miscellaneous	43	54	32	39	37	55
TOTALS	(668)	(240)	(101)	(58)	(208)	(61)

Interviewees could give more than one response, so percentages will not sum to 100 per cent.
These figures are based on the weighted results (see Chapter 2).

The broad category results confirm that 'social' activities were important for all groups except school students. 'Sport' was most popular with trainees – their most frequent leisure activity – and least likely to be mentioned by the employed and unemployed. The unemployed group gave the lowest number of responses relating to engagement in the 'media-arts: audience'. School students and the unemployed group were more involved in 'miscellaneous' activities.

The 'arts: participation' results reveal some interesting differences. Whereas the overall rate of participation in the arts (i.e. those doing a leisure art) for the sample as a whole was just less than one in four (23 per cent), the rate among post-16 students in full-time education was one in three (34 per cent). School students (29 per cent) were the only other group slightly above the percentage for the whole sample. The three remaining groups had relatively lower participation rates, with trainees as low as one in eight (13 per cent) and employees not much higher at 16 per cent. These findings parallel similar trends emerging from the analysis of current leisure interests by social class and educational attainment.

Leisure Interests and Educational Attainment

This section considers the relationship between young people's current leisure interests and their attainment in 16+ examinations, mainly GCEs and GCSEs. It obviously only concerns that section of the sample which had left school when interviewed. As the results show (see Table 3.14), educational attainment is closely related to social class and current status, in that those with greater numbers of GCSEs/GCEs are likely to enter higher education and those with fewer take up the training option.

Table 3.14 Selected leisure interests by educational attainment

Activity	Total sample %	Number of 16+ subjects reported as passed			
		None %	1-3 %	4-6 %	7 or more %
Socialising with friends	40	2	40	45	44
Clubs, discos, raves, parties	13	20	16	13	7
Swimming, diving	12	10	5	14	16
Tennis, badminton, squash	6	3	2	4	12
Football	12	19	11	7	11
Snooker, pool, table-tennis	4	6	8	0	2
Keep fit, aerobics, gymnastics	7	2	6	5	13
Mountaineering, orienteering and camping	5	2	0	8	7
Watching TV, videos	20	20	31	21	17
Cinema	19	13	15	22	23
Theatre	6	0	5	9	8
Reading	23	9	11	29	33
Playing a musical instrument	5	4	2	4	8
Painting, drawing	6	4	2	10	6
Writing stories, poems, plays	1	4	0	0	1
Sewing, fashion, textiles	2	0	0	6	3
Walking, messing around in street, town, woods	5	15	1	4	3
Youth club	3	12	1	0	0
Cubs, Scouts, Guides, Young Farmers	4	0	3	4	6
Cars and motorbikes	5	10	4	3	5
TOTALS	(437)	(101)	(74)	(93)	(152)

Interviewees could give more than one response, so percentages will not sum to 100 per cent.
These figures are based on the weighted results (see Chapter 2).
Approximately four per cent of the relevant post-16 sub-sample (N=437) constituted missing cases for this analysis.

Within the 'social' category, those with no 16+ GCSE or equivalent qualifications were least likely to mention socialising with friends as a salient leisure-time interest, but marginally most likely to refer to clubs, discos, raves and parties. Attendance at the latter diminished with an increase in the number of 16+ subjects passed.

In 'sport', the findings echoed those for social class. Football, for example, was highest for working class respondents and interviewees with no 16+ academic qualifications. The sporting categories most frequently cited by the high attainers group, particularly if compared to those with no qualifications or three or less, included swimming and diving, tennis, badminton, squash, keep fit, aerobics, gymnastics and mountaineering, orienteering and camping. Similarly, of the 'media-arts: audience' activities, cinema, theatre and reading followed the general trend of being mentioned more frequently by respondents with greater numbers of GCSEs/GCEs.

Most probably due to the smaller numbers involved, 'arts: participation' categories did not reveal such clear trends, but, as a general rule, more participants mentioning such artistic activities as playing a musical instrument, painting and drawing and sewing, fashion and textiles were to be found among interviewees with four or more GCSEs/GCEs than those with fewer qualifications.

Among the 'miscellaneous' category, it is noteworthy that virtually all the respondents who cited youth club as a main leisure pursuit were to be located in the group with no GCSEs/GCEs.

Finally, calculations of the average number of responses per respondent for each attainment group produced a noteworthy result. Whereas the averages for those without any 16+ qualifications, with 1-3 and with 4-6 were 3.1, 3.1 and 3.2 respectively, the average for the 7+ group was 3.7 per respondent. This latter average is well above any other rate produced in earlier analyses of other variables (e.g. the previous highest was 3.4 for Social Class I and II). As a result, explanations over and above the influence of social class are required to account for the additional element though care is required since, unlike other analyses, under-17 year olds have been excluded here. It may well be due to the presence of more forthcoming interviewees in this group. Alternatively, it may reflect a genuinely greater number of interests, stimulated by innate ability or by an educative process which has succeeded in stretching young people at school to the extent of nurturing a wider range of activities and pursuits in their leisure time. If the latter, it is pertinent to ask to what extent schools could make this process a more explicit part of their agenda for a wider constituency of young people.

Concluding Comments

Before leaving the analysis of the question posed at the beginning of this section, it seems appropriate to recognise that while the foregoing presentation of the results conveys a detailed picture of the quantity or frequency with which young people engaged in various activities, it does not capture the variations in the quality of leisure-time pursuits experienced by different interviewees. Lacking any sense that activities engendered deep personal meanings for them, some young people struggled hard to list a few things they did in evenings and at weekends. A typical response in this mould was:

> *Nothing much ... watch tele and go shopping with my friends on Saturday.*

In sharp contrast, others enthused about interests which were invested with high degrees of personal significance and which contributed greatly to their perceptions of their own individuality and self-identity. A lighting technician, for example, stressed on several occasions that his hobby, surfing, *'was everything to me'*. A 15 year old boy (the son of an agricultural contractor), who had not succeeded academically at school, gave an animated account of his secretarial work for two local Young Farmers Clubs; an A-level student was excited about all things artistic and in her spare time had recently attended drama workshops, drawn large cartoon stills, played the piano and a guitar, as well as written short stories. In all three of these examples, it was clear that their leisure-time interests were extremely important sources of fulfilment and self-esteem for them. Other interviewees illustrated how less 'participatory' interests in the arts can also be a source of personal meaning and identity:

> *Well, I suppose for me the arts is something that I'm interested in. It's an interest. It's something I'll go and find out about – read, watch, whatever, it's just part of my life. It's the major part of my life, I suppose. Doing things in the evening is going to have something to do with art if I go out. It's just there, you know. There's not physical involvement – it's kind of a framework of what I do.*
> (A 24 year old female in full-time employment)

> *Music is the most important thing in my life. Don't know what sort of a person I'd be without it. If I like it and it wasn't there, that would be a real problem.* (A 21 year old male in full-time education)

Although difficult to quantify, it was not uncommon for interviewers to meet young people who had strong attachments to either 'sports-oriented' or 'arts-oriented' self-images. These identities or definitions of themselves seemed to channel or predispose them towards a particular cluster of activities, and often set up antipathies or, at least, feelings of indifference, towards other types of pursuit. For instance, in response to questions about participation in the arts, many 'sports-oriented' interviewees would reply along the lines of *'No, I'm not into stuff like that, I'm more interested in doing sport'*. Young people with an arts bias expressed similar attitudes to sport.

Statistical analyses bore out these tendencies. Of the 187 respondents who were actively involved in at least one art form, 57 per cent of them did not participate in sport. Even more significantly, of the 389 respondents who participated in at least one sporting activity, only 21 per cent of them were also actively engaged in the arts. Moreover, the results consistently showed that the greater the number of activities young people did in either of the two spheres, the less likely they were to participate in the other.

As the following comment illustrates, part of this tendency can be explained by the simple fact that leisure-time is finite and choices on how to use the limited time available have to be made:

> *There are always opportunity costs. If you're doing the arts, you're not doing something else. If you're aiming for science-based stuff you'll be concentrating on that, so you're bound to do less arts.*
>
> (Male, 24 in employment)

However, limited time in itself does not account for the polarisation of 'sports' and 'arts' activities implicit in many of the interviewees' observations. For example:

> *I get annoyed with the way other people knock children who want to do something in the arts – just because they are into football. I feel people my age don't respect my interests* [arts-based], *but I'm over it.*
>
> (Male, 15 years, Year 10)

In many cases, this polarisation seemed to be bound up with a perception of distinct personality types which encouraged people to be either sports-oriented or arts-oriented. Traits associated with the former included a preference for being '*active*', '*physical*', '*out-of-doors*', '*competitive*' and '*having fun*', while the latter was related to cerebral characteristics such as '*airy-fairy weirdoes being all imaginative and creative*'. If more young people are to be drawn into the arts – or indeed if the aims of the National Curriculum to provide a broad and balanced education are to lead to the development of broad and balanced people – it may well be necessary for such stereotypes to be challenged at every opportunity – both in terms of their inaccuracy as descriptions of participants in both spheres, as well as in terms of the unhelpful boundaries and false dichotomies they perpetuate between sports and the arts.

4. Being Imaginative and Creative

This chapter focuses upon young people's perceptions on whether their evening and weekend leisure-time pursuits, and also what they did during the day (i.e. at work, school, training or college), were felt to be 'imaginative' or 'creative'. This question was deliberately asked before 'the arts' were specifically mentioned. The complex issue of recognition and definition of imaginative and creative activities is acknowledged and discussed.

The reported findings suggest that about half of the sample affirmed their leisure activities as creative or imaginative, and about three out of five viewed some aspect of their studies or work in this way. The chapter analyses which leisure pursuits and which work/school-related activities were nominated as creative or imaginative and then outlines variations in perceptions according to age, current status, gender, ethnicity, social class, educational attainment. It was found that the majority of young people from all social classes saw 'arts participation' as their main creative or imaginative outlet.

Introduction

Early in the interview, and immediately following the question discussed in the previous chapter, young people were asked whether they did anything in the daytime (for school, college, training or work – Item 18) or anything in the evenings/weekends (in their leisure time – Item 19) which they would call 'imaginative' or 'creative'. The responses to these two questions indicate which creative and imaginative activities, studies or work young people were involved in and, importantly, which they perceived as being 'imaginative' or 'creative'.

According to most dictionary definitions, art as '*practical skills, or its application guided by principles, human skill ... to the production of beauty*' is '*a work of creative imagination*'. This creativity and imagination is obviously inherent in the more traditional art forms, but it also needs to be recognised as an important force behind intellectual development, social and technological progression, and cultural renewal. Therefore, by collecting accounts of the creative and imaginative activities young people engage in before the term 'the arts' is mentioned in the interview schedule, it may be possible to gauge the range and direction of young people's creative talents and vitality, including artistic inclinations, without limiting them to formal, narrow and stereotypical images of 'the arts'. The term can be interpreted in a very restrictive and traditional manner: 'carapacial', according to Paul Willis (1990).

Perceptions of Activities as Imaginative or Creative

In response to the straightforward positive/negative questions of whether they did anything in the daytime or evenings/weekends which they would count as imaginative or creative, 61 per cent of the respondents (N = 643) indicated that they did something imaginative or creative during the day (for school, college, training or work), whereas 49 per cent of the respondents (N = 675) reported doing something imaginative or creative in the evenings/weekends (in their leisure time). The higher day-time percentage of those involved in activities they considered imaginative or creative is largely attributable to the fact that a substantial proportion (36 per cent) of those interviewed were at school in Years 9, 10 and 11 and were thus subject to such factors as encouragement and compulsion in a range of subjects. (Further details on this factor are presented later in the chapter.) However, it may not be discouraging that 61 per cent should find some aspect of their studies or work creative or imaginative. Perhaps more discouraging is the finding that only half of the interviewees felt they were involved in leisure-time activities which they considered imaginative or creative. It is worth stressing, though, that this does not necessarily mean that the other half did not do anything imaginative or creative – they may well have done so but considered it inappropriate to define it as such.

By cross-tabulating responses on day-time (Item 18) with those for leisure-time (Item 19) activities, it becomes apparent that less than a third (30 per cent) of respondents felt that they were imaginatively or creatively engaged in both (e.g. at school or work and in the evenings/weekends). Moreover, almost a quarter (23 per cent) of the interviewees indicated that they were not involved in any activities which they deemed imaginative or creative – neither during the day nor at the evenings or weekends.

Before going on to the reasons and factors affecting this degree of involvement, it is important to look in depth at the type of imaginative or creative activities engaged in by young people. Table 4.1 shows the responses to the question (Item 18) on day-time imaginative or creative activities. The upper section of the table refers to school subject areas deemed imaginative or creative, while the lower section presents the frequencies for the coded categories relating to respondents' perceptions of their degrees of creativity at work or in training.

Art (e.g. '*making up drawings*', '*doing paintings in the style of ...*') was the curriculum area most frequently mentioned (by 15 per cent of respondents) as an imaginative or creative activity engaged in. Design and Technology (11 per cent) and English (10 per cent) came next; the former was often related to '*solving problems*' or '*making things*', while the latter was linked to '*writing imaginative stories or essays*', or occasionally '*reading things like plays where you need to be imaginative*'. Music, as a major art form in the curriculum, was cited by only 5 per cent of respondents. Outside of the arts, it is interesting to note that mathematics and science – subjects studied by all students and for which the National Curriculum has emphasised problem-solving investigative skills and predicting-hypothesising processes – were rarely perceived to entail the use of imaginative or creative faculties (each mentioned by only two interviewees). This immediately provokes the question whether our education system does enough, not only to encourage imaginative and creative enterprises, but to foster awareness of the use of such cognitive processes in all areas of the curriculum.

Table 4.1   Day-time activities considered imaginative or creative

Subject area/approach to creativity in work or training	Respondents mentioning each activity %	As % of those taking the subject in Y10-11 %
Subject area associated with creativity		
Art	15	70
Music	5	48
Dance	3	66
Drama	8	40
English	10	27
Humanities	2	-
Design and Technology	11	-
Computers	2	-
PE, sport	1	-
Other subjects (e.g. maths, science, languages)	1	-
Perceived level of creativity in work or training		
Personal inventiveness (serious) in work or training	11	-
Personal inventiveness (trivial) in work or training	1	-
Course, training, work highly imaginative or creative	6	-
TOTAL	(681)	

Interviewees could give more than one response so percentages will not sum to 100 per cent.
These figures are based on the weighted results (see Chapter 2).
As shown in Table 4.5, 39 per cent registered no day-time imaginative or creative activities.

The percentages offered in Table 4.1 are useful in showing where there is most involvement in subjects which young people consider imaginative or creative. Their limitation, however, is that they do not disentangle two separate factors: the degree of actual involvement in a subject and the extent to which it was considered to be imaginative or creative. A subject like dance, for example, may be undertaken by only a small minority of students, yet still be considered highly creative by those taking part in it. Without removing the factor of frequency of involvement, it is impossible to compare actual levels of perceived creativity and imagination. This can be measured for art, music, dance, drama (see Item 33) and English (assuming all Year 10 and 11 students are taking this subject). Hence, for these subjects, Table 4.1 also shows the percentage of respondents in Years 10 and 11 who volunteered that they considered that these subjects were imaginative or creative as a proportion of the number of respondents who said they were studying these subjects (e.g. 40 per cent of those who did drama in Years 10 and 11 mentioned drama as something they do currently which they regard as imaginative or creative activities at school).

Art still remains the most frequently cited curriculum area, with 70 per cent of those taking it perceiving the subject to be imaginative or creative. Dance, which has now gained in significance at 66 per cent, comes a close second. On the other hand, less than half (48 per cent) of those studying music in Years 10 and 11 saw it as imaginative or creative. The significance of English (27 per cent) also falls, if the results are seen as a percentage of young people taking the subject. With the exception of English, however, these results should be treated as indicative and used for illustrative purposes only, because of the small numbers in the sub-samples for each area of the curriculum.

At one level, the results suggest that many young people interpret the concepts of 'imaginative' and 'creative' activities in quite a literal and concrete way. Their responses tend to focus on material rather than intellectual or emotional inventiveness: e.g. creating a visual object in art, the physical activity of dance, or the making of 3-D functional artefacts in technology. To this extent, the findings raise the issue of the extent to which all areas of the curriculum, not merely the arts-oriented subjects, could be doing more to develop and raise an explicit awareness of the importance of imagination and creativity as a less tangible and more cognitive quality. At a more direct level, the results certainly pose the challenging question of whether the teaching of, and the curriculum specifications for, subjects such as music, English and drama are failing to engage students' imagination and creativity, as it could be argued they should.

So far, the emphasis has been on the consideration of the perceived creativity at school – as explained later, students in Years 9, 10 and 11 formed the largest section responding in the affirmative to the question on day-time activities. Table 4.1 also includes trainees and employees who felt that their 'day-time' work engendered an element of imagination and creativity: 11 per cent of all respondents considered that their work or training programme was invested with a serious degree of personal inventiveness (e.g. shopkeepers and waiters referred to the need to be imaginative in their service to customers; secretaries liked to produce documents with a pleasing lay-out; nannies took pride in thinking of imaginative activities to do with the children in their care). In addition, 6 per cent of all respondents mentioned work, training programmes or higher education courses which demanded significant levels of imagination and creativity (e.g. graphic designers, hairdressing trainees, a film director, and a fine arts student).

Among the sub-sample (N = 58) of young people on training schemes, the occupational category with the highest proportion of trainees considering their work to entail imagination and creativity was skilled construction. Of those that saw some kind of personal inventiveness in their job, the largest groups were health and child care and secretarial work. Once again, the results partly reflect the preponderance with which young people entered specific occupational areas but, as with secretarial work, for several interviewees, especially those who liked their work, there was a certain amount of psychological resistance to acceptance of a view of their job as an occupation which allowed for few creative opportunities. They appeared to see subjective significance and meanings in jobs which, looked at from a more objective stance, appeared to be routinised and closely prescribed by the directives of supervisors.

Of those that indicated a high degree of creativity in their work, most were employed within the occupational category of literary, artists and sports. This group included journalists, designers, dancers, musicians and camera operators. Other prevalent groups were professional occupations such as teachers, trainee architects and social workers, as well as catering, travel and leisure/recreational workers.

Turning to leisure-time pursuits, the main area of youth activity considered to be imaginative or creative (see Table 4.2) was painting and drawing, which was cited by 11 per cent of all respondents. (It is interesting to put this finding alongside the later one that the 'visual arts' were the most common definition of 'the arts' proffered by young people.) The musical categories of playing a musical instrument and music-making and writing songs, along with writing stories or poems, were the next most frequently mentioned imaginative or creative pursuits. Other 'arts: participation' activities mentioned included sewing, fashion and textiles and drama, acting and theatre, and sculpture, making – all less than 5 per cent.

In the 'media-arts: audience' broad category, reading stood out as the activity most likely to be perceived as imaginative or creative by this sample of young people. Listening to music was referred to by only 1 per cent, cinema had fewer mentions, watching TV and videos still less and going to the theatre hardly any. In view of the frequencies with which listening to music and watching TV and videos were mentioned as general leisure-time pursuits in response to the question discussed in the previous chapter (see Table 3.1), it is difficult to avoid the conclusion that they were not referred to in replies to this question (Item 19) because they were not perceived to engender an imaginative or creative response or interpretation..

The only 'sporting', 'social' and 'miscellaneous' activity to be regarded as imaginative or creative by more than 3 per cent was cooking.

Table 4.2   Leisure activities considered imaginative or creative

Activity	Respondents mentioning activities %	Degree of perceived creativity as % of total involvement in activity %
Playing musical instruments	5	69
Music making, writing songs	5	97
Singing	1	44
Dancing (unspecified)	1	42
Drama, acting, theatre	3	86
Painting, drawing	11	88
Photography	1	64
Story, poem writing	5	100
Fashion sewing, textiles	4	82
Sculpture	3	91
Other arts	2	80
TV, films, videos	1	2
Cinema	1	5
Recorded music, radio	1	9
Reading	4	18
Pubs and drinking	1	3
Cubs, Scouts, Girl Guides	1	19
Computer games, club	1	18
Working, baby sitting	1	12
Cooking	4	73
Educational courses, activities	1	33
Practical making	1	87
Football	1	8
Aerobics, gymnastics	1	3
Boxing, wrestling, judo	-	9
TOTAL	(681)	

Interviewees could give more than one response, so percentages will not sum to 100 per cent.
These figures are based on the weighted results (see Chapter 2).
As shown in Table 4.5, 51 per cent registered no leisure-time imaginative or creative activity.

It is clear then that, according to young people themselves, participating in the arts was the most important outlet for young people's creativity and imagination, with about one in three (32 per cent) of all respondents referring to at least one arts: participation activity (see Table 4.3). Moreover, the vast majority of references were to traditional art forms. This percentage contrasts markedly with the 6 per cent for 'media-arts: audience' category, of which reading was the most prevalent. Similarly, sport and socialising were seldom perceived as imaginative or creative activities.

It is noteworthy that the participation rate for young people doing one or more arts activities deemed imaginative or creative (32 per cent) is higher than the corresponding rate which emerged from the question on young people's leisure interests, in response to which 23 per cent referred to at least one 'arts: participation' activity (see previous chapter on Item 17 and Table 3.1). This is understandable given that Item 17 asked interviewees about their main leisure interests and centred on all activities rather than the more specific probe on 'imaginative and creative' ones.

Table 4.3   Leisure activities in broad categories considered imaginative or creative

Activity Group	Respondents who mentioned at least one activity
	%
Social	0
Sport	3
Media-arts: audience	6
Arts: participation	32
Miscellaneous activities	14
TOTAL	(681)

Interviewees could give more than one response, so percentages will not sum to 100 per cent. The figures are based on the weighted results (see Chapter 2).
As shown in Table 4.5, 51 per cent registered no leisure-time imaginative or creative activity.

Before the above figures are explored further, it is interesting to compare the frequencies of reference to detailed categories deemed imaginative or creative with the percentages of those who actually took part in a given activity, hence removing the frequency of involvement factor. This has been calculated by taking those mentioning the activity in Item 19b (leisure-time imaginative/creative activity) as a percentage of those mentioning it at least once in Item 17 (leisure-time activities) or those in Item 19b. The results of this analysis are presented in Column 2 of Table 4.2 above, though it should be reiterated that, as with similar percentages in Table 4.1, the calculations are based on very small sub-samples and, thus, should be used for illustrative purposes only.

The analysis suggests that young people still appear to be quite traditional in their perception of activities they would count as imaginative or creative. For example, all of those who wrote stories, poems or plays in their leisure time considered it an imaginative or creative activity. Similarly, 97 per cent of those who did music-making or writing songs did so, in contrast to 69 per cent who played musical instruments. Sculpture or making is now brought to the forefront at 91 per cent, followed by painting and drawing at 88 per cent, and drama, acting and theatre at 86 per cent. Significantly, singing and dancing were least likely to be considered imaginative or creative.

With respect to 'media-arts: audience' categories, reading remained the most important (18 per cent) followed by a drop to 9 per cent for recorded music and radio. Watching TV and videos, theatre and cinema were the least likely to be adjudged imaginative or creative.

'Sport' and 'miscellaneous' activities in general ranged from 3 per cent (aerobics/gymnastics) to 18 per cent for computers and the scouts and guides. Again, the exception was cookery with a high percentage of 73 per cent, along with the making of practical things (87 per cent). 'Social' activities remained comparatively low.

It appears from these findings that young people's perceptions of what counts as imaginative or creative activities were very much oriented towards the accepted areas of the formal arts, though within these there was no doubt that alternatives and diversions from traditional forms were evident. At face value, the questions have not succeeded in showing up any convincing evidence of the phenomenon described in *Moving Culture* (Willis, 1990). By and large, imagination and creativity, as perceived by the young themselves, is not seen to any significant extent in everyday commonplace activities other than cooking. According to this evidence, those like Willis and others who maintain that young people's everyday informal behaviour is rich in vibrancy and creativity would need to provide data on why young people fail to recognise the level of imagination and creativity which is imputed by these researchers. In short, the proposition advanced by Willis would seem to require a false consciousness dimension. However, there is clearly a need for further analyses of these results, because when social class and attainment in 16+ examinations are taken into account, there appears to be a possible – though relatively minor – shift in perception of what counts as imaginative and creative activities among some interviewees with working class backgrounds and low attainment in GCSEs. (This will be discussed later in the section.) For the time being, what may be drawn from the results is that perhaps more emphasis could be placed on encouraging a wider appreciation of the importance of imagination or creativity in the 'consumption' of arts, rather than it being perceived as merely a mechanistic, passive and routine process.

At this point, it may be useful to summarise some of the key findings from these two questions by comparing the results for day-time activities with those for leisure-time. The fact that 'day-time' activities are influenced by a higher degree of institutional provision and compulsion, while leisure-time pursuits are more voluntary, is noteworthy. Art, mainly painting and drawing, was the most prevalent imaginative and creative activity for both daytime and leisure. Technology and the making of practical products also had high degrees of involvement in the daytime as well as leisure. On the other hand, music was considered to be less creative or imaginative at school than in young people's leisure time. A similar comparison could be made for English and the writing of stories and poems. Likewise with drama, which was also held to be more creative and imaginative in leisure time. Dance was an interesting exception to this trend in that it was more likely to be considered imaginative and creative at school. 'Dancing (unspecified)' in leisure time was rated as imaginative or creative by only 42 per cent, perhaps because much of it was viewed as light-hearted and social dancing in clubs, parties and raves rather than an outlet for artistic self-expression. However, creative dancing, ballet or tap was even lower at 28 per cent, perhaps reflecting an emphasis on the practising of simple and repetitive routines in many ballet and tap lessons. As for music, English and drama, the findings give rise to the issue of whether an appropriate balance in lessons and workshops is being struck between providing young people with the necessary technical knowledge and skills and stimulating an imaginative and creative engagement in the art form.

To take the analysis a step further, the responses to questions on day-time and leisure-time activities deemed imaginative or creative have been cross-tabulated with a number of key independent variables. For the first of these, the responses to Item 18 and 19 have been broken down by the interviewee's current status. The age cross-tabulation which follows directly after this section is closely related to current status.

Current Status

Understandably, the young person's current status is a major factor determining the levels of opportunity to be imaginative or creative in the daytime (see Table 4.4).

The table demonstrates that three-quarters (75 per cent) of the interviewees in Years 9, 10 and 11 at school indicated that they did an activity – nearly always a subject – which they would call imaginative or creative. Given the opportunities provided by compulsory schooling, it may be a cause for concern that a quarter felt that they didn't do anything at school which could be considered imaginative or creative. For those in full-time education (post-16), the tendency for increased specialisation and lack of breadth in curriculum coverage would suggest that there would be less chance of students considering their subjects imaginative or creative. Nevertheless,a relatively high figure of 62 per cent did so. In comparison to those in full-time education or training, young people in employment were less likely to view their day-time work as including a creative or imaginative dimension (47 per cent) (see the earlier discussion of Table 4.2 for a description of the occupational areas of trainees and employees most likely to be associated with imaginative or creative outlets). Only a quarter of unemployed respondents (25 per cent) reported doing anything imaginative or creative during the day (e.g. in voluntary work, hobbies or personal inventiveness in job-hunting).

Table 4.4   Existence of imaginative or creative day-time activities by current status

Any creative day-time activities?	Total sample %	At school Years 9-11 %	16+ FT education %	Training scheme %	In Employment %	Unemployed %
Yes	61	75	62	65	47	25
No	39	25	38	35	53	75
TOTALS	(628)	(239)	(92)	(58)	(208)	(31)

These figures are based on the weighted results (see Chapter 2).

Turning briefly to the specific imaginative or creative activities mentioned by young people in different positions, those at school in Years 9, 10 and 11 selected a wide range of subjects, but the main ones were art, English, technology and drama. The same four areas of the curriculum figured highly in the responses given by those in full-time post-16 education. Subjects such as mathematics, science, languages, social sciences and computers were hardly mentioned by either group of students. Half of those in employment who replied in the affirmative gave examples of serious personal inventiveness in their work, while just under a third were in jobs which entailed a significant degree of creativity and imagination (see earlier discussion for main types of occupation).

Age

As Table 4.5 shows, the age of the interviewee has an effect on the frequencies with which young people felt they engaged in an imaginative or creative activity during both the daytime and leisure time. It also influences the type of such activities they were involved in. As suggested in Chapter 3, this could be due to shifts in the attitudes of different age-cohorts or, more likely, the effects of maturation. Obviously, the current status of the interviewee (see previous section) is a major underlying factor affecting the day-time results.

The day-time frequencies revealed a slight 'U' shaped relationship with age. In keeping with the figures produced for the school group (in Table 4.4), three-quarters (74 per cent) of the under-17 year old group mentioned some school-based activities, nearly always subjects, which they deemed imaginative or creative. Compulsion, opportunities and encouragement in schools are clearly key factors in achieving this relatively high percentage. In contrast, the 17-20 year old group had the lowest percentage responding in the affirmative (49 per cent). The majority of this age band were in employment, many in routine and menial jobs, which allowed little scope for discretion and creativity. Consequently, the negative responses of this group, coupled with the replies of the unemployed, were sufficient to hold down the 17-20 year olds' percentage to 49 per cent in spite of the high percentages for those in this age group on training schemes and in 16+ full-time education. Within the 21-24 year old group, the percentage indicating that their day-time activities included imaginative or creative elements was 58 per cent. This was almost certainly caused by a greater proportion of employed respondents in this age bracket, many of whom were undertaking more professional and skilled work as a result of gaining qualifications or promotion. This interpretation is supported by the findings relating to the type of work activities considered imaginative or creative by different age bands. In contrast to 6 per cent of the 17-20 year group, 16 per cent of the over-21 year old group described their work as entailing high levels of creative and imaginative activities. Similarly, compared to 15 per cent of the 17-20 year group, 24 per cent of the older group found 'self-generated personal inventiveness' in their work.

Table 4.5   Existence of imaginative or creative activities by age

Any creative day-time activities?	Total sample %	Under-17 %	Age 17-20 %	21-24 %
Yes	61	74	49	58
No	39	26	51	42
TOTALS	(644)	(261)	(265)	(118)
Any creative leisure-time activities?				
Yes	49	49	44	60
No	51	51	56	40
TOTALS	(676)	(261)	(284)	(131)

These figures are based on the weighted results (see Chapter 2).

Turning to leisure-time activities deemed imaginative or creative, the under-17s (49 per cent) had a similar percentage registering involvement in some such activities as the 17-20 year old group (44 per cent) (see Table 4.5). However, among the over-21 year old group, there was a bigger proportion answering in the affirmative (60 per cent). In exploring the reasons why a greater share of the older group should participate in imaginative or creative pursuits, it is interesting to consider the results for the types of creative activity in broad categories disaggregated by age. The only broad category which produced significant differences according to age was 'arts: participation': whereas only one in four (24 per cent) of 17-20 year old interviewees were involved in imaginative or creative arts activities, a striking one in two (50 per cent) of the 21-24 year old group were so involved. Data on involvement in the detailed categories (deemed imaginative or creative) for 'arts: participation' show that, compared to the 17-20 year old group, the oldest group had higher rates of participation in playing a musical instrument, music-making and writing songs, photography, writing stories, plays and poems, sculpture, making and other arts, such as video-making. It is important to stress that these apparent increases in 'arts: participation' categories for the over- 21 year olds were not evident in the responses to the question on main leisure interests (Item 17). For some reason(s) the question under current discussion (Item 19), on leisure-time activities deemed imaginative or creative, elicited a particularly positive response in the 'arts: participation' category from the over-21 year old group. While the difference between the proportion of 17-20 year olds mentioning at least one 'arts: participation' activity as a main interest (Item 17) and those in same age group citing at least one 'arts: participation' activity as imaginative or creative (Item 19) was 6 per cent, the corresponding difference for the over-21 year old group was 26 per cent.

To tease out the possible reasons for this trend in 'arts: participation', it is helpful to consider some examples of responses from a few 21-24 year old interviewees. Firstly, it was frequently the case that, whereas in response to Item 17, interviewees listed their main (i.e. their most significant) interests and hobbies, Item 19 allowed respondents to allude to activities which did not constitute a 'hobby' and which were often undertaken quite rarely and irregularly. Perhaps because of their greater number of years and therefore experiences, the over-21 year old group seemed to include more respondents who were able to say they 'dabble' in something '*every now and then, when there was nothing else to do*'. This, for example, was a quite typical response to Item 19 (like most of the other examples given below it refers to an arts activity not identified in Item 17):

> *I wrote a short story a few weeks ago. My parents thought it was good*
> *enough to publish. I don't think it was. It was just something to do*
> *because I was bored.* (Female, 21, graduate seeking work)

There were also examples of young people, who having replied to Item 17 by mentioning 'media-arts: audience' categories as key interests (e.g. cinema), responded to Item 19 by describing how this interest had developed over the years to the point where they had managed to find ways of contributing in a more participatory way to the media or art form they had earlier referred to as a spectator role (e.g. making films and videos). Furthermore, there were signs that because more of the over-21 year olds had achieved more settled employment, and in the absence of easily accessible arts societies and facilities (such as those commonly found in institutions of higher education), they were taking a more pro-active and individualistic approach to their leisure, including participation in creative activities. Item 19 produced examples of a social worker, for instance, who '*wrote creative stories*'; a teacher '*wrote fiction*'; a students' union president did '*photography and jewellery-making*' but none of these activities were mentioned as main interests in response to Item 17.

Another factor which further increased the proportion of the over-21s who reported doing imaginative or creative artistic activities in their leisure time was the greater number of parents in this age group. Mothers and fathers often felt that sharing such artistic activities as painting, drawing, music-making and story-telling with their children involved imagination and creativity.

Most significantly, there were clear signs that young people in this age band were more willing than those in the 17-20 year old group to join societies, clubs and projects which could lead to participation in creative enterprises. A secretary (female, 24) had become very active in a group called Rotoact, which led to her involvement in video-making (e.g. writing story boards, filming etc.). An unemployed male (24), who had hardly ever done anything artistic before, described how he had recently participated in a sculpture project which involved building a facade of a Greek temple out of old tyres (featured in a television programme). By way of another illustration, an unemployed male (21), who was expelled from school when he was 15 for '*hoiking a teacher out of a classroom window*', had recently had a collection of poems published, having been encouraged to try writing poetry by a '*good wife*' (i.e. a lady) from a local community arts project.

Collectively, the above examples suggest several reasons why respondents in the over-21 year old group were able to mention more imaginative or creative arts activities: this group displayed an increased tendency to 'dabble' in art forms, including the occasional 're-visiting' of artistic activities they had enjoyed earlier in their lives; their higher education and employment patterns were more settled and less demanding, thus allowing time to organise their leisure time more purposively, often without institutional spoon-feeding; occupational and parenthood roles often stimulated involvement in the arts; and, most interestingly, after what was for many young people in the 17-20 year old category, a reaction against the institutional control experienced through compulsory schooling, the 21 and over group showed signs of a greater willingness to engage in organised events, societies and support agencies on a voluntary basis. It should be stressed, however, that this interpretation is very tentative, since a longitudinal cohort study is required to substantiate these hypotheses – the 17-20 year olds in this study could turn out to be dissimilar to the present 21-24 year old group.

Nevertheless, these findings, if confirmed, pose serious policy questions for arts funders and providers. Should, for example, youth arts provision attempt to sustain or stimulate involvement though the difficult 17-20 stage or could resources be better spent on the apparently more receptive over-21 year old group? Whatever the age group, how can arts funders and providers encourage young people to develop their sporadic 'dabbling' in imaginative or creative activities into fuller and more sustained experiences in arts participation?

Gender Variations in the responses to Items 18 and 19 according to gender may be associated with a wide range of factors: different interests and levels of enjoyment in specific activities, different levels of motivation, different levels and types of peer pressure to conform or deviate, different opportunities and different stereotyping influences. All these variations could affect the degree of involvement in activities for each sex, as well as the extent to which they may be perceived as imaginative or creative.

There were no significant differences in the proportions of the sexes that indicated involvement in leisure-time or day-time activities which were deemed to be imaginative or creative. There were, however, important differences in the type of activities considered imaginative or creative by each sex (though, as with all the cross-tabulations by key independent variables, it is difficult to establish whether these differences are due to variations in what is perceived to be imaginative and creative or to different levels of involvement).

For day-time activities (mainly work or educational courses), while males were more likely to nominate technology, and, to a lesser extent, computers as imaginative or creative, females were more likely to signal art, music, dance and drama as more imaginative or creative. Once again, it is noticeable that for leisure-time pursuits the enthusiasm and creativity of male young people for music-making, writing songs, playing a music instrument and singing have not been harnessed and developed in day-time activities (e.g. music lessons at school).

For leisure activities deemed imaginative or creative, males were more likely to mention indoor games and models, computers, football and, significantly music-making and writing songs (most probably linked to male preferences for playing in bands), while females were more likely to refer to cooking, dance categories, painting and drawing, and markedly, sewing, fashion and textiles. Reflecting these trends, females had a slightly higher participation rate in at least one imaginative or creative art form (34 per cent) compared to males (30 per cent).

Urban and Rural Areas As explained in the previous chapter, the difference between interviewees residing in urban or rural areas was greater for 'media-arts: audience' leisure activities than for 'arts: participation' pursuits, in which rural respondents had a slightly higher involvement rate (29 per cent participated in at least one art form) compared to their urban peers (21 per cent). It may be that ease of access to urban amenities affects spectator roles more than participatory ones, and that social class influences the different rates of involvement in the arts in that a relatively higher proportion of respondents from middle class families were to be found in rural areas. How, then, did perceptions of the extent to which leisure-time and day-time activities were considered imaginative or creative vary according to whether interviewees lived in urban or rural areas?

The results show that, although there was no difference in the overall proportions of urban and rural young people registering a day-time imaginative or creative activity, at school urban students were more likely to see English and the humanities as imaginative or creative, whereas rural students were more likely to see art and drama as such. For those in work or on post-16 full-time educational courses, a slightly higher percentage of urban (8 per cent) compared to rural (3 per cent) respondents suggested that their day-time activities entailed significant levels of creativity.

A higher percentage of urban interviewees (51 per cent) compared to their rural peers (43 per cent) mentioned at least one leisure activity which they judged to be imaginative or creative. Differences in the kinds of leisure activities considered imaginative or creative mirrored the differences identified in day-time activities: painting and drama and sculpture and making were mentioned by a higher percentage of rural respondents, while such activities as writing stories, poems and plays and reading were more likely to be cited by urban interviewees, as was sewing, fashion and textiles. Taken as a broad category, 'arts: participation' had very similar proportions of urban (32 per cent) and rural (31 per cent) young people registering at least one arts activity as imaginative or creative. Finally, the 'miscellaneous' category displayed an urban orientation, with such activities as cars and motorbikes, youth club, computers and general items being more likely to be seen as imaginative or creative by urban respondents – though the small numbers involved restrict the confidence that can be placed in this trend. The evidence suggests that the phenomenon of perceiving creative significance in everyday 'non-artistic' activities may be more likely to surface in urban cultures (although evinced by only a small minority: 16 per cent of urban compared to 10 per cent of rural interviewees cited at least one 'miscellaneous' activity).

Ethnicity

As with most of the other independent variables, the effects of ethnicity were not apparent in the proportions indicating an involvement in imaginative or creative day-time or leisure-time activities – which were virtually the same for white Europeans and the ethnic minorities – but in the kind of activities these two groups mentioned. For example, students (pre- and post-16) from a white European background were more likely to list English and art as creative subjects, while those from the ethnic minorities were marginally more inclined to mention dance. Such findings prompt questions as to whether the National Curriculum specifications for English and art are sufficiently encouraging of literary genres, visual imagery and symbolic traditions which would have cultural and imaginative appeal to members of ethnic minorities.

Consistent with these leanings among day-time activities there were significant variations of leisure-time involvement, especially with regard to the 'arts: participation' broad category. Whereas one in three white European respondents (33 per cent) mentioned at least one imaginative or creative 'arts: participation' activity, only one in four (25 per cent) of the ethnic minorities did so. In particular, the ethnic minorities were under-represented in painting and drawing, drama, acting and theatre involvement, music-making and writing songs, writing stories, poems and plays and playing a music instrument. The only art forms to show a slight bias towards higher ethnic minority involvement were dance and sewing, fashion and textiles. Cooking was also more likely to be considered an imaginative or creative activity by interviewees from the ethnic minorities sub-sample.

Social Class

The independent variable of social class, along with that of educational attainment (see next section), was found to have had an important bearing on the distribution of young people's leisure-time activities (see Chapter 3). As illustrated in Table 4.6, social class also appears to have influenced the proportions of young people indicating participation in imaginative or creative day-time and leisure-time interests.

Table 4.6   Existence of imaginative or creative activities by social class

| Any creative day-time activities? | Total sample % | Social Class | | |
		I & II %	III (N & M) %	IV & V %
Yes	61	68	57	63
No	39	32	43	37
TOTALS	(644)	(100)	(344)	(200)
Any creative leisure-time activities?				
Yes	49	57	47	48
No	51	43	53	52
TOTALS	(676)	(104)	(358)	(214)

These figures are based on the weighted results (see Chapter 2).

The results show a 'U' shape relationship between the three class-based groups and the extent to which mentions were made of imaginative or creative day-time activities. Social Class I and II respondents registered the highest percentage (68 per cent), followed by the Social Class IV and V group (63 per cent), with a dip for the Social Class III respondents to 57 per cent. The main contributors to this U-shaped relationship were students' (pre- and post-16) varying attitudes to English, humanities and art. The professional (I and II) and partly/unskilled (IV and V) groups were more likely to see these subjects as imaginative or creative than the middle skilled (III) group, which was more likely to so view technology as imaginative or creative. Given that the actual involvement in English and art in Year 10 and 11 was similar for all these groups, it seems probable that these variations were due to differences in perceptions as to what counts as imaginative or creative. The qualitative accounts garnered through the interviews suggested that these perceptual differences, which appear to be associated with social class and educational attainment, often centred on contrasting views on the standards implicit in definitions of what counts as 'imaginative' or 'creative'. Many middle class (I and II) respondents, for example, displayed a comparatively more rigorous and discerning view of activities which may be deemed 'imaginative or creative' (e.g. original responses to, and interpretation of, literature, creative approaches to texts, the production of structured and completed stories or paintings). In contrast, the responses of several interviewees in the partly/unskilled (IV and V) group were less demanding in their criteria of what counts as 'imaginative or creative', with more widespread references to commonplace activities (e.g. writing a letter, doodling, drawing a fantasy picture). Contrasting allusions to music-making as an imaginative or creative activity provide another example of these perceptual differences in criteria. Interviewees in the partly/unskilled (IV and V) group were more likely to consider playing with a toy musical instrument while child-minding as 'imaginative or creative', whereas those in the professional category, were not so likely to consider they were being 'imaginative or creative' until a song or a piece of music had been produced. In between these two extremes came respondents in the skilled category (which recorded the lowest percentage of day-time imaginative or creative activities). Their lower showing could be attributed to a tendency for more interviewees in this group to be aware of the 'higher' standards associated with being 'imaginative or creative', yet consider that their own involvement in such activities does not approximate those standards and criteria. In addition, there were signs that more young people in this group had an instrumental, applied and functional perception of 'imaginative or creative' activities, preferring to see 'creativity', which was often equated with 'problem-solving' outlets, in technology and design rather than English and the arts.

With respect to leisure-time activities, Table 4.6 shows that imaginative or creative pursuits were more frequently mentioned by interviewees from the Social Class I and II respondents. Furthermore, and most interestingly, 44 per cent of this group – compared to only 29 per cent of the other two groups – referred to at least one 'arts: participation' activity which they deemed imaginative or creative. The following 'arts: participation' activities were most popular with the professional group and received fewer mentions by the other two groups: playing a musical instrument, music-making and writing songs, drama, painting and drawing, photography, writing stories, poems and plays. In contrast, 'sporting' activities considered imaginative or creative were cited most by interviewees in the skilled (Social Class III) group and 'miscellaneous' activities most by respondents in the partly/unskilled group (IV and V). These results are consistent with the interpretation that, whilst a small minority of young people - with a slight bias towards those with working class backgrounds - perceived imaginative and creative potential in everyday, social and sporting activities, the majority in all three social class groups – but Social Class I and II respondents in particular – saw 'arts: participation' pursuits as the main imaginative and creative outlet. The 'moving culture' thesis (Willis, 1990) was thus only evident in the accounts of a very small minority, slightly more prevalent in working class cultures, and, from the participants' perspectives, appeared to be based upon a less rigorous criteria of what counts as 'imaginative and creative' than that typically applied by their middle class peers.

Educational Attainment

The analyses of the results for Items 18 and 19 by educational attainment were very similar to those for social class, especially for day-time activities, where an even more pronounced 'U' shaped relationship emerged. Involvement in day-time activities considered imaginative or creative varied from 5 per cent of respondents with seven or more GCSE/GCE qualifications to 44 per cent of those with between four and six and to 36 per cent of those with three or less. For those without 16+ qualifications, the percentage was 57 per cent. It is suggested that the most plausible reasons for these results are the perceptual shifts and variations in criteria posited in the previous section.

Concluding Comments

The section closes with a brief outline of some additional analyses carried out on the responses relating to day-time and leisure-time activities. To explore whether a 'two cultures' syndrome influenced the extent to which young people saw activities as imaginative or creative, sub-sets of (natural) science-oriented and 'arts oriented' (post-16) interviewees were created. Scientists are traditionally thought of as rational and logical people, but are not renowned, at least not from the popular stereotypical view, for their imagination. Consequently, it was considered worthwhile to investigate how young people with a science bias answered those questions in comparison to those with an arts bias.

Differences between the two groups did emerge. Of those whose GCSE/GCE qualifications displayed a science orientation (e.g. mathematics, general science, 'separate' sciences and technology), 41 per cent registered imaginative or creative day-time activities and 47 per cent did the same for leisure-time activities. The corresponding proportions for arts-oriented respondents (e.g. English, history, humanities, art and music) were 63 and 54 per cent. The differences give rise for some concern and the interviewees themselves gave testimony to the beneficial effects the arts may have on young people's personal, social and intellectual development that science and technology subjects find difficult to provide:

I don't think you can be regarded as learned or intelligent if you have no interest in the arts. (Male, 15 year old)

The arts are very important in today's society. As technology increases, the creativity is coming out of it and it's important to remember the human aspect of life and to have the balance.
(Male, 22 year old, Air Traffic Controller)

5. Participation In Specific Art Forms

This chapter focuses on responses to a closed question which asked interviewees to gauge their level of involvement, during their leisure time and also during day-time work/school/college, in some 17 pre-specified arts activities. The chapter presents a rank order of the art forms receiving the highest percentage of nominations for 'a great deal' or 'some' involvement (as opposed to 'little' or 'none'). In this ranking, dance, drawing/sketching and photography were the most frequently mentioned leisure-time participatory arts activities, while writing and drawing emerged as the two most cited arts activities at school. Statistical data, with accompanying illustrative qualitative material, are provided on these and a number of the other most commonly undertaken art forms – such as computer graphics, printing, drama and graffiti art.

Introduction

Thus far, the report has examined the main interests and activities of young people (including those they considered to be creative or imaginative), through questions that were open-ended and were aimed at collecting evidence which would provide a backdrop against which their arts participation could be set in context. In this chapter, analyses of responses to Item 24 in the interview schedule (see Appendix 1) are offered. Unlike the previous ones, this question was a closed item, and asked the interviewees to gauge their degree of involvement in a list of pre-specified art forms over the last year. The level of participation will thus appear high, as this form of questioning clearly 'prompted' for any arts participation, whereas the open-ended questions allowed interviewees to refer to those interests which came most readily to mind.

Interviewees were asked to indicate their degree of involvement in each art form through reference to a four point scale: (i) a great deal, (ii) some, (iii) a little, and (iv) none. Having responded to this closed item, respondents were given the opportunity in the next question (Item 25) to talk more openly about one art form in particular. The qualitative accounts generated by this question have been used to illustrate and widen the quantitative findings produced by Item 24.

The question looked at the degree of participation in 17 art forms during leisure time and also during the daytime (e.g. school/college/work etc.). Because of the fundamental influence of current status on the latter in particular, the overall frequencies and disaggregated results by current status are shown in detail in large tables (see Tables 5.2 and 5.3). These tables provide an overview of the responses to Item 24, but for ease of reading they are followed by the key points produced for each of the separate art forms. These summaries also contain analyses of the responses by key independent variables, as well as material from subsequent qualitative questions (especially Item 25). However, before considering each of the 17 art forms in turn, since school is the main area of day-time arts participation and an important arena for youngsters' art involvement, Table 5.1 displays the overall rank order of participation in leisure-time art forms for the full sample and the rank order of participation in day-time art forms for those still at school (i.e. the under-17 year olds).

Table 5.1   Art forms in rank order of participation in leisure time and at school (daytime)

	Leisure time			Daytime/school	
Art forms	% of all respondents indicating 'a great deal' or 'some'	Total answering each item	Art forms	% of all respondents indicating 'a great deal' or 'some'	Total answering each item
Dance	36	(678)	Story, poetry writing	82	(239)
Drawing, sketching	36	(678)	Drawing, sketching	66	(237)
Photography	32	(677)	Painting	49	(239)
Music-making	23	(680)	Drama, theatre	41	(238)
Story, poetry writing	23	(681)	Computer graphics	34	(238)
Arts events	21	(667)	Music-making	27	(239)
Painting	17	(680)	Sculpture	24	(238)
Computer graphics	15	(677)	Printing	23	(232)
Drama, theatre	14	(680)	Textiles	18	(239)
Fashion	13	(680)	Arts events	17	(234)
Video	9	(681)	Dance	15	(239)
Graffiti art	7	(680)	Fashion	13	(239)
Scratching, dubbing	7	(681)	Photography	7	(236)
Textiles	5	(680)	Graffiti art	6	(239)
Sculpture	5	(678)	Video	6	(239)
Jewellery-making	5	(681)	Jewellery-making	5	(239)
Printing	4	(674)	Scratching, dubbing	2	(239)

These figures are based on the weighted results (see Chapter 2).

It should firstly be reiterated that participation will appear higher than in Item 17, not only because this question is not restricted to main interests, but also because the art forms listed within it are very much open to the interviewees' interpretation. Furthermore, interpretation of the degree of their participation is also subjective. For example, the occasional doodle may be interpreted as 'a little' or 'some' drawing and holiday snaps as 'some' photography. Dance will often include dancing at parties or discos.

Thus cautioned, in leisure time, dance emerged as the activity with the highest level of involvement, along with drawing and sketching - drawing and sketching clearly being the most popular aspect of the previously used category, painting and drawing, in Item 17 (painting being 19 per cent lower). For this present item, drawing and sketching included references to sketching for technology and design. Undoubtedly, photography at 32 per cent was inflated by the number of allusions to snapshots as opposed to photography as a serious art form. The next most popular forms were poetry and story writing and music-making. Arts events featured surprisingly high up the list next, at 21 per cent, and higher than painting, which was perceived to be more time-consuming and needing more materials than drawing and sketching.

In contrast, the activities most participated in at school were those most commonly timetabled, and this clearly reflected the level of students' option choices at Years 10 and 11– e.g. story and poetry writing in English was highest (82 per cent). English being a core area of the curriculum, this was not remarkable but perhaps more surprising was the relatively high ranking for this activity in young people's leisure time (23 per cent). Drawing and sketching was next at 66 per cent, followed by painting at 49 per cent. Drama or theatre and computer graphics were both more common than music-making. Overall, it was clear that the ordering of these art forms reflected the availability and opportunity to participate in them at school rather than being a direct and sole indication of their popularity (e.g. scratching and dubbing being the lowest with only 2 per cent doing it 'a great deal' or 'some').

Having established the general ranking of art forms, Tables 5.2 and 5.3 show the results for each activity in detail and disaggregate the frequencies by current status both in leisure and daytime.

Table 5.2   Levels of day-time participation in different art forms

Art Forms	Total sample %	School (Y9-11) %	16+FE %	Training Scheme %	Employed %
Painting					
A great deal	11	20	5	12	3
Some	16	29	18	0	4
A little	13	18	14	3	10
None	60	33	63	85	83
(N = 646)					
Drawing, sketching					
A great deal	23	40	30	13	3
Some	16	26	12	14	5
A little	21	21	23	16	24
None	40	13	35	57	68
(N = 643)					

Art Forms	Total sample %	School (Y9-11) %	16+FE %	Training Scheme %	Employed %
Computer graphics					
A great deal	9	12	4	8	7
Some	17	22	19	0	19
A little	22	28	23	22	14
None	52	38	54	68	60
(N = 644)					
Printing					
A great deal	7	9	5	13	4
Some	9	14	9	9	5
A little	9	17	9	7	2
None	75	60	77	71	89
(N = 643)					
Photography					
A great deal	2	1	1	0	5
Some	5	6	10	0	4
A little	9	6	14	0	11
None	83	87	75	100	80
(N = 639)					
Sculpture					
A great deal	3	3	5	5	1
Some	11	21	10	7	3
A little	11	20	12	0	4
None	75	56	73	88	92
(N = 645)					
Drama, theatre					
A great deal	13	27	11	2	2
Some	8	14	9	0	6
A little	10	11	17	4	6
None	69	48	63	94	86
(N = 644)					
Dance					
A great deal	5	9	3	2	1
Some	3	6	2	0	2
A little	7	7	16	2	5
None	85	78	79	96	92
(N = 644)					

Art Forms	Total sample %	School (Y9-11) %	16+FE %	Training Scheme %	Employed %
Story, poetry writing					
A great deal	19	44	9	3	2
Some	21	38	29	4	3
A little	8	13	4	0	7
None	52	5	58	93	88
(N = 644)					
Video-making					
A great deal	2	1	4	0	2
Some	5	5	12	0	2
A little	9	15	12	2	5
None	84	79	72	98	91
(N = 636)					
Music-making					
A great deal	7	13	7	0	2
Some	8	14	5	3	2
A little	11	19	13	4	5
None	74	54	75	93	91
(N = 645)					
Scratching, dubbing					
A great deal	1	1	0	0	1
Some	0	1	0	0	0
A little	3	3	3	6	1
None	96	95	97	94	98
(N = 646)					
Fashion					
A great deal	2	4	0	2	0
Some	4	9	3	0	1
A little	8	15	5	6	1
None	86	72	92	92	98
(N = 601)					
Textiles making					
A great deal	3	7	0	0	0
Some	5	11	2	0	0
A little	6	11	6	6	1
None	86	71	92	94	99
(N = 645)					

Art Forms	Total sample %	School (Y9-11) %	16+FE %	Training Scheme %	Employed %
Jewellery-making					
A great deal	1	2	0	0	0
Some	1	3	0	0	0
A little	3	1	3	4	2
None	95	94	97	96	98
(N = 645)					
Graffiti art					
A great deal	0	1	0	0	0
Some	2	5	0	0	0
A little	5	8	6	2	2
None	93	86	94	98	98
(N = 639)					
Arts events					
A great deal	6	6	8	0	6
Some	9	11	16	5	6
A little	7	11	14	3	3
None	78	72	62	92	85
(N = 628)					

These figures are based on the weighted results (see Chapter 2).
Unemployed figures are not given, because many unemployed respondents preferred to answer only in terms of leisure participation. Hence, total numbers are less than those for the leisure-time version.

Table 5.3   Levels of leisure-time participation in different art forms

Art Forms	Total sample %	School (Y9-11) %	16+FE %	Training Scheme %	Employed %	Unemployed %
Painting						
A great deal	5	6	4	11	3	8
Some	12	11	11	24	11	11
A little	15	24	13	4	9	13
None	68	59	72	61	77	68
(N = 680)						
Drawing, sketching						
A great deal	14	18	18	19	3	17
Some	22	29	12	30	16	29
A little	25	26	36	14	25	16
None	39	27	34	37	56	38
(N = 678)						

Art Forms	Total sample %	School (Y9-11) %	16+FE %	Training Scheme %	Employed %	Unemployed %
Computer graphics						
A great deal	5	5	8	4	6	0
Some	10	14	13	9	5	4
A little	13	14	11	24	13	7
None	72	67	68	63	76	89
(N = 677)						
Printing						
A great deal	1	2	1	0	1	0
Some	3	5	3	4	0	0
A little	7	7	6	9	5	18
None	89	86	90	87	94	82
(N = 674)						
Photography						
A great deal	10	8	6	2	14	15
Some	22	22	27	9	25	19
A little	31	34	26	36	31	22
None	37	36	41	53	30	44
(N = 677)						
Sculpture						
A great deal	1	2	0	2	0	5
Some	4	3	5	0	3	7
A little	9	15	10	2	6	7
None	86	80	85	96	91	81
(N = 678)						
Drama, theatre						
A great deal	6	5	9	2	8	3
Some	8	8	12	2	5	13
A little	11	12	14	12	10	1
None	75	75	65	84	77	83
(N = 680)						
Dance						
A great deal	18	21	11	24	15	18
Some	18	9	27	21	21	21
A little	13	10	19	11	14	20
None	51	60	43	44	50	41
(N = 678)						

Art Forms	Total sample %	School (Y9-11) %	16+FE %	Training Scheme %	Employed %	Unemployed %
Story, poetry writing						
A great deal	9	12	10	0	7	7
Some	14	16	21	16	8	9
A little	18	28	21	4	12	12
None	59	44	.48	80	73	72
(N = 681)						
Video-making						
A great deal	1	3	0	0	0	0
Some	8	12	6	0	5	12
A little	12	12	7	22	11	9
None	79	73	87	78	84	79
(N = 681)						
Music-making						
A great deal	12	17	20	5	6	8
Some	11	9	10	13	12	13
A little	16	20	9	23	16	11
None	61	54	61	59	66	68
(N = 680)						
Scratching/dubbing						
A great deal	3	5	1	6	1	5
Some	4	3	3	10	3	2
A little	6	10	2	8	3	6
None	87	82	94	76	93	87
(N = 681)						
Fashion						
A great deal	5	7	1	2	6	5
Some	8	9	6	4	8	11
A little	14	14	13	19	12	11
None	73	70	80	75	74	73
(N = 680)						
Textiles making						
A great deal	1	2	1	0	1	4
Some	4	6	2	0	4	0
A little	7	10	3	9	5	5
None	88	82	94	91	90	91
(N = 680)						

Art Forms	Total sample %	School (Y9-11) %	16+FE %	Training Scheme %	Employed %	Unemployed %
Jewellery-making						
A great deal	1	2	0	4	0	0
Some	4	5	2	4	4	5
A little	11	13	14	12	10	6
None	84	80	84	80	86	89
(N = 681)						
Graffiti art						
A great deal	1	4	0	0	0	0
Some	6	7	3	11	2	10
A little	7	10	9	7	3	11
None	86	79	88	82	95	79
(N = 680)						
Arts events						
A great deal	6	8	11	0	3	4
Some	15	13	24	17	15	14
A little	8	12	12	6	5	4
None	71	67	53	77	77	78
(N = 667)						

These figures are based on the weighted results (see Chapter 2).

Drawing/ Sketching and Painting

♦ Drawing/sketching was the second most common activity in the daytime at school, and the most common in 16+ further education. In both cases, the proportion of participants taking part to the extent of 'a great deal' was high (i.e. they were more than mere dabblers!).

♦ For those in school or 16+ further education, participation was higher during the day than in leisure time, whereas for those on training schemes and in employment participation rates were higher in leisure time.

♦ Of those employed and involved in day-time drawing/sketching, three-quarters were only involved 'a little', suggesting that drawing was only an occasional and marginal part of their work.

♦ Drawing/sketching was the most common art form (i.e. it had the lowest percentages registering 'none') in leisure time for all categories of current status except the employed, though there was a smaller percentage drawing 'a great deal' in leisure time than in the daytime (i.e. there were more leisure-time dabblers).

♦ Painting received fewer nominations than drawing/sketching in leisure and daytime, though the difference between day-time and leisure-time painting was less significant.

♦ Additional analyses revealed that leisure-time painting was more popular with females and day-time drawing and sketching more so with males, more of whom mentioned sketching for design and technology.

♦ Ethnicity had little effect on painting in the daytime, though in leisure time (where cultural traditions will be especially influential), it was slightly more popular with white Europeans.

Some of the key reasons for drawing and sketching being so popular were suggested by a 19 year old male part-time joiner who enjoyed drawing in his spare time: '*It's quiet, you can do it on your own, you don't need to go out anywhere to do it, it passes time*'. In addition, materials are cheap and readily available.

Those that were involved in drawing at an older age often appeared to do so because of school influences and the experience of GCSE art. Although the following example was 'inspired' by school in a different manner, a 20 year old private in the army began drawing by '*being bored at school when I'm bored I fill a piece of paper with drawings and designs, people, houses, graffiti on a brick wall ... I enjoy it, it's cheap and it passes the time*'. He reiterated the cheap materials factor.

Boys often became involved in drawing and sketching through the design and technology side of the curriculum, which went some way to increasing its relevance to males. A 15 year old schoolboy provided a good example of this:

> it's basically designing, initially I put a few ideas down and then bring them together working towards a final idea ... I like drawing and enjoy sketching and doodling ... I'm not so hot at the making.

Many of the most enthusiastic respondents had been drawing since they were very young, often encouraged by parents or primary school teachers, or sometimes just 'coming to it' themselves. The following response from a 15 year old schoolboy was typical in many respects:

> I draw anything – anything that comes into my head – weird stuff from my imagination. I also draw still-life and things like that ... I've been drawing since I was little and have carried on because my parents said I was quite good at it ... I just enjoy it a lot ... it lets me express my feelings ...

The positive effect of perceived ability is very noticeable in this extract.

Painting, like drawing and sketching, is something often participated in from an early age. It is one of the first and most common artistic activities youngsters are encouraged to do by parents and primary school teachers. This was exemplified by two female interviewees who both described a particular love of painting.

One, an example from Social Class IV and V – a 23 year old not seeking work because of having two young children – explained, '*I try to paint whenever I have the opportunity. I want to go to college to finish a course I started before I became pregnant so I'm building a portfolio. I really work mostly in oils, but I also do some water-colours*'. Asked about how she became involved, she replied: '*I'm not very good at expressing my thoughts and feelings so if I didn't have my art it would all bottle up inside my head and make me crazy – I feel things very deeply you see*'.

The other, an example from Social Class I and II – a 20 year old occupational therapist who painted in water-colours, mainly animals, recounted how she became involved in painting and what she got out of it:

> *My junior school was madly creative. It went really modern - no sitting learning maths and English, every day we did something – maybe pottery or oil batiks – definitely what got me going (but made my maths and English dodgy!). I like the peace and quiet – your mind is not thinking about anything else – just on what you are actually doing. It takes your mind away from everything else – that's the nicest thing really ... I feel a bit embarrassed about putting them up* [her paintings] *.. I shouldn't really, other people would probably think they were all right – I do it for myself.*

Both these remarks illustrate the perceived therapeutic benefits of painting, which indeed was a common trend in young people's accounts of arts participation.

To conclude this sub-section, it may be noted that participation in painting, drawing and sketching frequently went hand in hand. By way of illustration, a 16 year old female school pupil, who was initially interested in drawing but developed through school and became involved in both drawing and painting for her GCSE art, which included imaginative pieces, set objects and life drawings, explained that it gave her pleasure, relaxation and allowed her to express herself.

Computer Graphics

♦ Almost half the day-time and leisure-time involvement in computer graphics was at the level of 'a little'. This suggests that for many respondents, it represents an activity with much occasional dabbling and little depth of involvement.

♦ Day-time computer graphics participation was highest among under-17 year olds at school, followed by students in 16+ full-time education. However, much of the student involvement was infrequent and at a low level (perhaps restricted to the presentation of written work).

♦ Similarly, trainees displayed a low level or quality of involvement in leisure-time computer graphics (e.g. they scored highly on 'a little') and the unemployed in particular stood out for overall lack of leisure-time participation (only one in ten had any sort of participation and none had 'a great deal').

♦ There were no significant differences for computer graphics between male and female day-time involvement. In leisure time, however, there was a marked increase in male participation through the different grades of involvement.

♦ Regarding age and computer graphics, there was a general, though quite gradual, decrease in leisure-time involvement with increased age. The under-17 year olds also had a higher involvement in computer graphics during the daytime.

♦ In the daytime, ethnic minorities were conspicuously more involved than white Europeans in computer graphics in that they had more participants at a level of 'some' and 'a great deal'. As a leisure interest, the involvement of ethnic minorities remained higher in the category of 'a great deal' but they also had a greater number of non-participants than white Europeans.

The impression from the statistics that computer graphics in day or leisure time are often just 'dabbled' in was frequently borne out by young people describing their participation in the qualitative follow-up question (Item 25). Participation often appeared to be a marginal aspect of a job or training, or little more than 'a bit of playing about/doodling' with computers in their spare time.

One 17 year old male on a training scheme, who started working on computers at school, had to do some *'printing from different sketches'* at work and some drawing at home, and reported: *'I just like doing it – it's like doodling really'*. Another trainee technician participated as a small element of his job without much genuine interest: *'part of my job ... not really that interested'*. It was also common among those at school. For example, a 16 year old male, who created pictures, graphs and leaflets for GCSE assignments, became involved through his older brother using a graphics programme for school work on the computer that they had at home.

There were, however, young people with a real passion for computer graphics and, not surprisingly, their involvement was not so superficial . For example, a 16 year old A-level student, who used utilities within computing systems to steal pictures from other programmes, responded:

> *I'll cut bits out from them and put them together to make a fairly strange sort of picture ... another form I've got into recently is ray tracing which is an interesting art form itself ... you set up a Virtual 3D space, a set of shapes and you tell the computer what you want the shapes to*

be like. You set up a picture – position and light sources etc. and the computer will draw a picture from that. I've created a couple that are written down in a book, they can take hours to calculate.

He explained that stealing pictures was easy and didn't take particular talent, but in the ray tracing there was thought to be *'creation in having the idea'* and being able to programme it correctly. However, he concluded that he got *'more a feeling of satisfaction than creation'*.

A 20 year old RAF flight controller perhaps put more creative energy into his computer graphics activities:

I make a basic design or cartoon ... on a piece of paper ... you programme them into the memory having drawn or coloured them first. You can then make the character move, talk etc. [He found his involvement] *a contrast to the Airforce where everyone seems stereotyped. It's nice to do your own thing and let your mind work towards something creative rather than my job.*

Occasionally, computer graphics was seen to bridge the gap between the arts, science and technology and also to offer scope for those who are artistically minded but lack technical skill. For instance, a 17 year old male science A-level student who had no interest in art or any artistic inclinations, was relatively enthusiastic. *'I have a computer in my room and I always design front covers, posters etc. for my school work – I prefer doing it on a computer than actually drawing it.'* A 24 year old unemployed male admitted, *'computers are a lot easier than a pencil ... I've always been artistically minded but my hands never agreed with me ... apart from the creative'.* He considered computer graphics to be *'about making a bit of a statement about the world in general – I hate politicians, they are in it for themselves'.*

The examples chosen illustrate the male predominance in leisure-time involvement.

Printing

♦ Overall, results for printing show only one in four were involved to any extent in the daytime and only one in ten were involved in leisure time. In day-time situations, the participation was fairly evenly distributed between 'a great deal', 'some' and 'a little'. However, in leisure time, it was mainly 'a little'.

♦ Day-time involvement was highest at school and lowest among the employed and unemployed.

♦ Leisure-time involvement was similar for all categories of current status, though the unemployed had the highest participation rate, albeit always at an infrequent and low level (i.e. 'a little').

♦ There was a general trend of less day-time involvement with increased age, probably due to fewer opportunities and compulsion on leaving education.

♦ Overall, in both leisure and daytime, printing was a more prevalent activity among ethnic minorities, especially at the level of 'a great deal' or 'some'. In particular, printing textiles was mentioned with increased frequency by respondents in Asian communities.

Generally speaking, the form of printing more often referred to in the interviews was the printing of cloth and clothes. One such example was an employed 19 year old female who printed T-shirts, some baby clothes and vests. She used textile pens or screen printing when she was at college and made the designs herself. She enjoyed it a great deal and found it enhanced her self-esteem and extended her competence.

Photography

♦ Overall, photography was one of the activities that was of minor importance during the day, but in leisure time it had the highest participation rate (63 per cent indicated 'a great deal', 'some' or 'a little'), although half of this was in the category of 'a little'.

♦ Photography in leisure time was the most important of the 17 nominated activities for those in employment. Likewise, it was the second most important for those at school and in 16+ full-time education.

♦ Photography appeared most common as a day-time activity among those in 16+ further education. Those in employment were most likely to be involved frequently or in depth (i.e. 'a great deal').

♦ Gender had no significant effect on photography in the daytime, but in leisure time females were more active at levels of 'some' and 'a great deal', whilst males were more likely to take part 'a little'.

♦ Photography seemed to be an activity that was particularly important to the 21-24 year old age group, especially in the category of 'a great deal' and in leisure time.

♦ Photography was comparatively more prevalent with Social Class I and II respondents, especially in their leisure time.

Participation in photography bears similarities to computer graphics insofar as it is more technological than traditional art forms. As such, the cost of equipment and materials becomes an important factor. For example, a 23 year old working class mother explained her involvement as follows: '*It's really since Thomas was born – I didn't like letting his childhood go by. I use about one 36 exposure film a fortnight ... I do enjoy it and would do more if I could afford an expensive camera*'.

A 19 year old student at university was involved for recreational reasons, '*personal reasons – mainly documenting holidays*'. As he said, '*it's a quick way of reproducing an image, I don't have time to sit down and draw*'.

The interviews, however, did produce examples of more creative and artistic forms of photography. A 16 year old A-level student for her skill component of the Duke of Edinburgh Award attended photography classes:

> *I process films in the dark-room. We will be learning about apertures ... I'm quite good at getting depth etc. right. I like to get scenery and appreciate landscapes and nature ... it's just pleasing to see a good quality print, it's fun – memories capture events for future reference – generally interesting and you end up with brilliant photos.*

An example of photography as part of work was provided by a 24 year old artist who took photographs as a '*subject matter for work*' and used it to record events. He explained he '*enjoys the interaction between me and the subject*'. As a record of events, '*it replaces your memory*'. Overall, 'capturing memories' was the phrase most frequently used about photography in Item 25.

Sculpture

♦ Sculpture had a greater level of participation during the daytime (even then only one in four partake) than in leisure, when nearly two-thirds of its participants were only involved 'a little'.

♦ Most of the day-time participation was at school, with very little among those employed and on training schemes (about one in ten).

♦ Day-time sculpture had lower participation rates for the older respondents, so that for the over-21 year old group, only 7 per cent participated during the daytime. However, half of that participation was in the 'a great deal' category.

♦ Trainees and the employed were the least active in sculpture within leisure time; students at school and the unemployed were the most involved.

♦ Consistent with this, leisure-time sculpture was most common among the under-17s, but mainly only at the level of 'a little', whereas the over-21s had a higher rate of participation at 'a great deal' and 'some'.

The participation rate for sculpture was comparatively high in leisure time among the unemployed (on a par with school pupils). An interesting and unusual example, which was referred to earlier in the report, was a 24 year old male, who previously was defined as having learning difficulties and had run away from school. He became involved in a project to build a Greek Temple from tyres and Portacabins. He stressed he would be very keen to do this again.

Drama and Theatre

♦ Drama and theatre ('drama' for short) had similar frequencies of participation in day and leisure time, though leisure time was a little lower and slightly more concentrated in the 'a little' level of involvement. Drama was the fifth most common day-time arts activity, largely due to school students having a non-participation rate of only 48 per cent.

♦ Drama was marginally more common among girls, especially in leisure time.

♦ There was a consistent and quite severe drop in involvement with age in daytime (certainly reflecting current status and day-time opportunity).

♦ Social class had a marked effect on drama and theatre in leisure time: participation rates were lower among Social Class IV and V respondents and higher among Social Class I and II interviewees.

♦ The Social Class I and II group also had the highest day-time participation (30 per cent indicating a 'great deal' or 'some'), but the partly/unskilled group were only 4 per cent lower; Social Class III respondents had the lowest day-time participation rate (17 per cent).

School accounted for the bulk of day-time participation in drama. The following is an example of a young man who had been stimulated by school drama:

I have done a school production of Macbeth and now I want to do it in my free time too. In lessons we make up scripts and work in groups to act them out ... ... I get a lot of pleasure out of it.

One 14 year old boy, who became involved through school, but then, through his own initiative, expanded his participation to leisure time reported:

We do it, for example, on holidays – we would set up something for ourselves and perform it in front of people ... ... I learnt to express myself a bit and just enjoy being with my friends.

Sixteen plus further and higher education institutions also gave opportunities for drama and theatre. For example, one 23 year old female, who was a member of her college drama group, became involved in producing, performing and writing comedy sketches. She found it '*satisfying and exhilarating*' and said she enjoyed the response of others to something she had written and performed. Another 17 year old female in 16+ further education directed and stage managed her college productions. She enjoyed the experience of working with other people, found it interesting and would like to do it again when she left college. Unfortunately, opportunities may not be so easily to hand and certainly the statistical evidence showed that most participation occurs within educational establishments. A number of respondents asked interviewers if the research project could provide them with information on opportunities in drama and theatre.

Dance

♦ In leisure time, dance, along with drawing/sketching, recorded the highest percentage registering 'a great deal' or 'some'. However, as explained earlier, a high proportion of this was reported to be dancing at discos, clubs and raves.

♦ In leisure time, half the interviewees participated in dance and of these, nearly three-quarters participated at levels of 'some' or 'a great deal'. Leisure-time dancing was most common among the unemployed, those in 16+ further education and those on training schemes – the groups that were found to be most frequent attenders at discos, clubs and raves. Dancing was least popular among the under-17s at school – again suggesting a link to social activities.

♦ In daytime only 15 per cent participated, though half of these participated at the two levels of 'a great deal' and 'some'. Day-time participation was highest among those at school and in 16+ further education. It was exceptionally low for those outside of education.

♦ In the daytime, females were more likely than males to take part in dance at the level of 'a great deal'. This was even more apparent in leisure time.

♦ Day-time participation in dance appeared to decrease with age and reflected current status.

♦ In leisure time, respondents from Social Class I and II had the lowest participation rate in dance.

Accounts collected in the interviews illustrated the wide variations in what constituted dance participation. As outlined above, dance was mainly a leisure-time activity and this ranged from popular discos and raves etc. to ballet. The following are two quite contrasting examples.

One 14 year old female had been dancing ever since she was little with her sister. They watched films like 'Dirty Dancing' or 'Footloose' and copied the movements: *'we won a dance competition at my Auntie's 21st birthday disco – just love to dance'*. The other was a 24 year old South African woman who became involved in contemporary and ethnic dancing through formal dance classes. She felt that she gained psychological liberation and that you *'feel like you're creating something with your whole being'*.

Similarly, a 17 year old A-level student was dedicated to a career in dance:

> *I started when I was three, so I have always done it. I do about 12 hours outside school of dance lessons. I teach adults and children in the evenings – tap, ballet and modern. I do competitions around England. I also do it in school instead of A-level which will hopefully give me my qualifications to teach ... ... my parents encouraged me, but were never pushy.*

However, it was disco and rave dancing which were more popular and some interviewees were adamant that it was an art form, as this 19 year old private in the army explained:

> *Rave is an art – everyone is in to their own kind of rave, everyone's rave is different... ... I go every weekend up and down the country ... ... you can mellow out and are free from army pressures ... you can be yourself and just, like, escape.*

Story and Poetry Writing

♦ Interestingly, there was nearly as much leisure-time involvement in story and poetry writing as in the daytime, but it was much less frequent and intensive.

♦ Story and poetry writing was the second most common activity in the daytime. Nearly half of the interviewees took part and of those, 83 per cent were involved at levels of 'a great deal' and 'some'. The exceptionally high school figures were mainly responsible for this finding – school pupils had only 5 per cent non-participation. The vast majority of participants in day-time writing were involved at the top two levels, although compulsion was much more of a factor than for other arts in schools and participation often seemed uninspired and unenthusiastic. Some 42 per cent of 16+ further education students participated. There was very little day-time participation outside of education.

♦ For leisure time, participation in writing increased for those not in education, but decreased for those at school.

♦ There was a slight female bias in both day- and leisure-time creative writing, particularly the latter.

- Reflecting current status and the leaving of educational institutions, the day-time participation for under-17s was much higher than that for 17-20 year olds which was similarly higher than that for the 21-24 year old group.

- There was also a marked decrease in participation with age in leisure-time participation. However, it was notable that the over-21 year olds that did participate were likely to do so at levels of 'a great deal' or 'some'.

- In leisure time, interviewees from the ethnic minorities had twice the amount of participation at the level of 'a great deal' than white Europeans.

- Respondents from the skilled class (Social Class III) were the group least likely to take part in story and poetry writing in both leisure and daytime.

An example of a respondent in 16+ further education was a 19 year old male at university who wrote short stories and descriptive pieces (often influenced by travel). He liked to personify ideas and describe dreams. He started writing at his first school and enjoyed it because:

there are not really any limits ... ... you can have method writing as opposed to method acting – interesting to see things from another point of view. Sometimes I have to get ideas out on paper – helps to disperse anger ... ... apart from dispersing anger, my thoughts become more clear, ideas or political argument can also be set out.

Unemployed participation in writing, compared to other activities, was certainly high. It was suggested that writing was a cheap and accessible way to express feelings and release pent up emotions or just pass time. One male 21 year old unemployed boxer, who was expelled from school at 15 years, wrote about 'living in the system', drugs, love, peace, crime, domestic violence, prostitution and his best and worst memories from childhood – believing that, '*it gets my feelings on to paper, gets it off my chest*'.

Another unemployed respondent (female, 20 years old) explained that '*basically, when I left school, I carried on because I like writing and things*', it gave her '*a sense of release – relieves boredom*' and allowed her a means of self-expression.

School participation obviously overflowed into leisure time, where it was less intense but still high overall. As one pupil said of her participation: it's '*mainly for school but I have done some in my spare time ... it gives me something to do*'. Another 15 year old male pupil found poetry writing was '*a relief from the stress of school work*'. As young people grew older, other priorities competed for attention in their leisure time. One 14 year old female enjoyed writing stories for her five year old cousin and poems for friends' birthday cards. She liked to do it '*in the evenings when not going out or if there was nothing else to do*'.

An example of an interviewee from a working class background participating at the level of 'a great deal' was a school age female, who enjoyed creative writing because of '*using your imagination, forgetting your own life*'. Indeed, as another of that class said of the 'arts' in general, there was '*fuck all else way for working classes to escape*'. Writing stories and poems were a particularly cheap and accessible form of arts participation.

As the quoted extracts start to show, story and poetry writing can be inexpensive and readily available. The data revealed that all types of young people can gain a variety of benefits. One other notable example of the extent of benefits of participation was a 14 year old male attender of a special needs unit for children with emotional and behavioural problems. He copied poems, read them out and wrote about what he thought: '*My teacher started me off – I had a little fight with her at the beginning*' but now he enjoyed it a great deal: '*... it's excellent ... about 201 poems in my file (an exaggeration – about 20!)*'. He gained from the experience of being able to sit and concentrate and '*getting on with poems helped my writing more*'.

Video-making

♦ Both leisure- and day-time participation were low: approximately one in five participated, with only one in a hundred indicating 'a great deal'.

♦ During the daytime, students in 16+ further education were slightly more likely to make videos than those at school, both overall and at the levels of 'some' and 'a great deal'.

♦ In leisure time, those at school were most involved and those in 16+ further education least.

♦ Video-making was more popular with girls at lower levels of participation during the daytime, but leisure time involvement was more male-oriented.

Video-making was not a common activity. In leisure time, it was found to be much more of an amusing pastime than a 'serious' arts form. For example, a 20 year old female secretary, who bought a camcorder before Christmas, commented: '*I did a lot of filming of the family at Christmas and on holiday at Scarborough – filmed scenery and things we did on holidays*'. She became involved through her father and liked to '*capture people on film when they are being stupid and for the memories*'.

Music-making

- For the overall samples, leisure-time participation in music-making (39 per cent indicating 'a great deal', 'some' or 'a little') was higher than day-time participation (26 per cent). Along with story and poetry writing, it was the fourth most popular art form in leisure time.

- Day-time participation in music was quite considerably higher among students in full-time education, especially those at school (where there was nearly one in two participating, compared to one in four for students in 16+ further education; trainees and employed having less than one in ten participating).

- In leisure time, participation was spread much more evenly among the current status groups. The most notable point was that school pupils and those in 16+ further education had very high participation at 'a great deal', whilst most of those outside of education were concentrated in 'a little' and 'some' (especially trainees).

- Daytime music-making was fractionally higher among females, whilst in leisure time there was a higher level of male involvement throughout all the levels, quite considerable at 'some' and 'a little'. This appeared to be due to more male participation in rock bands and occasionally 'messing with a guitar', compared with female involvement in choirs or orchestral music-making which were more likely at school.

- In daytime, compared with the under-17s, there was a lower level of participation among the 17-20 year old group, followed by a slightly smaller proportion of 21-24 year olds. In leisure time, there was an even, though less severe, decline through the age groups.

- Music-making in the daytime was markedly higher for middle class respondents (Social Class I and II), especially at the levels of 'some' and 'a great deal'. (Certain music-making activities, e.g. choir and orchestra involvement, tended to be more conspicuous among young people from middle class backgrounds.) The leisure-time involvement of Social Class IV and V interviewees, particularly at the levels of 'some' and a 'great deal', was lower than that of respondents from Social Classes I and II and III.

Arguably, this art form emerged as the broadest category of arts participation, including, as it does, a wide range of musical activities. Frequent testimonies to a deep love of music in general were collected, with interviewees often describing a variety of musical interests. For instance, a 19 year old female clerical assistant explained:

> I sing and play the trumpet in a band – modern/dance type music – but not mindless. Before that I was in the church choir from the age of six, [playing] school music, city jazz band singing and playing the trumpet. I started trumpet lessons at school, aged ten ... I love my music, the experience of it. Playing in a more intimate group and performing in an atmosphere that didn't involve parents and school.

Bands and groups of all types were a focus of enthusiasm for most young musicians and boys very commonly formed rock and pop groups, often when still at school. As one 16 year old male member of a rock group called 'Black Rose' put it:

> *I started when we chose our options ... we practice at dinner times, break and after school in the auditorium ... I enjoy it a lot – enjoy playing with the group, we compose tunes that we can all play, sometimes have lyrics with them. Do concerts – all the school concerts, but haven't had one outside school yet.*

Another example of a rock band involvement was a 24 year old employed male, whom school failed to inspire in all spheres including music. Of arts at secondary school, he said, '*I went to the classes but didn't learn anything ... just boring ... I wasn't interested*'. He now spent any moment of spare time on his music and, when asked about his enjoyment, he replied, '*I love writing words and feeling the flow of music, it really lifts me up*'.

Different again was this 21 year old employed female:

> *At the moment I've joined with Irish and Scottish musicians to sing and play. Have done two or three concerts at the Rising Sun Centre and the local pub ... My interest started at school and developed from there. I've done solo singing since the sixth form ... I find singing solo easier than violin solo – I enjoy singing very much – mostly folk and folk rock.* [She explained that she felt she gained] *personal expression, part of my identity, part of me, which is why I think creativity should be valued in people ...*

School and, very often, church choirs and orchestras provided considerable and influential opportunities for young people, especially females, e.g. a 15 year old female reported:

> *I play for the church quite a lot, inside school I've always played for the orchestra ... I started junior choir in school and am now in senior choir.*

Another 18 year old female told of her ten-year involvement in various church choirs and explained, '*I love music, love singing with other people, love having the commitment ... commitment more to the music than to religion, but don't tell the vicar!*'.

Parental support, in the form of private lessons and encouragement, often from an early age, may be a critical factor in shaping the social class results outlined in the key points. As examples, one 15 year old male played the piano and had enjoyed lessons since he was eight years old from various different teachers and since then had never wanted to give it up: '*once I can master a piece, I enjoy playing it. It's something creative, you're not left with an end result but there is still a feeling of accomplishment for me*'.

Another interviewee, having benefited from a high level of family encouragement and support (his father was a jazz musician and his brother is in a pop group) gave this testimony:

> *I have always had a piano and a load of instruments around me. I enjoyed them very much, although I didn't take the proper way of going through ... making sure I knew all the theory and things like that, just more experimentation ... My father didn't want me to follow in his footsteps, that wasn't what he was trying to do. He realised I had musical ability and without wishing to exploit it, I think he just wanted me to develop it into my own kind of way, and did that by providing me with instruments and things like that ... Because unfortunately my father died last year, and we had a jazz concert in memory of him ... some of my friends were invited along, all of which did GCSE music. Anyway, so after we got back to school we found we had a common interest in jazz and so with the help of a music teacher from the junior school we set up a jazz/soul group. After various complications, like some of us having a good ear for music but not being able to read music so well, we realised that we couldn't pick up songs if we wanted to do cover versions ... then we find there are too many part-time members of the band because we need a huge amount of people for one piece and then virtually none for another. You had people half stringing along and it meant they weren't fully committed to the group. So after we got over this complication, we decided to scrap this and move on to a kind of funk and the pop scene which just involved two regular guitarists, singer and a drummer, and there was a saxophone as well which I play ... I also sing as well. And basically we got some songs together and asked to have a pop concert ... at school. After this, one of my friends' friends asked if we could play at a party of hers. So we had to get our act into gear and then we got a reputation around and we've been asked to play in this club in London in the next holidays, which is basically as far as we have got.*

This was just one of many illustrations of how much easier and more likely musical advancement is when parental support, financial backing, 'cultural capital' and encouragement are present. This particular young man (Afro-Caribbean) had certainly had a privileged up-bringing and attended one of the country's top public schools. This case highlights one of the surprising ironies of the research findings: namely, that even rock music, which was expected to be associated with working class cultural creativity, was often found to be more accessible to those who had benefited from middle class upbringings which offered the resources and positive attitudes to encourage musical and artistic involvement from an early age. Similarly, some of the few interviewees who were professionally engaged in such alternative music-making forms as 'scratching and dubbing' (the subject of the next section) were middle class respondents who had experienced a classical musical education.

Scratching and Dubbing

♦ Scratching and dubbing, along with jewellery-making, was the least common activity in the daytime (with only 4 per cent participation), and was not a great deal more popular in leisure time.

♦ In leisure time, trainees had the highest participation rate (one in four), two-thirds of which was at the level of 'a great deal' or 'some'. Least leisure-time participation (with well under one in ten), was found among 16+ further education students and the employed.

♦ There was a clear decrease in participation in leisure time with age.

♦ There was a slightly higher ethnic minority participation in daytime and this was even more marked in leisure time.

♦ In leisure time, a slightly higher proportion of Social Class IV and V respondents were involved in scratching and dubbing than those from other social class categories.

One of the few examples of interviewees who participated in scratching and dubbing 'a great deal' was a 14 year old male who explained:

I go round all the shops and buy up records and at home I've two 'Technics' turntables connected up to a hi-fi and I like, scratch with one old one I don't like and with music beneath it ... mix them together ... I just enjoy music all the time ... if I'm really annoyed I just scratch up a record all the time! I just enjoy it.

An 18 year old employed female enjoyed a different aspect of scratching and dubbing. She commented:

I buy records that are unknown and hear bits from it – I take samples from it and make my own tapes. [She became involved] *at school listening to the radio. A kind of fashion in music through the various styles – acid, dance, rave things like that. ... It's fun to make it and let the group listen to it, and decide whether it's any good or rubbish.*

Finally, a 20 year old undergraduate, who had received a classical musical education and played the violin and piano, earned money at local clubs for his experiments in 'sound systems' and scratching and dubbing.

Fashion

♦ Fashion was one of the least participated in art forms, with only slightly more involvement than scratching and dubbing. Leisure-time involvement (27 per cent indicating 'a great deal', 'some' or 'a little') was higher than that of daytime (14 per cent).

♦ Day-time participation was mainly at school, nearly half of which was at the level of 'a great deal' or 'some'.

- School pupils were also the most involved in leisure time, closely followed by the unemployed, employed and trainees (who were most involved at a 'low' level). Those in 16+ further education were the least likely to be involved in leisure time.

- Females were slightly more involved in the daytime.

- Fashion participation was definitely more prevalent for the younger rather than the older respondents in both leisure and daytime. The most significant drop was from the under-17s to 17-20 year olds in the daytime, reflecting the effect of leaving school.

- Fashion was one of the art forms most markedly affected by ethnicity. The ethnic minorities had 13-14 per cent more involvement in both leisure and daytime. There was a particularly high ethnic participation in leisure time at the levels of 'a great deal' and 'some'.

Interestingly, the three examples of interviewees chosen that answered Item 25 on fashion are of Indian, Pakistani and Bangladeshi origin. Generally, when young people talked about their participation in fashion they referred to the making or designing of clothes, however occasionally it was modelling. A 21 year old part-time employed female, for example, who organised and modelled at fashion shows, enjoyed the social side of this activity, meeting people and seeing different venues. A 20 year old female sewing instructor was involved in designing and making clothes, having being taught in Pakistan. She found it '*very fulfilling to create a new idea or fashion*'. Another 14 year old female became involved in making clothes at school, though her family had always been involved in making clothes. She made clothes for her nieces and remarked that '*when it comes out well, it feels really good*'.

Textiles

- Participation was very low in both leisure and daytime.

- Participation was mainly in school during the daytime, two-thirds of which was in the 'a great deal' and 'some' categories.

- In leisure time school pupils were still the main participators, though this was less evident in the top two categories of involvement.

- Textiles was certainly a female-oriented activity in leisure time, with very little male participation.

- Looking at age, the 17 years and under group had the highest participation in both daytime and leisure time, but especially during the day.

◆ Overall, ethnicity had little effect, though ethnic minorities were noticeably more involved at the levels of 'a great deal' and 'some' in both daytime and leisure.

Most of the participation in textiles was at school and involved females. It frequently appeared to overlap with printing (e.g. screen printing) and was undertaken as part of GCSE courses in textiles.

Jewellery-making

◆ Jewellery-making (along with scratching and dubbing) was found to be one of the least common art forms in the daytime and leisure time.

◆ The only day-time participation at the levels of 'a great deal' and 'some' was to be found among school pupils.

◆ Leisure-time participation was again highest for school pupils, but also for those on training schemes.

◆ There was a noticeable, and not unexpected, orientation towards females participating in jewellery-making in both daytime and leisure time. The leisure-time figures, however, were particularly marked (female participation was 22 per cent higher).

One of the small number of young people who took part in jewellery-making to any great extent was a 15 year old female who became involved indirectly through school: '*We had to do a mini-business at school and we decided to make jewellery to sell. We did that and made quite a lot of money*'. This encouraged her to continue and she went on to say, '*I enjoy doing it ... when you just want to sit quietly and relax ... and I enjoy seeing what I get at the end of it – it gives some satisfaction (but I don't enjoy it as I do tennis!)*'.

Graffiti Art

◆ Participation overall was very small during the daytime (third least common activity of the 17 mentioned). However, in leisure time, albeit with a still relatively small participation of 14 per cent indicating 'a great deal', 'some' or 'a little', it was nevertheless not one of the least popular activities.

◆ The only day-time participation beyond 'a little' was at school.

◆ Leisure-time participation was slightly higher among school students and the unemployed.

♦ The popularity of graffiti art among males was very obviously shown in the leisure-time results, with male predominance throughout all degrees of involvement and a 16 per cent overall difference in participation at any level.

♦ Participation decreased though the age groups in both leisure and daytime and especially from the under-17s to the 17-20 year old group (on leaving school).

♦ Interestingly, graffiti art in daytime was marginally less common among the partly skilled/unskilled group (Social Class IV and V), whilst in leisure time there was a marked reversal of the situation with the latter group having 10 per cent overall higher participation than the professional group (Social Class I and II).

'*Being 13, I bombed the 'A' train in Brooklyn.*' This was a comment from a 19 year old unemployed male who was involved in graffiti art to the extent of 'a great deal'. 'Bombed' is terminology for spray painted, so in other words he spray painted the main Brooklyn [New York] commuter train. Art at school did not interest him, though graffiti appears to have raised enthusiasm – he described it as beautiful and when asked what he got out of it he said '*a thrill*'. He became involved through his brother and considered himself an artist. Apart from graffiti art, he appeared to live for rap and hip hop music and though unemployed, was not seeking work.

Arts Events

♦ Involvement in arts events was moderately common in both leisure and daytime.

♦ In both daytime and leisure time, participation was greatest among students in 16+ full-time education. The employed, unemployed and trainees all had similarly lower levels of participation.

♦ Increased age produced a slight decline in day-time participation. In leisure time, there was an overall low for the 17-20 year old group.

♦ Respondents from Social Class I and II had a markedly high overall participation in both day- and leisure-time arts events, but especially leisure where there was a difference of 20 per cent between themselves and other groups.

Reflecting the above average engagement in arts events by post-16 students, examples of involvement in arts events included an 18 year old student at university. She was involved 'backstage', setting up scenes in a theatre and doing costumes and make-up rather than actually performing. Her enjoyment stemmed from factors commonly experienced by other interviewees involved in such activities: meeting people, having fun, and interesting active involvement. An example of a performer at an arts event was a 14 year old girl who sang and danced with different groups which came together for festival days. She also performed in plays with the local drama group and went to drama festivals. She enthused, '*it really gives you a buzz, I suppose I like showing off a bit and like people to like me, see what I'm good at*'.

Final Comment

To conclude, this chapter has presented the results of respondents' reported participation rates in 17 specific art forms. Wherever possible, responses to the closed item have been exemplified with illustrative material from interviewees' open-ended accounts of their engagement in particular art forms. It was found that the leisure-time arts activities with the highest nominations of a 'great deal' and 'some' were dance, drawing/sketching, photography, music-making and story and poem writing. However, the responses of interviewees clearly indicated that the first three of these activities included participants whose motives were not so much artistic but more social and time-filling (e.g. disco dancing, doodling and taking holiday snaps).

It should be acknowledged that, with regard to certain art forms (e.g. dance, theatre, arts events), some interviewees may well have registered a degree of 'consumption' instead of strictly limiting themselves to active participation in arts activities, as the question asked. It is to the broader question of young people's consumption of the arts that we turn in the next chapter.

6. Encountering and Consuming the Arts

This chapter examines the young people's involvement in arts as 'receivers' or 'consumers' rather than active participants, although the difficulty of clearly distinguishing and defining such a mode of arts engagement is duly acknowledged. The findings from questions on whether the respondent had 'read, watched or listened to any arts' in their own leisure time or during day-time pursuits within the last year are reported, and variation according to age, gender, social class are identified. In leisure time, the main forms of 'consumed art' were reading literature, listening to music and going to the cinema. School students most often mentioned English as the forum for day-time arts engagement in an audience role.

Introduction

Although this research project has focused primarily on young people's arts participation in the sense of their active involvement as 'producers' or doers', the term 'participation' was considered broad enough to encompass more 'passive', 'consumer' or 'spectator' roles within the arts. Indeed, part of the difficulty of finding accurate words to distinguish these two roles is indicative of the fact that, in reality, there are often few clear watertight boundaries between arts 'production' and arts 'consumption' or 'reception'. As Paul Willis (1990) has illustrated, activities which appear to be 'consumer'-oriented (e.g. buying and listening to records) can be transformed and elide into 'production' roles (e.g. using them to compile 'scratched and dubbed' recordings). Similarly, Hargreaves (1989) relays Serafine's (1979) proposal that *'the productive and receptive aspects of engagement in the arts are opposite sides of the same coin'* and Gardner's (1973) theory that three interacting, and eventually indivisible, systems are evident: a making system (i.e. producing acts, actions or artefacts as creator or performer); a perceiving system (i.e. concerned with discriminations and distinctions as critic); and a feeling system (i.e. dealing with the affect as audience member) (p. 8). Consequently, as part of using a whole gamut of different types of questions to stimulate discussion about their involvement in the arts (e.g. 'evening and weekend' interests, activities considered 'imaginative or creative', participation in specific art forms etc.), it was considered important to include some items which allowed the interviewees to describe their level of engagement in the arts by starting from a more 'consumer'-oriented perspective.

Accordingly, young people were asked whether, within the last year, as part of their school work/training/course/job (i.e. day-time activities - Item 22) or outside of their school work/training/course/job (i.e. leisure-time activities - Item 23), they had read, listened to or watched any arts. The difficulty of identifying a comprehensive verb for these questions led to this rather clumsy compromise and reflects the problems experienced in picking a title for this chapter. To avoid the materialistic and passive overtones associated with the terms 'consuming' or 'receiving' the arts, the phrase 'encountering' has been used as an alternative, though there is no suggestion that non-production roles *vis-à-vis* the arts are inherently aggressive or confrontational. In a sense, the term 'encountering the arts' is used to incorporate Gardner's 'perceiving' and 'feeling' systems, whilst allowing for the close interdependency of these on the 'making' system. Finally, it should be stressed that the judgement as to whether activities such as watching TV or reading literature were considered to be engaging the 'arts' was left to the subjective interpretation of the interviewee, not the interviewer. As a final word of introduction, it is worth noting that at the point in the interviews when these questions were asked, the respondents had been encouraged by earlier items to interpret the interviewers' use of the term, the 'arts', as all-embracing.

Day-time Encounters with the Arts

Taking young people's day-time activities first (Item 22), a little over half (55 per cent) of the sample (N = 654) said that they had encountered (i.e. read, listened to or watched) the arts within the last year. Among the school students, 83 per cent responded in the affirmative, which means that approximately one in six (17 per cent) of school students felt that they had not encountered anything of an artistic nature over the course of the year preceding the interview. Whereas two-thirds (67 per cent) of post-16 full-time students considered that they had encountered the arts within their courses, a little over a quarter (27 per cent) of employees felt that their work had involved engagement in the arts in a non-producer or spectator capacity.

Given these findings, it is not surprising that the proportions of interviewees encountering the arts in their day-time activities show a considerable decline, as age increased and young people left full-time education (the proportions responding in the affirmative were 81 per cent of the under-17s, 44 per cent of 17-20 year olds and 23 per cent of the over-21s). The by now familiar 'U'-shaped relationship emerged again: this time in the relationship between affirmative responses on the day-time encountering of the arts and social class and 16+ educational attainment. To postulate possible causes of this association, it is necessary to consider the type of arts activities read, watched, or listened to in their day-time engagements.

The types of art activity encountered in educational institutions or at work (i.e. day-time activities) are set out in the first column of Table 6.1. The remaining columns of this table show the frequencies with which different types of arts were mentioned by interviewees in the various categories of current status. For students in schools, English was the subject area most frequently mentioned as providing an engagement with a work of art: 42 per cent said that they had read a poem, play or novel within the last year and 37 per cent referred to the watching of TV dramas or videos in English. No other subject area came close to these percentages. Undoubtedly, this reflects the fact that English was a compulsory area of the curriculum for all students, while other arts-related subjects usually formed part of option choices. Of these, art, music and drama attracted similar scores to one another. Only 8 and 4 per cent of school respondents mentioned a visit to the theatre and live concerts respectively and, moreover, the large majority of these were from middle class (Social Class I and II) backgrounds. Thus, even within school, the middle classes showed strong biases towards theatre and concert attendance. Theatre attendance, though not live concerts, was more likely to be cited by post-16 students in full-time education. For this group, the reading of plays, poems and novels remained the most common encounter with the arts – again by considerable margins.

Table 6.1   Day-time arts encountered by current status

Arts encountered	Total sample %	At school Years 9-11 %	16+ FT education %	Training scheme %	In Employment %	Unemployed %
Mainly in education:						
English: reading plays, novels etc.	21	42	35	0	2	0
English: videos, TV	16	37	9	0	3	2
Theatre visits	5	8	14	0	0	0
Drama	3	7	4	0	0	0
Humanities	2	2	6	0	0	0
Art: viewing works of art, gallery visits	4	7	5	4	0	0
Art: reading about	2	2	7	0	0	0
Music: listening to recorded	4	7	6	0	0	0
Music: concerts	2	4	1	0	0	0
Design	1	0	2	0	0	0
Languages	1	1	2	0	0	1
Another subject	4	5	11	0	0	3
Mainly at work:						
Theatre, drama	2	0	1	2	4	0
Visual arts, galleries	1	0	0	0	2	0
Dance	1	1	0	0	2	0
Concerts, live music	1	0	0	0	4	0
Recorded music	3	1	0	12	6	0
Videos, TV, films, computer graphics	2	0	1	3	4	0
Reading literature	3	3	0	0	8	0
Other arts at work, school	3	5	3	0	1	0
TOTALS	(668)	(239)	(101)	(58)	(208)	(61)

Interviewees could give more than one response, so percentages will not sum to 100 per cent.
These figures are based on the weighted results (see Chapter 2).
As explained in the text, 45 per cent registered no day-time encounters with the arts.

Listening to recorded music while at work was the most prevalent activity mentioned by young people on training schemes, and reading literature was marginally the most common arts form encountered at work by those in employment (prominent in this respect were occupations such as care assistants reading stories to children).

The U-shaped relationship between affirmative responses on the day-time encountering of the arts and social class and 16+ educational attainment is largely attributable to the comparatively high proportions of young people with no 16+ qualifications and Social Class IV and V backgrounds taking English, often as re-sits, in post-16 full-time education. Hence, by way of illustration, the proportions mentioning the reading of plays, novels and poems in their day-time activities were as follows: 16 per cent of those with seven or more GCE/GCSE passes; 7 per cent of those with between four and six passes; 0 per cent for those with one to three; and 10 per cent of those with no 16+ qualifications. The U-shaped relationship was even more pronounced for theatre visits in connection with studying English.

Finally, the analyses showed that white European respondents were more likely than members of the ethnic minorities to see the subject area of English as an arena for engaging works of art. This again suggests that schools could do more to include genres of literature with more relevance to ethnic minorities, though the latest National Curriculum orders for English have been criticised for not doing enough to encourage moves in this direction.

Leisure-time Encounters with the Arts

Turning to responses to the question (Item 23) on whether interviewees had read, listened to or watched any arts in their leisure time within the past year, the majority (79 per cent) answered in the affirmative (N = 679). Young people in employment (85 per cent) and post-16 full-time education (83 per cent) had the highest rates of involvement, while those in training (69 per cent) had the lowest.

The types of art form encountered by young people in their leisure time are displayed in Table 6.2

Taking the sample as a whole, music – in all its various guises - received more mentions than any other art form. Overall, two-fifths (40 per cent) of the sample mentioned listening to at least one type of music. Listening to recorded new/pop music (18 per cent) and live new/pop music (6 per cent) were the most popular specified categories; classical music – recorded (2 per cent) and live (2 per cent) – was much less common. After music, reading literature and cinema were the next most popular arts encountered. Some way behind these came theatre and watching TV and videos deemed artistic. Apart from going to galleries and exhibitions, other art forms (e.g. dance and ballet, poetry readings, spoken radio) were rarely mentioned.

Table 6.2   Leisure-time arts encountered by current status

Arts encountered	Total sample %	At school Years 9-11 %	16+ FT education %	Training scheme %	In Employment %	Unemployed %
Listening to music:						
Unspecified	10	8	6	14	15	6
Recorded classical	2	1	1	0	3	0
Recorded new, pop	18	20	12	20	17	22
Recorded music (unspecified)	2	1	0	7	2	2
Live classical	2	3	8	1	0	0
Live new, pop	6	3	11	4	9	0
Live (unspecified)	1	0	0	0	1	0
Radio music	2	3	0	2	4	0
% mentioning at least one type of music listening	(40)	(36)	(36)	(45)	(46)	(31)
Cinema	29	23	40	21	34	31
TV, videos	15	17	13	12	14	20
Galleries, exhibitions	7	2	6	4	11	12
Theatre	19	14	34	14	21	14
Dance, ballet	2	2	3	0	2	1
Radio (spoken)	1	0	0	0	0	2
Reading (literature)	30	25	34	26	36	33
Other reading	2	4	1	4	0	0
Poetry readings	1	0	0	2	0	0
Arts festivals, events	1	0	0	2	2	0
TOTALS	(668)	(239)	(101)	(58)	(208)	(61)

Interviewees could give more than one response, so percentages will not sum to 100 per cent.
These figures are based on the weighted results (see Chapter 2).
As explained in the text, 45 per cent registered no day-time encounters with the arts.

Most probably reflecting their relative lack of independent financial means, students at school were less likely than young people in other positions to attend live pop concerts, cinemas and theatres, galleries and exhibitions. They were also less likely to read literature in their leisure time. In contrast to any other group, students in post-16 education had the highest attendance rates at live pop concerts (undoubtedly, the frequency of live bands at college dances was a factor here), cinemas and theatres (one in three said they had been to the theatre). Interestingly though, respondents in employment mentioned reading literature and music more than any other group. In contrast, the unemployed group was lower on music and theatre, while comparatively high on TV and videos, and going to galleries and exhibitions.

Further analyses (see Table 6.3) suggest that three art forms show signs of increased involvement (in the capacity of 'spectator' roles) as young people grow older: reading literature, theatre attendance, and going to galleries and exhibitions (though it should be remembered that longitudinal research would be required to substantiate this inference). In so far as they show a distinct increase between the 17-20 year old group and the over-21s, the findings for these three art forms confirm earlier tentative interpretations that the older respondents seem more willing to engage in arts institutions and, as such, may represent a key target group for arts providers and sponsors. Cinema and music appear to increase beyond 16, but plateau between 17 and 20 rather than rising further, as in the previous three art forms. TV and videos (deemed artistic) is the only category which shows signs of decreasing with age.

Table 6.3   Leisure-time arts encountered by age and social class

	Total sample	Age			Social Class		
		Under-17	17-20	21-24	I & II	III (N & M)	IV & V
Arts encountered	%	%	%	%	%	%	%
Listening to music:							
Unspecified	10	8	10	17	12	11	8
Recorded classical	2	1	1	4	4	1	1
Recorded new, pop	18	19	20	13	9	17	25
Recorded (unspecified)	2	0	2	4	2	2	1
Live classical	2	2	3	1	7	2	1
Live new, pop	6	3	9	5	8	7	2
Live (unspecified)	1	0	1	0	0	1	0
Radio music	2	2	3	1	2	3	1
Cinema	29	21	34	32	32	28	28
TV, videos	15	18	13	14	16	18	10
Galleries, exhibitions	7	2	8	14	11	8	3
Theatre	19	15	19	26	32	17	16
Dance, ballet	2	2	1	3	7	1	1
Reading (literature)	30	23	30	46	39	30	28
TOTALS	(681)	(261)	(288)	(132)	(105)	(359)	(217)

Interviewees could give more than one response, so percentages will not sum to 100 per cent.
These figures are based on the weighted results (see Chapter 2).
As explained in the text, 21 per cent registered no leisure-time encounters with the arts.

With regard to variations by social class, the results (see Table 6.3) revealed a middle class bias towards listening to recorded and live classical music. Respondents in the Social Class IV and V group were the least likely to listen to live music, most probably because of fewer opportunities than college students and reduced finances. Theatre, dance and ballet were also found to have strong middle class orientations. Interestingly, with the exceptions of TV and videos, listening to recorded pop music and radio music, all the categories of art forms received their highest support from respondents in the professional class.

Indicative of these variations by social class and the likelihood that accessibility and physical proximity are not the major reasons for non-attendance, theatre-going was higher in rural areas, while cinema was higher in urban settings. Male respondents were more likely to mention listening to pop music, whereas female respondents were more likely than males to cite theatre attendance and reading.

This short chapter has summarised the evidence on respondents' participation in the 'perceiving', 'receiving' or 'consumption' of the arts. Overall, it appeared from the interviews that these variations in leisure-time arts consumption were more dependent on attitudes to the arts and cultural events than the availability of opportunities *per se*. For this reason, it is clearly essential to consider the range of attitudes young people displayed towards the arts. It is to this important factor that we turn in the next chapter.

7. Meanings and Values Attached to the Arts

This chapter provides data on the young people's perceptions and conceptions of 'the arts': particularly focusing on how they interpret the term 'the arts', and the importance which they attached to both the traditional arts (such as opera, music, literature, dance), as well as alternative arts (such as graffiti art, scratching and dubbing etc.). A number of findings are offered, including the type of young persons most likely to equate arts with only visual art (or another single art form), and the most notable variations in attitudes towards both traditional ('high') and alternative ('low') art forms. The chapter continues with evidence about how these attitudes towards the arts appear to be associated with certain definitions and also degrees of approval of the arts. It was found that appreciating the breadth of activities covered by the term 'the arts' was part of a cluster of attitudes which denoted a positive predisposition towards them. Those with a broader perspective were more likely to think highly of alternative arts.

Qualitative data are also presented to provide illustration of a range of attitudes and definitions. There is commentary on the key concepts and terms most frequently used by the young people when describing the personal significance with which they imbue the arts. Expression, creativity, communication and entertainment variously emerged, but the absence of aesthetics was particularly evident.

Introduction

Having studied the art forms that young people participated in (Chapter 5) and encountered (Chapter 6), we can now look at what the phrase 'the arts' meant to them – both in terms of what they understood by the concept and how important 'the arts' were perceived to be. This includes exploring attitudes towards traditional, as well as less traditional or alternative arts. It should be noted that while this chapter focuses on overarching attitudes to 'the arts' (e.g. how young people interpret and rate the arts), a tentative typology of more specific positive and negative attitudes to participation in the arts is offered in Chapter 11.

In considering young people's definitions of the arts (Item 20) and the personal significance they held for them (Item 21), it is particularly illuminating to place the qualitative data alongside the statistical results. It is also important to consider whether a relationship exists between a person's response to Item 20 (on their definitions of the arts) and their reply to Item 21 (on how important the arts were to them). For example, do those that have little understanding of the term 'the arts' tend to be those for whom they are less important?

It should be noted that much of the qualitative data generated by the questions reported in this chapter were volunteered by respondents in Social Classes I, II and III and by those approving of the arts. Young people in these categories were often more forthcoming, positive and lucid in their thoughts about the arts. Interviewees who held more negative attitudes to the arts tended to have less to say on the subject.

Young People's Definitions of the Arts

Item 20 in the schedule explored young people's understanding and interpretation of the term 'the arts': *'the term – the arts – can mean different things to different people. What does the term mean for you?'*. Though on the surface it may appear that how young people define the arts is of slight importance when compared with other factors such as the importance of the arts in their lives and the level of their involvement, it seems apparent that there are definite links and relationships between these aspects. Fundamental attitudes and definitions appear to be closely associated with involvement. How young people define and construct 'the arts' seems to have important bearings on their level of involvement in them – though, of course, the direction of causality is always open to question.

As will become apparent, young people perceived the arts in terms of similar defining qualities and characteristics, but there was one common, very notable addition to normal dictionary definitions of the arts, and one common, very notable omission. There certainly was a wide variety of meanings attached to 'the arts' by respondents, but the highest proportion of young people gave limited or uncertain answers.

To begin with, about one in eight respondents (13 per cent) were unable to give any meaning whatsoever to the term (see Table 7.1).

One in three (33 per cent) of the interviewees had a single perspective view of the arts (i.e. they defined 'the arts' through reference to only one art form). Well over two-thirds of these expressed that perspective in terms of visual art; solely visual perspectives amounted to 22 per cent of the whole sample.

In many respects, this is rather a worrying result insofar as 22 per cent of the respondents appeared not to differentiate between 'art' and 'arts'. To that extent, it is questionable whether their response can be considered an adequate definition of 'the arts'. On this basis, over a third of the respondents (13 per cent 'don't knows' plus 22 per cent 'visual arts') did not give an interpretation which would be widely accepted. Another significant group was the 7 per cent who saw the arts only as performance arts.

Just over one in five respondents (22 per cent) offered a double or dual perspective definition of 'the arts'. The biggest proportion of these interpreted 'the arts' as meaning 'performance and visual' art forms (9 per cent of the whole sample).

Recognising the breadth and diversity of art forms encapsulated within the concept, 22 per cent of the sample gave a multi-perspective view of 'the arts' (i.e. at least three art forms were mentioned). In addition, 7 per cent thought it was a 'collection of things', 10 per cent considered that 'creativity' was a defining factor, and 5 per cent thought that 'expression' was. Subsequent analyses showed that the vast majority who gave any of these three definitions, which in themselves indicated a broad perspective, also volunteered a multi-perspective answer. Table 7.1 displays these frequencies and gives details of further meanings young people attached to 'the arts'.

For obvious reasons, qualitative responses to this question were brief and rather limited when interviewees only offered the single and dual perspective answers. For example, a purely visual perspective (one of the most common answers) went along the lines of *'painting and art galleries'*. A fuller example of a purely visual perspective, but less typical, was collected from a 14 year old (Social Class I and II) female – *'I suppose – art work, everything to do with art, clay work, drawing, sketching, sculpture, painting ... suppose modern arts and history of art'*. The most frequent dual perspective answer, 'performance and visual', was typically given in a form such as *'art galleries and theatres'* (a 14 year old school pupil).

Those with multi-perspective views, apart from very typical answers such as *'well ... writing, drama, music, dance and obviously painting and sculpture'* (from a 20 year old student), produced a variety of thoughtful and perceptive answers. It was these answers that often included references to the defining characteristics of expression, creativity and communication.

A male 22 year old student from a working class background suggested, *'it denotes the branches of creative activity, i.e. art, music, film, writing, which communicate ideas'*. A 23 year old male social worker simply stated *'pleasurable, conceptual awareness of the world'*. An interpretation frequently given was neatly expressed by a female 24 year old in employment, *'it indicates anything non-scientific allowing creative expression'*. Likewise, a 24 year old male teacher answered *'a collection of mediums of expression'*. A reply in line with the theory of grounded aesthetics, but very atypical, was, *'it can mean art/music or a concept which refers to a creative way of producing experience of the everyday'*. A 20 year old trainee electrician felt that the arts were *'a different way of living from work, a way of expressing yourself'*.

The final example is taken from a 15 year old working class school girl:

> *I think art's a skill that you have to do something that's creative and put somebody in a position where they know what you mean, but it is not like you are talking, it's what you are doing – in a sort of play. If you are doing an art it's like when you are doing drama, you have to feel the part.*

Table 7.1   Meanings attached to 'the arts'

Perceived meanings	%
Don't know	13
Single perspectives	
Performance arts	7
Visual arts	22
Music	1
Literature	1
Contemporary art	1
Crafts, pots, textiles	1
(Sub-total offering single perspective)	(33)
Dual perspectives	
Performance and visual	9
Performance and music	4
Performance and literature	1
Performance and contemporary	1
Visual and music	4
Visual and literature	1
Visual and contemporary	1
Music and contemporary	1
(Sub-total offering dual perspective)	(22)
Multi-perspective	
Multi-perspective (three or more art forms)	22
Additional meanings	
Includes crafts and arts	2
Not science	1
Social science and humanities	2
Anything creative	10
Expressing yourself	5
Collection of things	7
Things at school	1
Students	1
Too broad to define	1
Pejorative implication	2
Other	5
TOTAL	(681)

Interviewees could give more than one response, so percentages will not sum to 100 per cent.

These figures are based on the weighted results (see Chapter 2).

Approximately 1 per cent of the sample (N = 681) did not respond to this item.

Looking at the results for this item with regard to different biographical variables, it can be seen that disaggregations by the current status of the respondent produced several significant points.

Firstly, 21 per cent (one in five) of those at school answered '*I don't know*'. In contrast, only 4 per cent of those in post-16 further education and 6 per cent of those in employment gave that response. Those on training schemes and the unemployed were also less likely to give an answer.

Respondents who offered an eclectic or multi-perspective view of the arts tended to be in employment or post-16 further education, e.g. 34 per cent of those in post-16 further education gave multi-perspective answers, whilst only 17 per cent of those in school and 10 per cent of those on training schemes did so. Young people on training schemes seemed to think of the arts especially in visual terms – 54 per cent of them interpreted 'the arts' as visual art. School pupils and the unemployed also displayed this tendency, but to a lesser extent.

These results are broadly consistent with those for age, namely that the older the interviewee the more likely they were to be able to suggest an answer, and the less likely it constituted a purely visual perspective. For the older respondents, it was also more likely to be a multi-perspective interpretation (e.g. 37 per cent of the 21-24 year old group gave multi-perspective answers, whilst only 17 per cent of the under-17s and 20 per cent of 17-20 year olds did). The older interviewees were also more forthcoming in defining the arts in such terms as 'anything creative' or a means of 'expressing yourself'.

Two significant trends are conspicuous in the above findings. Firstly, just under half (46 per cent) of those still at school were either unable to answer the question or equated 'the arts' with 'art'. Secondly, a greater proportion of the older group were able to give more sophisticated interpretations of the term. As suggested in previous chapters, it was this older group which showed signs of greater receptivity to the arts and increased participation in them. As will be seen later in this chapter, there was also a positive association between having a multi-perspective view of the arts and perceiving them to be important. Once again, it needs to be stressed that no direction of causality can be inferred from this, but it does suggest that appreciating the breadth of activities covered by the term 'the arts' is part of a whole cluster of attitudes which denote a positive pre-disposition towards them. Hence, returning to the first and rather disappointing trend mentioned above, it seems pertinent to ask whether fostering a broader appreciation and understanding of what 'the arts' entail among school students, would help encourage greater involvement in them. To this end, considerable benefits may be gained by schools adopting a unitary concept of 'the arts' in much the same way that schools currently offer students a collective image of 'science'. It seems pertinent to note that a broad image of 'science' is firmly embodied in the National Curriculum, but not so 'the arts'.

The main variations according to gender were that males were more likely to see the arts from a visual perspective (30 per cent did so compared with 15 per cent of females). Females, on the other hand, were more likely to have a multi- perspective view – (26 per cent compared to 18 per cent of males).

The only point of significance which the disaggregated results by ethnicity produced was that white Europeans were more likely to have a multiple perspective of the arts (23 per cent compared with 13 per cent of ethnic minorities).

Social class produced marked and consistent differences. Middle class respondents were more likely to offer multiple perspectives: 38 per cent of the professional group (Social Class I and II) answered thus, compared with about 19 per cent of the skilled (Social Class III) and partly/unskilled (Social Class IV and V). Conversely, working class interviewees were more likely to answer '*I don't know*': 28 per cent of the partly/unskilled, 6 per cent of the skilled (Social Class III) and 3 per cent of the professional group; or with a solely visual perspective: about 25 per cent of the partly/unskilled and the skilled and 10 per cent of the professional group. Middle class interviewees were also more likely to mention 'creativity', 'expression' and a 'collection of things'.

GCE/GCSE (16+) attainment produced very similar results to the social class analysis, but they were even more striking in terms of the visual only responses. Significantly, 27 per cent of those with no GCSEs answered '*I don't know*', compared to 6 per cent of those with one to three and less than 2 per cent of those with four or more. Moreover, 50 per cent of those with no qualifications gave solely a visual perspective; this decreased through the attainment groups to 7 per cent for those with seven or more GCSEs. Alternatively, of those with no GCSEs only 3 per cent gave a multi-perspective answer, which increased through the attainment groups to 34 per cent of those with seven or more GCSEs. Again, increased GCSE attainment was associated with a greater likelihood that interviewees saw 'the arts' as a form of 'expression', 'creativity' or a 'collection of things', or that they could articulate their perceptions through such concepts.

Thus the results show that there is a clear and strong tendency for those of middle class families, those with higher 16+ qualifications, older interviewees, and those in post-16 further education or employed, and also females, to define 'the arts' with a broad perspective. Conversely, those from working class backgrounds, those with lower GCSE attainment, younger interviewees and those at school, and to a lesser extent males, were more likely either to have not volunteered a definition of 'the arts' or to see them from a single perspective, mainly visual. Obviously, there were many exceptions to this general trend.

The Significance of the 'Traditional' Arts

Although previous chapters have alluded to the importance of the arts in some young people's lives, suggested either by statistics or glimpsed at in qualitative extracts, Item 21a asked young people directly how important the 'traditional' arts were to them. A range of art forms were used to exemplify the 'traditional' arts rather than mention the word 'traditional' itself: *'for some people, 'the arts' include music, dance, drama/theatre, film, literature (novels, poems etc.), painting, sculpture and so on. How important are those kinds of arts to you?'*.

One in three of the young people (33 per cent) who provided codable responses to this question considered the arts as a whole were not important to them. On the other hand, one in five (20 per cent) felt that the arts were a very important part of their lives. In between, 47 per cent of the sample indicated that the arts were quite important or sometimes important (see Table 7.2).

Table 7.2   The importance of the 'traditional' arts

Responses	%
Very important	20
Quite important	47
Not important	33
TOTAL	(604)

These figures are based on the weighted results (see Chapter 2).
The responses of approximately 11 per cent of the sample (N = 681) were uncodable in these categories.

With regard to particular art forms, music stood out by a considerable margin as a particularly significant form. Virtually one in three (31 per cent of the full sample; N = 681) said that music was an important aspect of their lives. Next came painting, drama, film, and literature at approximately 6 per cent each.

Further analyses revealed an interesting fact about the respondents who mentioned music and film: those who said that the arts in general were of little importance to them were most likely to say that music or film was important. This suggests that music and film often may have little overt or conscious artistic value or significance to the young people involved. Moreover, music and film were often distinguished from the other arts so that these particular forms could be valued without considering them as part of 'the arts'. One male 21 year old clerical assistant (with a single perspective of the arts) goes some way to illustrate this distinction: *'film is important to me, and music, but the others – I don't really have an interest in them'*, and this 24 year old clerical assistant also did: *'not interested at all; music – yes, but not the rest ... dance music, hip hop, rap – yes!'*.

Policy-makers may find it helpful to consider whether by encouraging young people to perceive popular cultural forms such as rock music and cinema as art, a more positive attitude to 'the arts' could be engendered.

As expected, those who saw the arts as very important were much more likely to stress its significance through reference to 'creative expression', 'enjoyment' or a 'feel-good' factor. Of the 20 per cent that considered 'the arts' very important, there were many interviewees who gave vent to strong emotions and deeply-held beliefs and values in their answers. A 24 year old art design student, for example, stated: '*I think they are the most important thing and they should be important to more people*'. Moreover, it was not just 'artistic' young people who recognised their value: a 16 year old A-level student explained:

> Well, I am more a scientist than an artist ... however, a question once asked of me by an English teacher of mine was: if you were given the choice – all scientific knowledge was to be destroyed or all artistic work was to be destroyed, which would it be? I had to say the scientific knowledge because it can be found out again, the things that are in the 'artistic data bank of the world' are very important as far as I'm concerned.

Another A-level student (middle class, female) answered, typically: '*very ... it's a way of expressing yourself to convey ideas and so can poems and music. It's like leisure, but educational at the same time*'. A 23 year old social worker of a working class background was more direct in his answer: '*important because they are areas of my life where I find pleasure*'. Again a typical answer of a 24 year old male teacher was: '*very, because they are therapeutic and stimulating*'. A final example, a 23 year old unemployed female, stated, '[they're] *vitally important. Arts are an interpretation of other people's opinion expressed in a unique way*'.

Unfortunately, those who declared that the arts were not important to them tended to have little to say. Rather than being 'positively' critical, they were generally brief and dismissive in their answers. Typical answers included '*not a lot*', '*just not interested*', '*not important to me*' or '*don't really mean that much to me*', '*I'm not really that interested*'. Similarly, a 17 year old male A-level student answered '*not that important ... it all seems the same ... it doesn't do anything for me*'. A 19 year old (racehorse stable 'lass') replied '*not very, I'm not really arty*', but added '*if people want to, then go for it*'. Slightly less dismissive, but again quite typical, was a 20 year old self-employed female who answered '*not very, music is quite important to me, but not the sort of music I would call art. I would enjoy the theatre if I had time, but it is of no major importance to me*'. The general thrust of the responses of those for whom the arts held little importance was personal indifference rather than outright anti-artistic attitudes.

Some interviewees rejected the arts on the grounds that they felt excluded due either to social attitudes, perceived 'snobbery' or expense. For example, a 15 year old male simply answered the question by saying: '*too expensive, so they exclude me*'.

Obviously, there were a lot of 'middle of the road' answers, with those who indicated '*quite important*' in the majority. Typical answers in this category went as follows – a 21 year old part-time employed female replied: '*I go to the cinema quite a bit, and also read. Music is important, but mainly pop music, so yes, they are quite important*'. Another reply which summed up the attitudes of many was given by a young person wanting to go to university: '*I enjoy it when I come across it, but it isn't of great importance. I enjoy watching a good play, looking at a good painting and listening to classical music, but it's not really meaningful for me*'. Thus, 'quite important' or 'sometimes important' answers were generally lacking in any depth of enthusiasm or commitment. Sometimes, the interest was indicative of a non-artistic perspective, as this 20 year old male explained: '*... it's just a social interest ... going to the cinema and theatre with friends*'.

As the statistics show, music was very commonly mentioned as possessing particular significance for young people, even though frequently 'the arts' were not imbued with meaning for them. Three typical comments were:

> *I don't think the world'd be anywhere without music ... music is the best art anybody could have made.* (15 year old working class female)

> *... music is very important – mostly rock and pop but also opera.*
> (19 year old student)

> *music is really important to me, as that's all I do.*
> (15 year old middle class schoolboy)

However, as mentioned earlier, a lot of those who cited music as important, described their appreciation in somewhat more superficial terms:

> *I suppose music because, when the telly isn't on, music is.*
> (23 year old middle class female, employed)

Looking at the responses to this item cross-tabulated by the current status of respondents, those in full time post-16 education had the highest percentage considering the arts to be very important to them (40 per cent, compared with the next highest, those in employment with 19 per cent and the lowest, those at school, with 12 per cent). They also had the lowest percentage considering them not important. The unemployed and employed groups both had quite similar results and were closest to, though significantly far behind, full-time education students in terms of overall consideration of the arts as important. Those on training schemes considered them least important. Despite this, 52 per cent of those on training schemes mentioned music as being important; the inference being that they did not consider their taste in music as artistic. Literature was least likely to be mentioned as important by those on training schemes. The same applied for drama and theatre.

Disaggregation by age revealed that the number of interviewees considering the arts as important increased significantly with age. The three age groups had similar percentages considering the arts 'quite important', but the over-

21s were conspicuous in having the least saying that they were of little or no importance. The over-21 year old group was least likely to refer to film as important. This was quite remarkable as actually going to the cinema increased appreciably with age, perhaps illustrating that the perceived importance of an activity as an art form may bear little relation to frequency of involvement. Painting had the highest percentage of 17-20 year olds mentioning it as important (9 per cent), mainly by students in post-16 full-time education. References to drama as important decreased with age from 11 per cent for the youngest interviewees to 3 per cent for the oldest group. Literature was judged to be particularly important to the over-21 year olds: 4 per cent for the 17-20 year olds compared with 14 per cent for the over-21 year olds.

There were no major gender differences in response to this question, although slightly more females than males found the arts very important. Males attached considerably more importance to music: 39 per cent considered it was important compared with 23 per cent of females.

Although interviewees in urban and rural areas produced equal proportions considering that the arts were very important to them, rural interviewees were more likely to consider the arts 'not very important' – (47 per cent of the latter compared with 28 per cent of urban respondents). Hence, within the rural sample, there was for this question a greater tendency to polarise to the extremes.

Social class analyses generally produced a similar effect to the age results, with, for example, the proportion considering the arts very important increasing with social class from 12 per cent for the partly/unskilled group to 35 per cent for the professional group. All groups had similar percentages replying 'quite important' but Social Class III and Social Class IV and V respondents were much more likely to consider the arts of little or no importance (36 per cent and 37 per cent) than Social Class I and II interviewees (17 per cent). Also of note is that middle class respondents were more likely to rate drama and theatre as important and the skilled group (Social Class III) were least likely to mention literature as important.

As might perhaps be imagined from the findings so far, the GCSE or 16+ attainment results show that those with seven or more GCSEs contained a high percentage of interviewees who considered the arts 'very important' (34 per cent). The 1-3 GCSE group had the lowest figure for very important (5 per cent) and the highest for not important (36 per cent). So in general, attaching significance to the arts increased with GCSE attainment, though as with earlier 'U'-shaped relationships, those with no GCSEs did not fit the pattern exactly, notably the 12 per cent of non-GCSE interviewees who answered 'very important'. The 4-6 GCSE group appeared markedly less likely than the other groups to consider painting important and also the seven or more GCSE group were significantly more likely to consider art important for the enjoyment and feel-good factor. Those interviewees with no GCSEs were noticeably most likely to see film as an important part of their lives.

To summarise, those most likely to see the arts as very important were those of middle class background, those who were well qualified, those in post-16 full-time education or older interviewees. Examples holding most of these characteristics included a 24 year old teacher with a philosophy degree who gave the previously cited quotation: '*very, because it's therapeutic and stimulating*'; a 20 year old female who was reading French at university (with 12 GCSEs and three A-levels) answered: '*important, music especially, I do all of them!*' and, thirdly a 20 year old female doing a biology degree (with 11 GCSEs and five A-levels) from a middle class family who answered: '*very ... I think it's just the thing about ideas ... new ideas ... presenting different ideas in different ways. It's very important, just the whole creative process*'.

Most likely to see the arts as less important were respondents with fewer GCSEs, from working class backgrounds, those who were younger, those on training schemes (or at school) and those in rural areas. With all these criteria, a 17 year old male trainee with no GCSEs answered, '*don't like painting, reading or drama*', though he did appear to like Bob Marley and going to the cinema. Similarly, a 14 year old school pupil from a working class family and a semi-rural area answered simply, but very typically: '*not at all*'.

The Significance of 'Alternative' Arts

As the last but one extract suggests, many interviewees rated the 'traditional' arts as not important to them, yet expressed an interest in cultural activities which they did not class as 'the arts' or even 'music', 'drama', 'literature' and so on (e.g. '*I don't like the arts, but I like Bob Marley*'). In an effort to ascertain how personally significant these 'informal cultural activities' or 'youth arts' or 'low/popular arts' were perceived to be, interviewees were invited to indicate how important these kind of artistic activities were to them (see Item 21b): '*some young people make up their own arts activities (e.g. scratching/mixing, devising their own fashion clothes, computer graphics, graffiti art). What do you think about those kinds of arts?*'. In this section, these kind of 'low' arts have been called 'alternative arts'.

From Table 7.3, it can be seen that 46 per cent of the respondents who volunteered codable responses 'quite approved', and only 9 per cent actually 'disapproved' or 'rejected' them, with 12 per cent 'highly approving'. Fifteen per cent had 'personal reservations' and 18 per cent 'approved for others'.

In addition to these core categories, of the full sample (N = 681), 16 per cent volunteered that the 'alternative' arts were valid art forms, and 8 per cent added that it was a valuable form of self-expression. Six per cent were concerned about the legality of it, graffiti art in particular. A further 3 per cent believed that such art forms were especially important and appropriate for young people.

Table 7.3   Views on the 'alternative arts'

Responses	%
Highly approves	12
Quite approves	46
Approves for others	18
Disapproves, rejects	9
Personal reservations	15
TOTAL	(644)

These figures are based on the weighted results (see Chapter 2).
The responses of approximately 6 per cent of the sample (N = 681) were
uncodable in these categories.

It should be noted that graffiti art, the last of the listed examples of alternative arts given in the question, was often picked up by the interviewees and thus responses were often angled towards it.

Among the 12 per cent who highly approved, typical answers included, '*again, I think that is very important because you are doing something for yourself – you are creating something. You haven't copied, you are doing something on your own – make it different, it's original*', from a 14 year old middle class school girl and from a 19 year old, employed female with no qualifications, '*very clever and creative*' or '*I think they are wonderful, I love graffiti art – beautiful. I like computer art – photo realistic. There is a million things you can do with a computer*' – the reply from an 18 year old Social Class III A-level student. Another common response was '*graffiti is as important because people are given a creative outlet*' – this from a 24 year old teacher. A frequent viewpoint from those who were aware of social class and status differentials in the arts was '*they're good, much more interesting, not so stuck up, more street level*'. Finally, the next three extracts briefly illustrate particularly common attitudes: '*they enable people to express themselves*' (15 year old school girl), '*gives a means of communicating*' (an 18 year old male in post-16 further education) and '*easier to express yourself instead of letting your frustration out in other ways*' (another 18 year old male in post-16 further education).

As shown in the table, the majority of young people 'quite or sometimes' approved. Such responses ranged from qualified approval through indifference to moderate or unenthusiastic approval. Typical examples included, '*some's all right, don't like graffiti over buildings – I like it when it's where it should be*' (18 year old female) and showing increasing approval, '*I suppose you'd have to call them arts because they are a creative way of doing something*' (from a male, 16 year old, middle class A-level student), '*they've got their place - creativity in society*' (the answer of a 24 year old demolition worker) and '*as long as you're able to express yourself it's all right. All art is a form of expression*' (from a Social Class III female 17 year old A-level student). A typical example of 'sometimes' approving was volunteered by a 16 year old middle class sixth former:

> *I think some of it is quite interesting. Some graffiti art is quite good – not vandalism ... it's not something that just anybody could do, so I think they deserve credit for it. I'm not so keen on mixing* [similar to scratching and dubbing] *but it's personal taste.*

Those who 'approved for others' often answered along the lines of '*It can be positive to people who do it, but it doesn't have any effect on me*' (a 15 year old female) or '*if they like doing it then that's good*' (14 year old male) or more indifferently '*they are OK if that's what they want to do with their time*' (male 18 year old trainee).

Personal reservations took the form of '*they are arts, but it's not my thing, I'm more into classical stuff*' from an 18 year old female in post-16 further education.

Disapproval (only 9 per cent) varied from mildly – '*don't really count it as art*' from a 19 year old working class male accounting technician, to '*I think it's crap, no good at all ...*' from a 21 year old, unemployed, working class male. Another example fairly typical of the negative answers was: '*not that good really, I don't like scratching, I don't know if you can call all the vandalism art, I suppose you have to be good at it, but I don't like it*'. One response, and indeed exceptionally atypical for this sub-sample, was, after initially saying '*sorry, I don't know anything about those*' and that they were not arts – '*people call them art – but people miss the basics, only then can you start experimental art which I think these are. If you avoid the hard work first it doesn't count as art*'. However, this view was a minority one, since a significant number of people mentioned the hard work, talent, skill, and time involved, for instance, in graffiti art. Disapproval took the form of either no particular dislike or rejection by not considering them art or artistic, or, much more uncommonly, outright rejection or dislike.

When considering views on the 'alternative' or 'low' arts held by respondents in the different current status groups, those on training schemes (18 per cent) and in post-16 further education (15 per cent) were marginally most likely to approve highly. Trainees were also more likely to state that the alternative arts were a valid art form – 23 per cent of them mentioned this.

As well as those on training schemes and in post-16 further education, the over-21 year olds were also more likely to highly approve. Gender had little effect or significance on young people's feelings towards alternative arts. Females, however, were more likely to see the alternative arts as a valuable form of self- expression, though the legality of graffiti concerned females more. Ethnicity produced similar results.

Looking at the effect of social class on attitudes towards alternative arts, some noteworthy results emerge. Approving highly of the alternative arts increased both noticeably and consistently as the status of social class increased (16 per cent of the professional class approved highly, in contrast to 9 per cent of the partly/unskilled class). Conversely, the social class most likely to disapprove was the Social Class IV and V group – though personal reservations throughout the classes were very similar. In addition, there was a marked increase in the proportions mentioning alternative arts as valuable for self-expression with increased status of social class and a substantial increase (4 per cent for Social Class IV and V to 32 per cent for Social Class I and II) in those referring to the alternative arts as a valid art form.

Further analyses also revealed that those with four or more 16+ qualifications were more likely to approve highly of the alternative arts than those with fewer qualifications.

In general, approval of the alternative arts was most likely among those in post-16 further education or on training schemes (although trainees were least likely to value self-expression), those in the middle classes and those with over four GCSEs. Whilst disapproval was most likely among the unemployed, and among males, those who are in Social Class IV and V and those with few GCSEs.

Having looked at interviewees' responses to the three separate questions, it was considered worthwhile to inquire whether patterns emerged when looking at all three questions together, e.g. are people that define the arts in a certain way (Item 20) likely to rate the significance of 'traditional' and 'alternative' arts (Item 21a and b) in a similar manner?

Associations between Attitudes and Definitions

Although based on small sub-samples, a cross-tabulation between Item 21a (views on the 'traditional' arts) and Item 21b (views on 'alternative' arts) produced the following 'broad-brush' points:

♦ Of those that felt that the traditional arts were very important, less than 1 per cent disapproved of alternative arts.

♦ Similarly, only 2 per cent of those that disapproved of alternative arts thought that traditional arts were very important.

♦ Conversely, 47 per cent of those that disapproved of alternative arts felt that traditional arts were also not important to them.

♦ Of those that highly approved of alternative arts, 84 per cent felt that traditional arts were important or very important to them.

♦ Of those that felt traditional arts were not important, only 5 per cent approved highly of alternative arts.

Perhaps rather surprisingly, and certainly very noteworthy is that, in general, believing that the traditional arts are important and approving highly of alternative arts tend to go hand in hand, as do disapproving of them. This is significant since the Willis thesis tends to polarise 'traditional arts' and informal cultural activities like graffiti, scratching/dubbing etc. Our evidence suggests that young people's attitudes towards them are not consistent with a polarisation and that many perceive them as being part of a continuum covering a broad collection of activities subsumed under the umbrella term 'the arts'.

A cross-tabulation between Item 20 (definitions of 'the arts') and Item 21a (views on the 'traditional' arts) also disclosed a significant trend by highlighting the following points:

♦ Of those that felt the traditional arts were not very important to them, nearly two-thirds (65 per cent) didn't know what the term meant or gave a single perspective answer, and only 15 per cent offered multi-perspective answers.

♦ Of those that felt the traditional arts were very important, nearly three-quarters (74 per cent) gave dual or multi-perspective answers.

In general, therefore, it seemed likely that the less important the arts were considered to be, the narrower one's perspective of the arts and, vice versa, the more important the arts were deemed to be, the broader the interpretation associated with them.

Lastly, significant points produced by a cross-tabulation of Item 20 (definitions interpretations of 'the arts') and 21b (views on 'alternative' arts) included:

♦ Of those with multiple perspectives of 'the arts', only 5 per cent disapproved of or rejected alternative arts.

♦ Of those who disapproved, only 14 per cent volunteered a multiple perspective.

♦ Of those that disapproved of alternative arts, 29 per cent didn't know what 'the arts' meant.

♦ Of those that approved highly of alternative arts, 39 per cent had a multiple perspective of the arts.

In short, those with a broad perspective were more likely to think highly of alternative arts and least likely to disapprove; those who disapproved of the alternative arts were most likely not to know the meaning of the term 'the arts'.

Thus, in conclusion to this overview of the three questions considered together, the statistics point to the possibility that there may be two main types of young people or manifest attitudes. The two types cluster around those with broad perspectives of 'the arts', who approve of alternative arts and feel that traditional arts are very important to them, and those who don't know what 'the arts' entail or perhaps have limited ideas, and disapprove of alternative arts and find that traditional arts are of little or no importance to them. Obviously, there are many exceptions and there is much merging in the middle ground, but the following two responses to the three questions from the same two individuals illustrate the two different attitudinal and value positions:

[Q20]: *Anything that can create a feeling or expression, a mood of someone else – music, theatre, literature, art, anything like that.*

[Q21a] *A lot ... they are all important in different ways depending on my mood ...*

[Q21b] *Yes, they are expressing feelings and emotions – just a modern form – I don't agree with those who say it is not art ...*

and

[Q20] *Nothing*

[Q21a] *Not at all*

[Q21b] *Stupid*

or the following, which goes a little further in illustrating how restrictive definitions can isolate young people from the arts:

[Q20] *Opera, ballet, theatre*

[Q21a] [he stated that they were] *of little importance*

[21b] *I don't really class them as art, they are everyday stuff – wouldn't class it as art.*

It is open to conjecture to what extent a broad perspective and understanding of the arts leads people to see them as an important aspect of their lives or if, for whatever reasons, finding the arts important develops broad perspectives. Even if the former is not entirely the case, it does appear from the evidence that how people define the arts may have major implications for how they value it.

In this section, the qualitative data have so far been used to illustrate statistical results, but before reaching the final conclusion of this important aspect of the research, a closer and fuller look should be taken at the available qualitative accounts.

Qualitative Data on Attitudes to the Arts

One observation immediately apparent when reading the comments offered by respondents is that very few mentioned aesthetics or beauty as important dimensions in the arts. Instead, significance was placed on expression and creativity. Typical references to these qualities included: '*anything that can create a feeling or express a mood of someone else*', '*anything that anybody does that is creative*' and '*people expressing themselves in the way they want to*'. Many such comments began to illustrate the depths to which young people feel the need to express inner feelings and the scope or outlet that the arts can provide for this. These responses extend this point a little further:

'*personal freedom of expression*',

'*express your thoughts and desires – freedom of expression*',

'*expressing and experiencing one's inner self*',

'*personal expression*',

'*an important representation of expressions, forms that you cannot express in school and other routine day to day life*',

'*being able to express one's self in the fullest way we want to*'.

The phrase, '*expressing things the way we want to*', often surfaced in the interviews. This suggests that the arts were seen as an area, unlike others, where young people don't feel restricted or constrained: '*everyone should be able to express themselves in the way they want*', and finally the arts '*have built my self-expression*'.

Another feature that became apparent in young people's accounts is that the arts are seen not just as a means of expression, but they also involve a process, perhaps prior to expression, of coming to terms with yourself, defining yourself, developing and discovering your ideas and feelings. The following illustrate this aspect:

'*Imagination, creating your dreams and interpreting them*',

'*help to formulate ideas*'

and

'*it is what is inside the person*'.

This is shown at the receptive level by comments such as:

'*art shows you many new aspects, opens up new vistas*',

'*very important to see other people's outlook*',

'*awareness, opening up horizons*',

'*conceptual awareness of the world*',

and also

'*the arts tells you about processes governing art and focuses on things contradictory and tells you about things in society.*'

'Communication', as distinct from expression, was another concept that resonated throughout young people's definitions and statements on the importance of the arts.

'Talent' and 'skill' were conspicuous as perhaps the next most important aspect (after expression and creativity) of young people's definitions: '*I think it's talents really – simply, – skills and expressing yourself*'. Very often, the key criterion for judging whether alternative arts were valid art forms was whether or not their execution demanded 'skill' and 'talent'.

Imagination also proved a significant element in the definitions and importance of art to young people. A typical reference was: '*creating and using your imagination for your own thing*', or '*just things with your hands, imaginative things*'.

Looking more at interviewees' perceptions of the importance of arts, 'entertainment' was a word that was frequently used. It was generally voiced more by 'consumer' or audience-oriented respondents, whilst aspects of fulfilment and satisfaction were more often used in answers from 'producers' or 'doers', e.g. '*extremely important for self-fulfilment*', '*pleasure*', '*fun*', '*enjoyment*', '*recreation*', '*would be boring without them*', '*therapeutic*', '*relaxing*', '*social*', and '*a relief from everyday life*'.

The fact that definitions and views on the importance of the arts often reflect a consumer's and producer's perspective is relevant to the theory of making, perceiving and feeling systems mentioned in a previous section. An example of the latter two systems is the following response: '*important – but I'm not very musical or into giving inputs into the arts – I'm more of a listener/ appreciator rather than a provider*'. A comment from someone using the perceiving system was: '*I like looking at stuff and think people have to be talented and know what they are doing to be able to do the things as well as they do*'. The feeling system is well illustrated by: '*I enjoy the theatre ... I like music, I just love it, it's really pop music, what's going on in the charts – I love going to the cinema*'. Whilst someone who sees the arts more from a making perspective answered '*important because you are doing something for yourself, you are creating something*', and another who exhibits using the making system stated, '*my art work is very important, I like expressing myself*'.

An art student pointed out how functioning in one of the systems helps development with another: '*I think if more people could create things ... it is only through doing it yourself that you appreciate what other people are doing*'. A 15 year old working class girl captures all three systems in the following comment: [some of the comments have already been presented in other sections]

> *I think that art is a skill that you have to do something that's creative and put somebody in a position where they know what you mean, but it's not like you are telling them, it's what you are doing – in a sort of*

play. If your doing an art, like you're doing drama when you have to feel the part ... I don't think the world would be anywhere without music – music is the best art anybody could have made up – sometimes it makes you feel happy, sometimes it makes you sad ... when I was little I used to paint and make up poems to go with the paintings but I stopped doing that as I got older!

It was evident that although the feeling system was the most frequently articulated by this sample of young people, the most enthusiastic answers tended to come from the makers; this system was cited least.

Attitudes and definitions that surfaced in these questions also included factors that excluded or alienated young people from the arts. On a very basic level, a perceived lack of knowledge tended to exclude young people from using the perceiving and making system, and restricted them to the feeling system. This problem was acknowledged by one respondent's reply to Item 21a: *'very important. The arts are a form of entertainment. Life would be dull without them. Music and theatre because that's what I like. I've not enough knowledge to appreciate a lot of it'*. And also by a 17 year old unemployed male with no qualifications: *'I like graffiti, but the rest is too confusing for me ... I like the sort of graffiti that says something – you know what it means'*.

Money was obviously another barrier to many aspects of the arts. This was illustrated by several respondents who simply stated that the arts were inaccessible for them, because of the lack of financial resources and expense of many arts activities.

Another very important barrier, particularly for the working class interviewees, revolved around the perception that the arts were for 'snobs' and the middle classes e.g. *'I hate snobbery in art',* and one definition stated *'ballet, opera, that sort of thing, upper class posh things'*. Both lack of knowledge and understanding, along with feelings of exclusion due to perceived snobbery (social barrier), either alone or combined, created a significant attitudinal barrier. Some interviewees, not only avoided both these barriers, but were equipped with the cultural upbringing which offered positive attitudes and the appropriate knowledge and understanding. Young people who had been inducted into or surrounded by the arts, took it as a common place and possessed an inherent understanding and appreciation of it. For example: *'what I've done for the whole of my life'* or *'a necessary outlet, I've always been exposed to the arts'*.

Occasionally, some interviewees showed great awareness and insights into the difficulties and barriers restricting access to the arts:

[the arts are] *extremely important, our culture either makes it snobbish or says it's totally superfluous and removes it from daily life, which is wrong. People's creativity gets squashed, especially in working class backgrounds; important in that anything that inhibits human nature is a crime really.*

Although the statistics show that the most common tendency was for those who disapprove of traditional arts to also disapprove of alternative arts, there was a significant minority who felt excluded from traditional arts but found an outlet in alternative ones. For example: *'they are good, much more interesting, not so stuck up – more street level'*, and *'more valid than so called proper art – it should be more valued as part of everyday life'*.

Looking at the qualitative data on alternative arts, again the keyword appears to be 'expression'. Many of the young people who defined traditional arts as 'expressive' or 'creative' went on to say that those alternative arts were also valid art forms. For example: *'as long as you're able to express yourself it's all right'*, *'all art is a form of expression'*, or *'no clear cut limits to what art is – it's any creative activity'*. It was often in their references to expressive qualities that approval or acceptance of alternative arts surfaced: *'if someone wants to express themselves in that way, no problem, everyone should be able to express themselves in the way they want'*.

As with traditional arts, it appears from the qualitative evidence that those who highly approved of alternative arts were the ones most likely to particularly value and appreciate them for their expressive qualities. The answer *'they are expressing feelings and emotions in just a modern form'* is indicative of the frequent references to the alternative arts as encompassing 'modern(ity)', 'modern society' and 'youth'. For example *'more like a young person's art than sculpture etc. – yes it is art, it's their personal view'*, and *'I think they have their place in modern society'*. One interviewee went further: *'I think it is important that every generation has its own identity through these things'* and similarly *'I don't agree with those who say it's not art, they are putting old opinions on new talent'*. Another talked about *'images projected by people my age, for example, spray paint or promotion for bands is art ... images you notice and think about'*, putting the emphasis not just on expression, but extending it to communicating ideas and thoughts rather than emotions and feelings alone. Modern art, perhaps more than traditional forms, was considered to communicate the social and political messages of young people:

I think they are ways people can get over their views, what they think, especially graffiti writing – it's a way of expressing art – what goes on in their mind, what they think about, what goes on in the world.

Taking these thoughts on alternative arts further, one respondent answered, though not typically:

They have great potential, because they [the 'traditional' arts] *are the dominant art, and people who control it dictate the status quo.*

Alternative art is able to subvert by portraying things from a different perspective.

Alternative arts were commonly recognised as different, even though considered a valid art form:

I think it's personal preference – what you like really. I've not got a low view of street art or mixing, or dance music or anything, it's just that they're less traditional – so they are less accepted by people,

or

they are not traditional arts but they are contemporary arts that have to evolve with current society,

and also a little more grudgingly

I suppose it's a kind of art – I wouldn't see it in the same light as Shakespeare.

The general drift seems to be that it's a matter of personal taste: '*different tastes, beauty is in the eye of the beholder*', and that it is a valid art form, but different. These were particularly common feelings among those who 'quite approved'.

Apart from the small level of outright disapproval, there were also objections expressed against illegal graffiti. Common reactions were '*... don't like graffiti over buildings, I like it where it should be*', and '*I don't agree with spray and that on private property*'.

Although the freedom to paint graffiti wherever the artist chooses may be cause for concern for some, the 'freedom' of alternative arts in other senses, such as 'doing your own thing', with a feeling of originality, was often referred to: '*again, I think they are very important as you are doing something for your self, it's original*', '*I don't see much difference, anything original is art, isn't it? Anyway, art should be accessible – I hate snobbery in art*'; '*A good idea because anybody could do it*'; and also '*I think they're better than the others, they're doing your own thing*'.

This final comment suggests more approval of alternative arts than traditional ones. It illustrates how the alternative arts sometimes attract young people who, for whatever reason, feel excluded or exclude themselves from more traditional arts. However, it is important that it is realised that this is atypical and the general trend (as already outlined) is that those that approve highly of traditional arts, also approve of the alternative.

To summarise and conclude, a major point to be taken from the qualitative data is the general absence of mention of aesthetics and the importance put upon expression. For example, '*all graffiti is an art form because it's expressive whether it's well painted or not*'. As pointed out by one interviewee, alternative arts are the media with greatest potential for expression. The evidence also suggested that for the large majority of young people who offered a broad interpretation of the arts, approval of one branch of the arts commonly extended to approval of the other.

Broadminded attitudes and interpretations seemed to be linked to the valuing of the arts by young people. This was clearly evident in the perceptions of young people with relatively high numbers of 16+ qualifications.

As discussed, schools (school pupils being the least likely to approve highly and most likely not to know the meaning of 'the arts') may be seen as critically important institutions in the efforts to increase broadmindedness and break down attitudinal barriers and thus greatly reduce the prevalence of young people being dismissive on negative grounds alone. Lack of skills and artistic knowledge (a feeling that it is 'over their heads' or they are not talented enough) were often found to be barriers to involvement. As such, it is at least pertinent to ask whether schools could be doing more to erode such barriers. At this point, it seems appropriate to move on to consider young people's perceptions of their arts experiences in schools.

8. Arts During The School Years

This chapter examines the data from questions posed to interviewees about their arts experiences in the primary and secondary phases of their school careers. About three quarters of the sample had positive recall of primary school arts, and a similar proportion reflected positively on their secondary school arts experiences. Drama and acting in plays were recollected as the most enjoyable and valuable primary school arts activities, and this preference was repeated in the sample's recall of arts at secondary school. The chapter also presents young people's views on the learning outcomes of school arts, and examines how these amounts of the effects of arts involvement at school differ according to such variables as gender, social class and age.

The chapter concludes with findings on arts specialisation (i.e. the continuation of arts subject study beyond Year 9 or equivalent). It was evident that just over half of the sample took at least one arts subject as a separate or specialised discipline. However, analysis shows notable gender differences in the particular subjects, as well as the number of arts subjects taken.

It should be noted that, given the age of the interviewees (14-24), the era of primary school arts recollected will be the mid-seventies to 1990. The sample's recollections of secondary school arts will cover the period of 1980 to the present.

Primary School Arts Experience

I don't think you'd ever realise what you learnt out of the arts at primary school really ... but you could've learnt something which wouldn't hit you because you're too young to realise and, asking me now, I'm too old to remember. You might think with your friends 'that's daft, I'm not acting as an elephant again' – but there was probably something somewhere: yet it's too late to remember now.

(Male, 19, in employment)

This circumspective response raises a central dilemma in recollecting the value of primary arts experiences: namely 'too old to remember now, too young to know then', and thus perfectly summarises why there may be a need for considerable caution when looking at the findings in this area of the investigation. Nevertheless, the data do reveal – or confirm – trends in arts participation which show that, even at an early stage in their school career, certain categories of young people might already be exhibiting signs of what might be termed an '*arts by-pass*', that is, are less likely to feel they have found the arts which they experienced either enjoyable or valuable.

Positive or negative recall of primary arts?

In response to the first closed question (Item 28a): *'can you remember any arts activities (including drama, visual, music, literature etc.) which you particularly enjoyed or valued at primary school?'*, just over a quarter (27 per cent) of the total sample (N = 681) responded negatively (i.e. felt they had not particularly enjoyed or valued their primary school arts), and approximately three-quarters (73 per cent) affirmed positive views when recollecting their arts experiences in this period of schooling.

Additional analyses revealed that this approximate three to one ratio of positive recall on primary arts experiences was fairly consistent across the variables of location – urban/rural residency, ethnicity and age band, although the sample showed a slightly higher than average positive response from the under-17 year olds (76 per cent compared to about 71 per cent for the other two age groups).

However, when the variables of gender and social class were looked at, there were some significant differences in positive and negative responses. Table 8.1 demonstrates a higher incidence of negative responses to primary school arts among males (about one-third) and shows a notably higher proportion of young people from professional backgrounds (Social Class I and II) recording a positive recall on their primary school arts experiences than those from the other two social class categories.

Table 8.1   Primary school arts recall by gender and social class

Recall on primary arts	Total sample %	Gender		Social Class		
		Female %	Male %	I & II %	III (N & M) %	IV & V %
Positive	73	68	78	81	73	70
Negative	27	32	22	19	27	30
TOTALS	(680)	(336)	(344)	(104)	(358)	(218)

These figures are based on the weighted results (see Chapter 2).

When positive recall of primary school arts was broken down by both gender and social class together, the most likely candidates for 'arts by-pass' were males from Social Class IV and V backgrounds (over a third were negative about primary school arts). In contrast, females whose parent(s) were in the Social Class I and II category ranked highest in frequency of positive recall: only about one in six girls felt they did not value or enjoy their arts experiences during the primary years of school.

Finally, the results of this closed question on positive recall of primary school arts were broken down by 16+ educational attainment. Here again, it seemed that a small – though perhaps notable – difference emerged, with the highest achievers in educational attainment (those with seven or more GCSEs or equivalent) more often registering positive recall of primary school arts. Over three-quarters (77 per cent) of high educational achievers affirmed their enjoyment or valuing of primary arts, compared to around two-thirds (66 per cent) in the categories of lower achievement (three or less GCSEs or equivalent).

Reasons for negative recall of primary school arts

Of those 183 respondents who replied 'no' to the closed question on valuing or enjoying primary arts, 154 answered a follow-up question. This supplementary question (Item 28b) inquired whether there was a particular reason for the negative recall, worded as *'was there any particular reason why'* [you didn't enjoy or value primary arts]? The reasons given were coded, and eight main categories of response emerged. The rank order of these – with examples of verbatim replies for each category – are given below.

Category of response	Example of comment *[The reason I did not enjoy or value primary arts was ...]*
Can't remember	*... nothing sticks in my memory as to what they were offering me.* (Male, 18) *I can't even remember doing it.* (Female, 14)
Arts disliked, boring	*wasn't keen on any of these things. They didn't interest me..* (Male, 21) *Didn't like them, I found them boring.* (Male, 19)
Not much done	[Where I went to school] *it was very basic – they concentrated on the work side of it – there wasn't much. There were plays put on every three years but I was too young.* (Female, 19) *We didn't get the chance.* (Female, 14)
Didn't like school	*At that age I was* [only] *into rushing home from school.* (Male, 19) *Hated school, we didn't do anything.* (Male, 24)
Not good at it	*I found it very difficult.* (Female, 16)
Peer influence	*The crowd I was in just didn't want to know.* (Male, 18)
Negative social, emotional effect	*I was rather shy.* (Female, 16) *... hated performing on my own when people watching.* (Female, 17)
Poor teaching	*The teacher didn't bother with us much.* (Male, 15)
Other reasons	The respondents declared that they did not like particular activities such as music or drama, or that they preferred sport.

The actual percentages of respondents mentioning each type of reason are set out in Table 8.2.

Table 8.2   Reasons for negative recall of primary school arts by gender

Response	% of respondents who answered follow-up questions on negative recall		
	Total sample %	Gender	
		Male %	Female %
Can't remember	36	29	48
Arts disliked, boring	28	30	24
Not much done	9	7	11
Poor teaching	5	8	0
Didn't like school	5	5	6
Not good at it	3	4	2
Peer influence	3	5	0
Negative, social emotional effect	3	1	4
Other reasons	8	10	5
TOTALS	(154)	(96)	(58)

These figures are based on the weighted results (see Chapter 2).

In this way, almost two-thirds (64 per cent) of the sample who indicated negative recall either couldn't remember or specifically did not enjoy primary school arts. Breaking down this group of respondents by independent variables again shows some interesting differences. As Table 8.2 shows females were more likely to suggest they could not remember their primary school arts experiences, while male respondents were marginally more likely to nominate their own lack of enthusiasm for the arts as the major reason. Of course, this gender difference may reflect an inherent diplomatic politeness by girls in response to an interviewer or it may be further confirmation of a general non-arts orientation by many males which begins even in the earliest stages of schooling. It could be important for future research with larger samples to inquire whether there is any significance in the fact that no females volunteered 'peer influence' or 'poor teaching' as a reason for not valuing their primary arts experience. Qualitative evidence described later in the report (see Chapter 11) suggests that peer influence factors were particularly important in affecting male attitudes to the arts.

Though again numbers of respondents are very small, cross-tabulations by social class suggested that young people from professional backgrounds (Social Class I and II) emerge as the group who most frequently nominated lack of opportunities for arts activities within their primary years of schooling. It is possible to speculate that this may reflect the academic orientation of some educational establishments attended by professionals' children or a retrospective awareness on the part of this category of young people themselves that there is a rigour and complexity in acquiring arts skills which the primary school did not address.

Valued primary arts activities

Following the previous questions on perceptions of primary arts, interviewees were asked a subsequent question (Item 28c) *'what arts did you enjoy and why did you enjoy them?'*. This double question allowed interviewees to focus on particular art forms and/or cite any general aspect of the experience of primary school arts participation which contributed to their positive views. Coding allowed up to three responses to be registered.

Table 8.3 shows the ranking of 'enjoyable' primary arts experiences which the sample of young people nominated, and also shows the variation between males and females. It includes all primary school art forms nominated by more than five interviewees.

It was apparent that dramatic performance ('acting in plays') and also general or unspecified drama sessions/lessons (coded as 'drama') were often recalled as a particularly enjoyable primary arts activity. It is very striking that more than a third of the sample registered their valuing of at least one form of drama. This is considerably higher – almost double – the references to music and the visual arts. Furthermore, 19 per cent of respondents mentioned at least one musical activity (e.g. 'learning a musical instrument', 'choir', 'singing' or non-specific references to 'music'). This parallels the number of nominations for 'painting/drawing'. The very low number of references to 'writing' may also be significant: it appears to be rarely associated with the arts.

Looking at the differences between male and female responses (see Table 8.3), most significantly there was a noticeably higher number of girls nominating musical aspects of their primary education as an art form they valued or enjoyed. 'Learning a musical instrument', 'singing', 'music (unspecified)' and participation in a 'choir' were more likely to be cited by females. The collation of figures for males and females mentioning at least one musical activity show this gender difference particularly starkly. The low incidence of males mentioning dance as an art form enjoyed at primary school is also evident (though the small numbers involved require caution). Male respondents' positive recalls of 'drama', 'acting in plays' and 'visits to the pantomime' are noticeable, as is their selection of 'painting and drawing'. Possibly the sociability, performance and physical aspect of drama and play acting had particular appeal.

Table 8.3   Primary school arts experiences enjoyed or valued by gender

	Total sample	Gender	
		Male	Female
Activities	%	%	%
% mentioning at least one dramatic activity	(37)	(37)	(37)
Acting in plays	25	26	24
Painting, drawing	19	21	17
% mentioning at least one musical activity	(19)	(12)	(25)
Drama	15	14	16
Learning musical instrument	7	4	10
Reading literature	7	6	7
Music (unspecified)	6	5	8
Choir	6	4	8
Dance	5	2	9
Singing	4	2	6
Unusual art techniques	3	1	4
Clay, pottery	3	2	3
Pantomime trips	2	3	2
Writing	1	1	2
English	1	1	1
TOTALS	(681)	(338)	(343)

Interviewees could give more than one response, so percentages will not sum to 100 per cent.
These figures are based on the weighted results (see Chapter 2).
As shown in Table 8.1, 27 per cent of the sample (N = 681) registered that they had not enjoyed or valued any aspect of primary school arts.

Perceived benefits of primary arts

Interviewees were also asked to nominate what they thought they had 'learnt or got out of' these art activities (Item 28d). The rank order of categories of response to this question are shown in Table 8.4 and the chart overleaf offers examples of comments from young people for each category.

Category of response	Example of comments *[What I think I learnt from or got out of primary school arts was ...]*
Excitement, enjoyment	*... it was more to do with fun* (Male, 24)
Overcoming shyness	*drama – I talked more – it brought me out of my shell a bit* (Male, 19) *... like public speaking, sort of confidence building I suppose.* (Female, 18)
Learnt nothing	*Nothing ... I can't think of a single thing that I got out of school when I was younger.* (Male, 23) *Nothing – I liked to show off.* (Male, 14)
Acquiring technique	*I suppose I got it together in music when young.* (Male, 18) *Painting: you learnt how to hold your brush and use it.* (Female, 16)
Social aspect, mixing	*I'd certainly say it increased the scope of what you thought you'd want to do at school rather than just doing the basic subjects. You'd certainly a lot more friends.* (Male, 19) *And it helped me to get on with other people because I tended to be a loner, but dancing you have to work with others.* (Female, 14)
Don't know, can't remember	*I've never had any lasting memory of it.* (Female, 24) *Haven't a clue!* (Female, 15)
Experience of acting	*Acting in front of loads of people – I thought it would be scary but it wasn't.* (Male, 19)
Sense of achievement	*Made me feel at least I could do something.* (Male, 20)
Self-expression	*Yeah, I suppose I learnt to express myself through the music that we do.* (Female, 14)
Started my interest	*I went from learning the recorder on to the clarinet – so it started me off.* (Female, 16)
Insights	*I quite liked writing poetry – it made me understand things.* (Female, 14)
Language, vocabulary	*I'm not sure – better vocabulary I suppose for literature.* (Male, 16)
Discovering talent	*... in primary school I think I decided I knew art was what I wanted to do in my life. I found out I was good at it.* (Male, 17)
Not at that age	*I suppose at that age I can't remember.* (Female, 21)

Table 8.4   What young people got out of/learnt from primary school arts

Responses	Total sample %	Male %	Female %
		Gender	
Excitement, enjoyment	17	13	22
Overcoming shyness	11	11	11
Learnt nothing	10	12	8
Acquiring technique	8	8	9
Social aspect, mixing	8	7	10
Don't know, remember	4	3	6
Experience of acting	4	4	4
Sense of achievement	4	4	4
Self-expression	3	2	4
Started my interest	3	1	5
Insights	3	3	3
Language, vocabulary	3	2	3
Discovering talent	1	0	2
Relaxing	1	1	1
Communication skills	1	1	1
Free choice activity	1	1	1
Not at that age	1	1	1
Using imagination	1	2	1
TOTALS	(681)	(338)	(343)

Interviewees could give more than one response, so percentages will not sum to 100 per cent. These figures are based on the weighted results (see Chapter 2).
As shown in Table 8.1, 27 per cent of the sample (N = 681) registered that they had not enjoyed or valued any aspect of their primary school arts.

Thus, the sample of young people predominantly recollected that 'enjoyment and excitement' was the main dividend accruing from primary school arts. Following on from this, it is notable that specific arts skills, knowledge or understanding were mentioned by a very small minority. Indeed, the third highest ranking response was that they had felt they had not learnt anything (10 per cent of the total sample). The evidence suggests that less than one in ten (8 per cent) remembered primary arts as comprising any significant skill acquisition ('acquiring technique'); and only one in a hundred (1 per cent) felt it had been an occasion for realising any specific 'talent' within the arts. 'Insights' also ranks quite low. It was more frequent for the primary school arts to be recollected as a contributor to young people's personal and social development: notably 'overcoming shyness', 'a sense of achievement' and 'self-expression', or more generally as an opportunity for social interchange and communication.

Breakdown of this ranking by the variables shows some interesting trends in gender and class responses, though in many aspects there was, in fact, little variation recorded.

However, some interesting gender differences did emerge in the numbers of male and female responses nominating 'excitement and enjoyment' (see Table 8.4). Additionally, male respondents rarely mentioned they had 'discovered an arts talent' at primary school and females were more likely to suggest that the social/mixing aspect was something they learnt or got out of their primary arts experiences. Males were also more likely to express the opinion that they had 'learnt nothing' through their arts experiences. All in all, it perhaps indicates a tendency for females to more readily discern that their primary arts experiences were an opportunity to acquire, or realise artistic and social skills.

Analysis showed two interesting differences between the white and ethnic sample on the range of responses describing any learning retrospectively associated with primary arts. Eight per cent of the interviewees from the ethnic minorities (N = 67) felt they had 'discovered a talent', compared to only 1 per cent of white interviewees (N = 608). As well as that, while 11 per cent of white young people did not think they had learnt anything, only 5 per cent of ethnic minority respondents replied in this way.

Table 8.5   What young people got out of/learnt from primary school arts by age

Response	Total sample %	Under-17 %	Age 17-20 %	21-24 %
Excitement, enjoyment	17	20	15	18
Overcoming shyness	11	12	12	8
Learnt nothing	10	9	13	6
Acquiring technique	8	10	5	13
Social aspect, mixing	8	7	10	6
Don't know, remember	4	7	3	3
Experience of acting	4	4	4	3
Sense of achievement	4	4	5	3
Self-expression	3	3	3	5
Started my interest	3	2	3	5
TOTALS	(681)	(261)	(288)	(132)

Interviewees could give more than one response, so percentages will not sum to 100 per cent. These figures are based on the weighted results (see Chapter 2). As shown in Table 8.1, 27 per cent of the sample (N = 681) registered that they had not enjoyed or valued any aspect of their primary school arts.

The most noticeable differences in Table 8.5 emerge in the relatively low ranking of positive learning outcomes from primary arts as nominated by the 17-20 age range: certain categories of response such as 'excitement and enjoyment' and 'acquiring technique' are nominated less by this age band than by the under-17s and over-21s. Equally, the response 'learnt nothing' is offered most by the 17-20 year olds. Seventeen to 20 year olds were also more likely to suggest primary arts had social benefits. Interestingly – and perhaps not a little paradoxically – the youngest band, i.e. those less than 17 (and therefore those who are closest chronologically to their primary arts experiences) showed the highest percentage of those claiming not to remember what they had learnt or got out of such activities.

It is, of course, only possible to speculate on the reasons underlying these trends which appear to suggest primary arts are seen as valuable learning opportunities either by those furthest or nearest to experiencing them, but are recollected least by the youngest sub-sample. Does time alter perceptions, with mid-term memory proving least kind to early arts experiences? Was the early eighties (when the 17-20 age-band would have been at primary school) a particularly under-funded or under-valued period for arts education? Whatever the cause, this age-band represents a section of arts participants and consumers who may require particular support. As a group, they no longer are offered institutional arts support nor are likely to be significant wage-earners who can readily finance the development of their own arts interests. Alternatively, are the results a further indication that it is the over-21s which evince signs of increased positive attitudes and receptivity to the arts, and that, therefore, they would make a more fertile target for support and additional resources? The fact, however, that the 17-20 year old group are the sub-sample most likely to give negative accounts of the benefits of arts experiences during their formative primary years may give pause for thought.

Further analyses also looked at the responses to this question disaggregated by social class. Most noticeably, it was the young people from a professional background (Social Class I and II) who most frequently felt that their primary arts experiences were enjoyable and exciting. Indeed, more than one in four (29 per cent) gave this response, compared to only about one in seven (15 per cent) of those young people from skilled (Social Class III) and partly/unskilled (Social Class IV and V) backgrounds.

An overview of primary arts experiences

As a final question (Item 28e) in the section on primary arts, all interviewees were asked: '*looking back what did you think of the arts at primary school?*'. Of course, most interviewees would have already given some elaboration on their particular recall – positive or negative – of the arts activities available at primary school: this question was intended to help the respondent draw together their own summative and evaluative overview after having been encouraged to describe the details and causes of those recollections.

The overall ranking of these summative overviews (which were categorisable into ten codes) is given in Table 8.6. The ten categories of response, with examples of comments, are given first in the chart below. The actual percentages in this rank order are set out in Table 8.6.

Category of response	Example of comments *[Looking back, what I thought of arts at primary school was ...]*
All right, quite good	*Good enough – I did it because I had to, it wasn't interesting teaching.* (Male, 14) *It was average – it wasn't anything special, but it was average.* (Female, 18)
Enjoyable, fun	*At that time, it was basically all good fun – nothing serious – it was a giggle, that's what it was there for, nothing more, nothing less.* (Male, 18) *They were good – at that age you're not interested in anything serious – you just want to learn things and get enjoyment out of it – you didn't want to be bored by anyone lecturing you – just wanted to get enjoyment out of it.* (Female, 21)
Boring, not good	*I hated it ... it was boring.* (Female, 14)
Not unified	*You don't understand at that age what it's done for.* (Female, 20) *I never saw it as the arts – it was just school.* (Male, 23) *I don't think they're terribly 'there' in my mind. There wasn't a consciousness ... you know of 'the arts'.* (Female, 24)
Not enough time spent	*The less academic kids did art (painting etc.) – if you were bright, we had to do English and maths.* (Female, 19) *We didn't do much. We had about one art lesson every three months or something like that.* (Female, 14)
Not enough variety	*Limited – you had to do what the teacher said – you didn't have a choice – if the teacher liked it you'd do it, but there was no choice ... I didn't like that lack of choice at all.* (Male, 19)
Not enough depth	*We used to do a lot of painting but just to put paint to paper which usually turned out a mess.* (Male, 14) *At the time they were all right but now they seem limited – but at that age they didn't – after the comprehensive [primary school arts] seem limited and pointless.* (Male, 15)
Expressive, imaginative	*Primary school got us to open up our right hemispheres.* (Male, 19)
Worse than secondary	*OK – not as good as secondary school.* (Female, 19)
Better than secondary	*Great fun, could get stuck into it, not so detailed as secondary school.* (Female, 15)

Table 8.6   Summative overview of primary school arts by gender

Response	Total sample %	Gender Male %	Female %
All right, quite good	21	22	20
Enjoyable, fun	18	16	20
Boring, not good	18	23	13
Not unified	16	14	17
Not enough time spent	15	14	17
Not enough variety	10	9	12
Not enough depth	9	10	8
Expressive, imaginative, educational	7	5	9
Worse than secondary	2	1	2
Better than secondary	1	1	2
TOTALS	(681)	(338)	(343)

Interviewees could give more than one response, so percentages will not sum to 100 per cent.
These figures are based on the weighted results (see Chapter 2).
Approximately 12 per cent of the sample (N = 681) did not respond to this item.

Looking first at the ranking from the total sample, it would appear from the top three responses – where qualified approval, non-specific enjoyment or outright negative judgements prevail – that primary arts are not recollected or defined as a major opportunity for developing arts skills nor for recruitment to the ranks of committed arts consumers. Indeed, only 7 per cent chose to pinpoint that primary school arts had been educational or developed their imaginative and creative capacity. Of course, it must be remembered that the association of primary arts with enjoyment – and likewise its receipt of qualified approval – does not preclude the possibility that arts experiences at this age actually did achieve highly educational outcomes, even if not directly recollected as such by the young people themselves. Nevertheless, there is a prevalence of responses which indicate that young people reflected critically on the quality of their arts education. In an open question, a significant proportion of young people elected to mention some shortcoming in the opportunities for arts at primary school: suggesting either that they did not recall primary school as a place where the arts as a unique but collective discipline of human endeavour was relayed to them; or that they had not had sufficient time spent on the arts in primary school; or that they did not encounter sufficient types of arts; or that the primary school arts did not provide enough rigour in developing arts skills.

When the sample is broken down by gender, as Table 8.6 shows, there is again the noticeable tendency for a higher share of males to comment that the primary arts were 'not good', and for slightly more females to discern an educational value 'imaginative and expressive' in their arts experience at primary school.

Looking at the breakdown by social class in Table 8.7, there were significantly more young people from professional backgrounds expressing a recollection of primary school arts providing 'enjoyment'; fewest of these suggesting the arts activities were 'boring'; and yet, in all of the specific criticisms of their primary arts curriculum (relating to its inadequate opportunities and substance), again this social class registered the highest percentages. It was noticeable that the age-band under-17 also registered consistently high percentages in these specific criticisms.

Table 8.7   Summative overview of primary school arts by social class

Response	Total sample %	Social Class I & II %	III (N & M) %	IV & V %
All right, quite good	21	17	22	21
Enjoyable, fun	18	28	16	16
Boring, not good	18	10	18	21
Not unified	16	20	13	18
Not enough time spent	15	20	17	11
Not enough variety	10	17	13	3
Not enough depth	9	14	8	9
Expressive, imaginative	7	11	9	2
Worse than secondary	2	0	0	5
Better than secondary	1	2	1	2
TOTALS	(681)	(105)	(359)	(217)

Interviewees could give more than one response, so percentages will not sum to 100 per cent.
These figures are based on the weighted results (see Chapter 2).
Approximately 12 per cent of the sample (N = 681) did not respond to this item.

However, it is the breakdown by educational attainment which shows the starkest contrasts in the evaluative overviews of primary school arts (see Table 8.8).

Table 8.8   Summative overview of primary school arts by educational attainment

| | Total sample | | GCE/GCSEs | | |
| | | None | 1-3 | 4-6 | 7 or more |
Response	%	%	%	%	%
All right, quite good	22	25	31	24	17
Enjoyable fun	18	17	9	10	23
Boring, not good	16	24	26	12	8
Not unified	14	7	11	19	18
Not enough time spent	15	7	11	22	20
Not enough variety	8	2	8	10	12
Not enough depth	9	2	5	4	17
Expressive, imaginative	8	0	4	4	18
Worse than secondary	1	0	0	0	2
Better than secondary	1	0	1	0	1
TOTALS	(437)	(101)	(74)	(93)	(152)

Interviewees could give more than one response, so percentages will not sum to 100 per cent. These figures are based on the weighted results (see Chapter 2).
Approximately 4 per cent of the relevant post-16 sub-sample (N = 437) constituted missing cases for this analysis.

Thus, it is high achievers who were most likely to pinpoint the specific shortcomings of the primary school arts; who most frequently can identify an educational value; and who were least likely to take the overview that primary arts were 'boring and not good'. Indeed, it is noticeable that this latter response is particularly frequent among the two bands of low educational achievers. However, those with no formal qualifications rank, along with highest achievers, as the sub-sample who most readily register their recollection of enjoying the arts. (The 'U' shape finding thus emerged again.)

In sum, the categories of young people who, in retrospect, most often stated they valued primary school arts appear to be females, from the professional classes, and those with high academic ability or those who have most obviously not succeeded in the arena of educational attainment.

Secondary School Arts Experiences

This section of the chapter considers the data on young people's recollections of arts experienced at school from the age of 11 upwards. Given that identical questions were asked, it directly parallels the data discussed in the previous section on recall of primary school arts. Hence, where relevant, comparisons between the arts experiences in the two educational sectors will be made. However, in doing so, it is worth drawing attention to the fact that while all respondents had completed primary education, a third (33 per cent) of the respondents were still at secondary school when they were interviewed.

Positive or negative recall on secondary arts?

The data again confirm trends in arts participation which show that, recalling this later stage in their arts school career, certain categories of young people continued to exhibit signs of what was termed an 'arts by-pass', that is, they are less likely to feel they have found the arts they experienced either enjoyable or valuable.

On the first closed question (Item 32a): '*can you remember any arts activities (including drama, visual arts, music, literature etc.) which you particularly enjoyed or valued at secondary school?*' a quarter (25 per cent) of the sample (N = 674) replied negatively (i.e. felt they had not particularly enjoyed or valued their secondary school arts), and three-quarters (75 per cent) affirmed positive views on their arts experiences in this period of schooling. This division remains quite consistent with primary arts recall.

This three to one ratio of 'positive recall' on secondary arts experiences was fairly consistent across the variable of location – urban/rural – just as was the case for primary.

However, the sample showed a significant decrease in positive responses among the over-21 year old interviewees and ethnic minorities, with just less than two-thirds of respondents in these categories indicating that they had enjoyed or valued their secondary arts experiences. Table 8.9 shows this more than one in three negative recall, which is noticeably higher in these two categories than was the case with responses to the parallel question in the primary arts section.

Table 8.9   Secondary school arts recall by age and ethnicity

Recall on secondary arts	Total sample %	Age			Ethnicity	
		Under-17 %	17-20 %	21-24 %	White European %	Ethnic Minorities %
Positive	75	77	77	63	76	60
Negative	25	23	23	37	24	40
TOTALS	(675)	(260)	(283)	(132)	(603)	(64)

These figures are based on the weighted results (see Chapter 2).

As with primary school arts, when the variables of gender and social class were looked at, some noteworthy differences in positive and negative responses emerged. Table 8.10 demonstrates a higher incidence of negative responses to secondary school arts among males (still about one-third) and shows notably more young people from professional backgrounds having positive recall of their secondary school arts experiences than those from the partly/unskilled category.

Table 8.10 Secondary school arts recall by gender and social class

Recall on secondary arts	Total sample %	Gender Male %	Female %	I & II %	Social Class III (N & M) %	IV & V %
Positive	75	69	81	82	76	69
Negative	25	31	19	18	24	31
TOTALS	(674)	(335)	(339)	(104)	(359)	(211)

These figures are based on the weighted results (see Chapter 2).

When positive recall of secondary school arts was broken down by both gender and social class together, the most likely candidates for 'arts by-pass' remained males from partly/unskilled backgrounds (over a third were negative about secondary school arts). Again, females whose parent(s) were in the professional category ranked highest in frequency of positive recall, though the numbers involved for this kind of analysis are obviously on the small side.

Finally, Table 8.11 shows the results of this closed question on recall of secondary school arts broken down by educational attainment. Here a greater difference emerged, with the two higher bands of achievers in educational attainment (those with four to six or seven or more GCSEs or their equivalents) registering positive recall of secondary school arts more frequently. Around four-fifths of high educational achievers affirmed their enjoyment or valuing of secondary arts, compared to around three-fifths in the two categories of lower achievement (i.e. three GCSEs or less). Indeed, those who had obtained no GCSEs were less likely to register their enjoyment of secondary arts than was the case with primary arts, while those with four to six GCSEs showed a higher proportion indicating positive recall.

Table 8.11 Secondary school arts by educational attainment

Recall on secondary arts	Total sample %	GCE/GCSEs None %	1-3 %	4-6 %	7 or more %
Positive	73	58	61	78	83
Negative	27	42	39	22	17
TOTALS	(431)	(98)	(74)	(91)	(152)

These figures are based on the weighted results (see Chapter 2).
Approximately 4 per cent of the relevant post-16 sub-sample (N = 431) constituted missing cases for this analysis.

Thus, unlike recall on primary arts experience, the 'arts by-pass' in secondary school arts seems more consistently to include young people from the lower bands of educational attainment.

Reasons for negative recall of secondary school arts

As with the section on primary school arts, the 171 respondents who replied 'no' to the closed question on valuing or enjoying secondary arts were then posed the supplementary question *'was there any particular reason why* [you didn't enjoy or value secondary arts]?'. Though not all interviewees gave explanations, the total sub-sample (N = 143) nominated nine major categories. Examples of comments for each of these categories are given first, in rank order of frequency. Table 8.12 then shows the percentages of negative recall.

Category of response	Example of comments *[The reason I did not value or enjoy secondary school arts was ...]*
Disliked arts	*Same as before, I wasn't interested in them. I liked PE more than drama or art and music.* (Male, 19) [I was] *not into art at school.* (Male, 17)
Didn't like school	*Because I hated school. Hated the environment and set up of school.* (Female, 24)
Not much done	*Probably most I got out of art was during my A-levels when our teacher was in the Civic Theatre Play Company – we used to go and see a lot ... apart from that we didn't do much ...* (Male, 20)
Poor teaching	*I didn't enjoy English literature, art or CDT. It was the way we were taught – the teachers should've been more patient with those who couldn't do it very well. We weren't given much practice or guidance.* (Male, 23)
Not good at it	*I was bottom of the class for three years in a row ... I was accused of being naff at art, none of my friends were into the arts.* (Male, 18) *I can't do it. I can't draw.* (Female, 14)
Peer influence	*None of my friends liked the arts ... it wasn't the done thing.* (Male, 18)
Negative social, emotional effect	*I preferred academic lessons, I used to get shy if we ever did anything like drama.* (Male, 16)
Can't remember	*I mainly remember science at secondary school – 'cos it was good. I can't remember arts.* (Male, 19)
Not all art forms experienced	*There was no drama, no music, definitely not those subjects.* (Female, 18)
Other reasons	The respondents disliked specific art forms (e.g. CDT, music, literature).

Table 8.12   Reasons for negative recall of secondary school arts by gender

| | % of respondents who answered follow-up questions on negative recall | | |
| | Total sample | Gender | |
Response	%	Male %	Female %
Disliked arts	45	51	35
Didn't like school	13	14	10
Not much done	7	5	11
Poor teaching	6	8	3
Not good at it	5	5	6
Peer influence	3	4	0
Negative social, emotional effect	3	3	4
Can't remember	3	1	6
Not all art forms experienced	2	0	5
Other reasons	13	9	20
TOTALS	(143)	(94)	(49)

These figures are based on the weighted results (see Chapter 2).

In this way, 45 per cent of those who indicated negative recall specifically stated this was due to a lack of enjoyment of secondary school arts: unlike primary school arts, 'can't remember' was very rarely mentioned as a reason. (It should be remembered that the under-17 year olds were within the secondary phase of schooling at the time of the interview.) Equally, a considerably higher proportion of respondents felt that their lack of enjoyment of secondary school arts was related to their general dislike of school. Looking at gender differences, also outlined in Table 8.12, again the prominence of males stating their lack of enjoyment of secondary school arts is evident.

Though again numbers of respondents are small when breaking down the numbers for social class, it does seem that disliking secondary school arts experiences *per se* was, as with primary school arts, least likely to be mentioned by young people from professional backgrounds as a reason for negative recall. Rather, they again emerge as the group who most frequently nominated lack of opportunities for arts activities ('not much done'). This may reflect an acknowledgement by young people from professional backgrounds that there are 'opportunity costs' in secondary specialisation (selecting sciences and humanities). Equally, along with this group's high ranking for 'poor teaching' it may suggest an awareness of what arts education *could* have offered, but in their particular case didn't. Interestingly, young people from professional backgrounds rarely indicated that negative recall of the secondary arts was part of a general dislike of school (only 2 per cent did so).

Table 8.13 shows a breakdown of negative recall of secondary arts experiences by age of respondent. Here, in contrast to the equivalent primary question, those over-21s who expressed negative recall were least likely to suggest it was because they disliked their secondary school arts experiences or found them boring. Just over a third gave this reason, compared to almost two-thirds of those under-17. Conversely, this top age-band did not nominate 'not much done' as a reason for negative recall, but were more likely to mention 'poor teaching' or 'didn't enjoy school'.

Table 8.13   Reasons for negative recall of secondary school arts by age

| | % of respondents who answered follow-up questions on negative recall | | | |
Response	Total sample %	Under-17 %	Age 17-20 %	21-24 %
Disliked arts	45	62	41	37
Didn't like school	13	0	16	19
Not much done	7	10	10	1
Poor teaching	6	4	4	11
Not good at it	5	4	5	7
Peer influence	3	9	0	0
Negative social, emotional effect	3	5	0	5
Not all art forms experienced	3	0	0	5
Can't remember	2	0	4	3
Other reasons	13	6	20	12
TOTALS	(142)	(38)	(54)	(50)

These figures are based on the weighted results (see Chapter 2).

Valued secondary arts activities

As with recall of primary school arts, the interviewees were also asked the question (Item 32c): *'what arts were recollected as enjoyable and why did you enjoy them?'*. Coding allowed up to three responses to be registered.

Table 8.14 shows the ranking of 'enjoyable' secondary arts experiences which the respondents nominated, and also shows the variation between males and females. It includes all secondary arts forms nominated by more than five interviewees.

Table 8.14 Secondary school arts experiences enjoyed or valued by gender

| Activities | Total sample % | Gender | |
		Male %	Female %
% mentioning at least one dramatic activity	(30)	(29)	(32)
Drama	22	22	23
% mentioning at least one musical activity	(19)	(19)	(19)
Painting, drawing	17	17	18
Reading literature	12	7	17
Music (unspecified)	12	11	12
Acting in plays	11	12	11
Learning musical instrument	5	5	5
Theatre trips	5	4	6
Clay, pottery	5	3	6
Dance	4	2	6
Choir	3	3	4
English	3	1	5
Writing	3	2	4
Craft, design and technology	2	3	2
Textiles	2	1	2
Poetry	2	1	2
TOTALS	(681)	(338)	(343)

These figures are based on the weighted results (see Chapter 2).
Interviewees could give more than one response, so percentages will not sum to 100 per cent.
As shown in Table 8.9, 25 per cent of the sample (N = 681) registered that they had not enjoyed or valued any aspect of secondary school arts.

Just as in primary, 'drama' was most often recalled as a particularly enjoyable secondary school arts activity, although the specific response of 'acting in plays' was very much less often mentioned. Visual arts, namely 'painting and drawing', again ranked very high, but music quite markedly increased its proportion of nominations in comparison to the corresponding results for primary school arts. All these three art forms, as experienced in secondary school, rank equally high with males and females, and this means there is a marked increase in male enjoyment of the music curriculum at secondary school compared with primary.

Other noticeable gender differences emerge in the area of 'reading and literature', with small differences for 'English' and 'writing', which perhaps confirms the language orientation of females. 'Dance' is another art form which, perhaps not surprisingly, has a higher positive response rate from females.

Perceived benefits of secondary arts

Interviewees were also asked (in Item 32d) to nominate what they thought they had '*learnt or got out of these art activities*'. The following chart gives the rank order of total responses, and some typical examples of actual comments. It is followed by Table 8.15, which displays the frequencies for these categories.

Category of response	Example of comments *[What I learnt or got out of secondary school art was ...]*
Excitement, enjoyment	*I got excitement, it was fun.* (Female, 21) *It was a buzz, I liked it.*
Learnt nothing	*Not much really.* (Female, 20)
Acquired technique	*I started doing it* (art) *seriously, learning techniques and about the arts.* (Male, 17) *I learnt to understand music more, being able to read music and stuff like that.* (Male, 14) *How to do perspective and how to mix colours.* (Female, 17)
Social aspect	*Working with others in a group, got to know other people, we're doing your own thing, no-one telling you what to do.* (Female, 21)
Sense of achievement	*I'd feel proud afterwards ... it was satisfying to know you could do something.* (Female, 16) *Suppose the sense of knowing I could do things that I'd had doubts about.* (Male, 18)
Overcome shyness	*... perhaps it opened me out a bit.* (Male, 19)
Insights	*In drama, we learnt how other people feel about things and how they see things differently to how you see them.* (Female, 15)
Self-expression	*It was the self-expression in drama ... expressing what you were thinking and feeling.* (Male, 16)
How to make things	*Making things with wood.* (Female, 15)
Communication skills	*I learnt about communicating to my peer group – social involvement.* (Female, 23)
Builds concentration	*To listen to music more carefully. The dance especially helped because you have to listen to where you are.* (Female, 14)
Using imagination	*I got more imaginative with writing and making up songs.* (Male, 16)
More appreciation	*I suppose I realised that I could enjoy that sort of thing, whereas before I didn't really know.* (Male, 18) *More appreciation of music, records and tapes.* (Male, 16)
Relaxing	*It was easier, more gentle on the brain than maths.* (Male, 17)
Experience of acting	*Putting on shows for parents.* (Male, 14)
Started my interest	*That I knew what I wanted my career to be.* (Male, 18) *Drama – did it for GCSE, so school started me off.* (Female, 16)

Table 8.15   What young people learnt/got out of secondary school arts

Response	Total sample %	Gender Male %	Female %
Excitement, enjoyment	18	16	19
Learnt nothing	12	14	10
Acquired technique	12	9	14
Social aspect	8	7	9
Sense of achievement	8	5	11
Overcome shyness	7	5	9
Insights	6	5	7
Self-expression	4	4	4
How to make things	3	4	2
Communication skills	3	2	4
Builds concentration	3	3	3
Don't know	3	1	4
Using imagination	2	3	2
Relaxing	2	3	1
More appreciation	2	2	2
Experience of acting	2	2	2
Started my interest	2	1	3
TOTALS	(681)	(344)	(338)

These figures are based on the weighted results (see Chapter 2).
Interviewees could give more than one response, so percentages will not sum to 100 per cent.
As shown in Table 8.9, 25 per cent of the sample (N = 681) registered that they had
not enjoyed or valued any aspect of secondary school arts.

As for primary school arts, the predominant recollection of those expressing positive recall of secondary school arts was again 'enjoyment and excitement'. In comparison to positive recall on primary arts, it is possible to detect an increase in responses suggesting that specific arts skills, knowledge or understanding were felt to be delivered: 'acquiring technique' was mentioned by almost a third more respondents than was the case for primary; 'how to make things' entered the rankings; and double the percentage of respondents suggested 'insights' was a benefit of their secondary arts experiences. Equally, 'a sense of achievement' had doubled the number of respondents.

Breakdown of this ranking by the variables showed a few interesting trends in gender and ethnic response. As illustrated in Table 8.15, the very obvious gender difference in the proportions of male/female responses nominating 'excitement and enjoyment' which was evident in primary school arts did not emerge in comments on secondary school arts. However, wider gender variation did arise in some instances: twice as many girls as boys nominated a 'sense of achievement' (11 per cent and 5 per cent) and 'overcome shyness' (9 per cent and 5 per cent) as outcomes of secondary arts activities. Also 'acquiring technique' and 'communicating skills' were mentioned more by girls than boys. All in all, it perhaps again indicates a tendency for females to discern that their secondary arts experiences were an opportunity to acquire, or realise artistic and social skills. Indeed male responses were higher than female in only two categories of response: those indicating they had 'learnt nothing', and in the pragmatically defined 'how to make things'.

Analysis showed two significant differences between the white and ethnic sample on the range of responses describing any learning retrospectively associated with secondary arts. Only 6 per cent of interviewees from the ethnic minorities felt they had 'learnt nothing', compared with 13 per cent of white European interviewees. One per cent of young people from the ethnic minorities defined the benefits as 'insights' compared with 6 percent of the white young people.

In breakdown by social class and age, variation in discerned outcomes of secondary arts was more evident, and Tables 8.16 shows the variation in those categories which rated 20 or more responses.

Table 8.16   What young people learnt/got out of secondary school arts by age and social class

Response	Total sample %	Age Under-17 %	Age 17-20 %	Age 21-24 %	Social Class I & II %	Social Class III (N & M) %	Social Class IV & V %
Exciting, enjoyable	18	18	19	13	18	16	20
Learnt nothing	12	13	14	7	5	13	15
Acquired technique	12	11	12	12	15	15	6
Social aspect	8	5	12	5	16	6	7
Sense of achievement	8	6	7	13	10	7	8
Overcome shyness	7	5	9	8	14	7	5
Insights	6	9	5	3	8	7	3
Self-expression	4	3	3	8	6	5	2
How to make things	3	2	4	4	3	2	6
Communication skills	3	2	4	4	4	2	4
Builds concentration	3	2	4	1	2	4	2
TOTALS	(681)	(261)	(288)	(132)	(105)	(359)	(217)

These figures are based on the weighted results (see Chapter 2).
Interviewees could give more than one response, so percentages will not sum to 100 per cent.
As shown in Table 8.9, 25 per cent of the sample (N = 681) registered that they had not enjoyed or valued any aspect of secondary school arts.

Most noticeable differences in these findings, when compared with responses on the benefits of primary arts, are the higher ranking of positive learning outcomes from secondary school arts nominated by the 17-20 age range. However, the response 'learnt nothing' ranked highly for the 17-20 year olds, as in the equivalent question on primary arts, and again it is the 17-20 year olds who were more likely to suggest secondary arts had social benefits.

The over-21s offered responses pinpointing what might be seen as personal development rather more than the other age-groups: namely, 'sense of achievement' and 'self-expression'. Of course, the reasons for this trend can only be surmised but it is at least possible that older respondents perceive opportunities and long-term benefits for personal development in the secondary arts curricula which are not so apparent to those who are still, or have very recently, been experiencing it. If such benefits cannot be 'measured' or always fully understood by young people at the time they are experienced, this over-21 age-band may be providing important testimony for those who wish to defend the place of the arts in secondary schooling.

With regard to social class it is evident that the partly/unskilled sub-sample were less likely to nominate 'acquiring technique' than was evident among young people from professional and skilled backgrounds. Young people from professional classes were the sub-sample which more often mentioned secondary school arts as offering social and personal development advantages ('overcome shyness' and 'mixing with others').

An overview of secondary arts experiences

As a final question in the section on secondary arts (Item 32e), all interviewees were asked: '*looking back what did you think of the arts at secondary school?*'. As with the equivalent question in the primary school arts section, this question was intended to help the respondent draw together his or her own summative and evaluative view, even though the details and causes of negative or positive recall had already been elicited.

The overall ranking of these summative overviews (which were categoriseable into ten codes) is given in Table 8.17. First, examples of responses in the ten categories are given, and then Table 8.17 shows the percentages within each category.

Category of response	Example of comments *[Looking back, what I thought of secondary school arts was ...]*
Boring, not good	*I never tried to paint or draw, I didn't like it at the time.* (Male, 18) *They were available, I just didn't want to do them ... they were boring.* (Male, 18)
Enjoyable, fun	*Just that they're not all boring and it's a lot of fun.* (Male, 14) *Liked and enjoyed them – I wanted to do more. I was told not to by mum – won't get a job.* (Female, 21)
All right, quite good	*Quite liked, 'cos they used to take us to different plays.* (Female, 14) *There wasn't that much on offer, but of what we did, it wasn't bad, it was fairly good.* (Male, 14)
Not enough time spent	*We did some arts but not enough.* (Male, 16) *Not enough – should've been more time for them.* (Male, 16)
Expressive, imagination	*When I was actually introduced to them I found them very interesting. Helped broaden your mind, enlarge perspective on things.* (Male, 20) *I think I've learnt more about them and done more ...* (Female, 14)
Better than primary	*A lot better than primary school. There was more time to do it as well. You have a certain lesson for a subject.* (Female, 15) *Knew more about them so they were more interesting.* (Female, 14)
Not enough depth	*They didn't try to tell you enough about the arts ...* (Male, 23) *Personally speaking the way they teach art at secondary school I don't really agree with – it's very much 'There's a peach – draw it'.* (Male, 16)
Not unified	*Didn't really think of them as 'the arts', just something I enjoyed doing.* (Male, 17)
Worse than primary	*Not as good as at primary school, but still very expansive.* (Male, 19) *Did less at secondary school than primary, that is bad.* (Female, 14) *Good, but not as good as primary.* (Male, 20)

Table 8.17 Summative overview of secondary school arts by gender

| | Total | Gender | |
Response	sample %	Male %	Female %
Boring, not good	21	26	16
Enjoyable, fun	20	18	22
All right, quite good	19	17	21
Not enough time spent	12	10	15
Expressive, imaginative	11	9	14
Better than primary	10	8	11
Not enough depth	7	8	7
Not enough variety	5	5	6
Not unified	2	2	2
Worse than primary	2	4	1
TOTALS	(681)	(338)	(343)

These figures are based on the weighted results (see Chapter 2).
Interviewees could give more than one response, so percentages will not sum to 100 per cent.
Approximately 13 per cent of the sample (N = 681) did not respond to this item.

Looking first at the ranking from the total sample, it would appear that two of the top three responses again suggest either qualified approval or non-specific enjoyment of secondary arts, while outright negative judgements now just rank as the most common response. However, secondary school arts would seem to be rated higher than the primary school arts curriculum (some 10 per cent of the sample chose to compare the two sectors and state the superiority of their later years of arts education) and a slightly higher percentage of young people defined secondary arts as educative to their imagination and creativity (11 per cent for secondary compared to 7 per cent for primary).

Of course, it is important to repeat the caveat that the association of secondary arts with enjoyment – and likewise its receipt of qualified approval – does not preclude the possibility that arts experiences at this age actually did achieve highly educational outcomes, even if not directly recollected as such by the young people themselves. However, it is worth noting that responses suggesting a lack of 'variety' of secondary school arts experiences; or their lack of 'depth'; or a lack of awareness of the arts as a unique sorority of related disciplines features very much less in interviewees' summations of secondary school arts, if compared with parallel overview responses about primary school arts.

When the sample is broken down by the variables of gender, as Table 8.17 shows, there is again the noticeable tendency for more males to comment that the secondary arts were 'not good'. Females seemed more likely to specify an educational value – 'imaginative and expressive' – in their arts experiences at secondary school, and to suggest inadequate time was given to the arts.

Looking at the breakdown by social class in Table 8.18, a number of noticeable differences emerge. As with the overview of primary school arts, young people from managerial and professional backgrounds were marginally more likely to summarise their secondary school arts as providing 'enjoyment'.

Table 8.18 Summative overview of secondary school arts by social class

Response	Total sample %	Social Class I & II %	III (N & M) %	IV & V %
Boring, not good	21	12	22	24
Enjoyable, fun	20	24	21	17
All right, quite good	19	21	20	17
Not enough time spent	12	17	14	6
Expressive, imaginative	11	17	12	7
Better than primary	10	10	8	12
Not enough depth	7	11	7	7
Not enough variety	5	12	6	1
Not unified	2	2	1	5
Worse than primary	2	2	4	1
TOTALS	(681)	(105)	(359)	(217)

These figures are based on the weighted results (see Chapter 2).
Interviewees could give more than one response, so percentages will not sum to 100 per cent.
Approximately 13 per cent of the sample (N=681) did not respond to this item.

A slight increase in the negative summation of arts as 'boring/not good' is evident in all three categories of class, though the differences in percentage between these three categories remains very much the same as for the equivalent primary school arts data. Again, as with primary school arts data, the professional and managerial class ranked the highest response rate in all the specific criticisms of their secondary arts curriculum (namely, lack of opportunities, substance and multiformity).

A breakdown of summative overview responses by age of respondent revealed a trend for the over-21s to pass specific critical comment rather more than the other age bands (e.g. on lack of opportunities and substance). It was noticeable that it was the under-17 age band which registered consistently high frequencies in these specific criticisms in their summative comments on primary school arts.

Finally, turning to an analysis of the responses by educational attainment, it was higher achievers (those with more than four GCSEs) who were most likely to pinpoint the inadequate amount of time for secondary school arts as well as the arts curriculum's 'lack of depth'. As with primary, it was the highest achievers who most frequently nominate an educational value in their arts experiences; and who are least likely to take the overview that secondary arts were 'boring and not good'. Indeed, it is again noticeable that this latter response was particularly high among the two bands of lower educational achievers.

In this way, the categories of young people who, in retrospect, stated the most positive overview of secondary school arts appear to be females, from the professional classes, with high educational attainment. Those who have most obviously not succeeded in the arena of educational attainment (i.e. with fewer GCSEs) do not appear to offer such a positive overview of their secondary arts experiences as was evident in the same question relating to primary school arts.

This trend is further borne out by the results of cross-tabulating responses to Items 28a and 32a. (The identical closed questions on whether there were any arts at primary and then secondary school which were particularly valued and enjoyed.)

Here, it was evident that only about one in eight (12 per cent) of the total sample did not recall enjoying arts activities at either primary or secondary school, while almost 60 per cent had positive recall of the arts offered in both educational sectors. However, around 20 per cent of those in the lower educational achievement categories (0-3 GCSEs) registered enjoying neither primary nor secondary school arts. In contrast, this negative viewpoint was registered by only about 7 per cent of those in the categories representing higher educational achievement (four or more GCSEs).

Breakdown by the variable educational attainment further showed that those with four or more GCSEs were more likely to register valuing secondary school arts but not those offered in primary school, while those with lower educational attainment (three or less) showed the reverse of this, with positive recall of primary school arts, but not those available in their secondary education.

These findings may suggest a number of issues regarding entitlement and rigour in the arts curriculum. Of course, low educational attainers may simply be expressing these negative responses to arts as part of a negative attitude to school generally, while high attainers include arts as a positive overview of schooling with its associations of success and achievement. However, this trend does at least raise the issue of the need for a differentiated curriculum in order to ensure a genuine arts entitlement at all stages of schooling.

Arts in Years 10 and 11

This final section of the chapter looks specifically at the numbers – and categories – of young people who continue with some aspect of the arts in their later secondary years, after the options choice which faces most 14 year olds.

All interviewees were asked an appropriate version of the question (Item 33a) *'did you/are you going to do any of the following subjects in the 4th/5th year or Years 10 and 11?'*. Five arts subjects were then mentioned – art; music; drama; dance; media – and the respondent was asked to state whether the continuation with study of each art form was as a *'separate subject'*; or *'as part of'* another subject; or was *'not* [undertaken] *at all'*.

Overall involvement in arts subject in Years 10 and 11

Overall, the results of this closed question showed that almost a third (32 per cent) of the total sample felt they did not do any arts in these years of schooling, either as a separate subject or as part of another (such as humanities, English). Sixty-eight per cent indicated they encountered one or more of the five arts forms in some aspect of their studies. However, nearly half (45 per cent) of the total sample stated that they did not take any arts as a separate subject during this period.

Looking more specifically at which arts were most frequently studied, Table 8.19 outlines the total percentages of young people continuing with each of the five art forms in Year 10 and 11 (or equivalent) either as a separate subject or as part of another.

Table 8.19   Participation in arts subjects in Years 10 and 11

Arts subject	Subject in its own right %	As part of of another subject %	Not taken %	N
Art	37	5	58	(681)
Music	14	3	83	(681)
Drama	15	12	73	(681)
Dance	3	6	91	(681)
Media	4	12	84	(681)

These figures are based on the weighted results (see Chapter 2).

Thus, art (i.e. visual arts) ranked as the most undertaken subject experienced by just over two-fifths of the sample, whereas drama was experienced by about a quarter of the sample. However, music and media were undertaken by only one-sixth and dance by less than one-tenth. Put another way, the figures of five-sixths of this sample of young people not encountering music or media education, and nine-tenths having no educational involvement with dance, between the ages of 14 and 16 may illustrate the issue more starkly.

When the distinction between undertaking the arts as a separate subject or as part of another is made, again some interesting interpretations emerge. Thus, art and music were more rarely encountered in a multi-disciplinary capacity, while the majority of those young people experiencing media or dance education in Years 10-11 did so by its inclusion in another subject. Drama and media were, not surprisingly, most often mentioned as part of the English curriculum in these years, while dance was predominantly experienced through PE. 'Expressive or creative arts modules' accounted for a tiny number of young people's arts experiences during these years of schooling: indeed, a total of only five respondents reported doing dance through this particular type of Years 10-11 curriculum organisation, while six referred to such modules offering visual art opportunities and eight stated that they had encountered music in this way.

Trends in arts specialisation

Just over a half of the sample (55 percent) continued with their study of at least one arts subject as a separate or 'specialised' discipline after Year 10. The vast majority of this sub-sample who studied a separate arts subject in Year 10 and 11 did so by taking only one subject (see Table 8.20). The taking of more than one subject in the arts was comparatively rare: only 12 per cent of the respondents studied two or more arts subjects compared to 43 per cent who took one. Table 8.20 also shows that females were markedly more likely than males to study one or more arts subjects in the last two years of compulsory schooling.

Table 8.20   Number of separate arts subjects taken in Years 10 and 11 by gender

Number of separate arts subjects (taken in their own right)	Total sample %	Gender	
		Male %	Female %
0	45	51	39
1	43	39	47
2	7	6	8
3	4	2	5
4	1	2	1
TOTALS	(681)	(338)	(343)

These figures are based on the weighted results (see Chapter 2).

Further analyses revealed that those on training schemes had the highest proportions (65 per cent) not taking any arts subjects and that respondents from professional backgrounds had the lowest percentage (40 per cent) not studying an arts subject.

Interestingly, differences surfaced when the kinds of arts subjects studied were disaggregated by gender. Table 8.21 shows that, whereas music had an equivalent proportion of males and females taking it or not taking it, art (as a subject in its own right) was studied by a higher percentage of females. In fact, none of the five arts subject were studied by more boys than girls.

Table 8.21   Individual arts subjects by gender

		Subject in its own right %	As part of of another subject %	Not taken %	N
Art	Males	34	6	60	(338)
	Females	41	3	56	(344)
Music	Males	14	3	83	(338)
	Females	14	3	83	(344)
Drama	Males	13	11	76	(338)
	Females	16	14	70	(344)
Dance	Males	2	3	95	(338)
	Females	4	10	86	(344)
Media	Males	2	12	86	(338)
	Females	5	13	82	(344)

These figures are based on the weighted results (see Chapter 2).

The breakdown of arts specialism in Years 10-11 by both gender and social class together also shows some interesting trends (see Table 8.22).

Table 8.22   Arts subjects studied in own right by gender and social class together

	Social Class I and II		Social Class III		Social Class IV and V	
	Male %	Female %	Male %	Female %	Male %	Female %
Art	34	41	34	38	34	46
Music	17	20	14	12	13	13
Drama	13	18	10	17	19	13
Dance	1	2	1	4	3	7
Media	2	1	2	7	1	5
TOTALS (N = 681)	(53)	(52)	(175)	(184)	(110)	(107)

The figures are based on the weighted results (see Chapter 2).

Most noticeably, both females and males from the professional (Social Class I and II) class registered the highest percentages in music specialism. More marginally, females in the skilled and partly/unskilled classes referred most to specialism in dance and males from Social Class IV and V backgrounds registered the highest percentage of drama study.

Table 8.23   Arts subjects studied in own right by educational attainment

| | GCE/GCSEs | | | |
| | None | 1 - 3 | 4 - 6 | 7 or more |
Subject	%	%	%	%
Art	36	44	31	28
Music	9	7	10	17
Drama	8	9	12	8
Dance	1	0	1	0
Media	3	0	8	4
TOTALS				
(N = 437)	(101)	(74)	(93)	(152)

These figures are based on the weighted results (see Chapter 2).
Approximately 4 per cent of the relevant post-16 sub-sample (N = 437) constituted missing cases for this analysis.

From Table 8.23, it is apparent that the higher educational attainers (four GCSEs and above) recorded the lowest percentages of art specialism, and those in the top attainment band (seven or more such qualifications) registered the highest percentage of music specialisation. Such variations suggest interesting biases in the clientele for those subjects: it would appear, for example, that music in Years 10 and 11 attracts a disproportionately higher share of the more academically able and middle class students.

Reasons for the biases in music specialisation can only be speculated about – is music, for instance, a subject increasingly dependent on parental support and finances for instruments, tuition etc.? Do young people require additional teaching beyond the primary and secondary school music curriculum to ensure the acquisition of music skills and knowledge? It may be a distinct concern that studying music can appear to be so consistently associated with social class advantages, particularly since the commitment to music forms such a significant part of young people's cultural preferences and tastes.

Finally, each respondent was asked to outline 'any particular reason' for taking the arts specialisms they had in Years 10-11. Seven main reasons emerged. Some interviewees referred primarily to their 'enjoyment' of the arts, or acknowledged they had some 'talent' in the art specialism chosen (e.g. '*I was good at it*', '*... it comes easy to me*'). Others referred to the limitations of choice and option constraint in selecting specialisms for Year

10 form (e.g. *'it was the only subject available to me'*). The view that arts were an easier, or *'lighter'*, *'practical'* subject, to take alongside, or instead of, more demanding, academic subjects was also proffered; while some respondents saw arts subjects having a distinct 'career purpose' (or at least providing additional qualifications). 'Self-expression' was also mentioned (*'... a chance to get some personal satisfaction'*, *'a way of being myself'*, *'it offered freedom ... gave me creative potential'*). Also suggested was the influence of a particular arts teacher, or the teaching/learning approach which the art form offered – such as group work in drama. Table 8.24 shows the rankings and percentages of responses by gender.

Table 8.24   Reason for arts selection at Year 10 by gender

Reasons	Total sample %	Gender Male %	Gender Female %
Enjoyed it	36	29	44
Talent for it	13	14	12
Limited choice	11	11	11
Careers, additional qualifications	6	4	9
Lighter subject	5	5	6
Self-expression	3	4	3
Teacher influence	2	1	2
TOTALS	(681)	(338)	(343)

The figures are based on the weighted results (see Chapter 2).
Interviewees could give more than one response, so percentages will not sum to 100 per cent.
As shown in Table 8.20, 45 per cent of the sample (N = 681) were not in a position to respond to this question since they had not selected an arts subject in Years 10 and 11.

Thus, Table 8.24 shows the re-emergence of females' assertions of 'enjoyment' of the arts, which is consistent with the earlier finding that females were appreciably more likely than males to study one or more arts subjects in Years 10 and 11. It also accords with a key point to emerge from the evidence outlined earlier in this chapter which showed that female respondents were less likely than their male counterparts to view their primary and secondary school experience as *'negative'* and *'boring'*. On a wider level, these results echo the general trend of higher female participation in leisure and day-time arts (e.g. see Chapter 3). Given this, it is pertinent to ask whether there is an equal opportunity issue to be addressed by schools in that in seeking to enrich young people's engagement and education in the arts, the problem of male reluctance may deserve special attention.

Having focused in this chapter on respondents' views of their arts experiences in primary and secondary schools, we now return to consider further evidence on their involvement in the arts beyond and outside of formal education.

9. Arts Beyond School

This chapter focuses on young people's arts engagement beyond school: including youth club opportunities and arts experiences after leaving secondary education.

It emerged that about a third of the sample felt that any arts participation had declined in their immediate post-school years, but for some, this was followed by an increase in their later teens and early twenties. The chapter provides analysis and illustration of the reasons given for increased or decreased participation. Overall, it was found that a third of the sample suggested that their arts involvement had increased, though a considerably higher percentage of young people from professional and managerial backgrounds nominated this trend.

Clear evidence on social class variation in youth club attendance is reported and also the perceived opportunities for arts participation at youth club. It was found that, while over half of the activities undertaken in youth clubs referred to sport, only about one in ten referred to arts participation. Finally, views on the outcomes and effects of youth club arts activities are relayed.

Introduction

Having examined young people's recollections and evaluations of the arts in schools, in this chapter we turn to present evidence on the sample's experiences of the arts beyond and outside the secondary phase of schooling. The first part of this chapter offers evidence on respondents' perceptions of their degree of involvement in the arts since leaving school. In some respects, this section can be viewed as 'filling the gap' between interviewees' accounts of their current arts participation (see Chapters 3, 4 and 5) and their school-based experiences of the arts (see the previous chapter). Obviously, it only concerns the 64 per cent of the (weighted) sample who had left school (see Chapter 2 for details).

The second part of the chapter provides an interpretation of the evidence on respondents' perceptions of the arts within youth clubs. It presents the results of questions which were put to respondents who were still at school, as well as those who had left.

Post-school Involvement in the Arts

Relative to other day-time current status positions, attendance at school has been shown to be a period of comparatively high involvement in the arts. It is, of course, common to all young people of school age and it provides varying degrees of opportunity, encouragement and compulsion for everyone. In Item 35 in the schedule, interviewees were asked whether since leaving school their involvement in the arts had *'gone up, gone down or stayed the same'*. In a supplementary question, they were requested to explain their answers. For example, involvement in the arts may have declined owing to a lack of compulsion or have blossomed with a new-found choice and independence. Indeed, as we shall see, it was not uncommon for a later growth in participation to be preceded by a diminution in arts involvement in the immediate years following compulsory schooling.

Before presenting the quantitative and qualitative findings produced by this item, it should be stressed that only respondents who had left school were asked this question. Approximately 427 respondents (64 per cent of the weighted sample) were eligible for this question, though as can be seen from Table 9.1, the total number of coded replies was 387. The majority of non-responses came from interviewees who had completed Year 11 only a year or two prior to the interview and felt that the question had little relevance to them. Finally, it should be noted that interviewees' replies to Item 35 included both 'producer' and 'consumer/receiver' involvement in the arts.

Variation in patterns of involvement since leaving school

The overall picture to emerge from the responses to this item (shown in Table 9.1) is that approximately a third of the respondents felt that their arts involvement had increased since leaving school, a third thought it had gone down and a third considered that it had stayed the same.

Table 9.1   Post-school arts involvement by gender and urban/rural residency

Involvement since school	Total sample %	Gender		Residency	
		Male %	Female %	Urban %	Rural %
Gone up	33	37	27	36	23
Gone down	32	33	32	33	31
Stayed the same	35	30	41	31	46
TOTALS	(387)	(188)	(199)	(282)	(106)

These figures are based on the weighted results (see Chapter 2).

Contrasting these results by urban and rural residency (see Table 9.1), it is apparent that, compared to 23 per cent of rural respondents, 36 per cent of urban respondents indicated that their involvement in the arts had gone up since leaving school. Additionally, while 46 per cent of rural respondents said that it had stayed the same, 31 per cent of urban respondents gave that response. Given that earlier evidence indicated that young people's leisure-time 'arts-participation' (Item 17) was higher in rural than urban areas, and vice versa for 'media-arts: audience', it is suggested that much of the greater proportion of urban respondents declaring that their involvement had gone up is due to increased interest in, and consumption of, 'media-arts: audience' activities (e.g. going to the cinema, listening to music). In part, it may also suggest greater opportunities and facilities which encourage post-school participatory involvement in urban areas. The comparatively high proportion of rural respondents replying 'stayed the same' seems to reflect a characteristic of rural young people's participation in the arts: much of it was due to middle class involvement in the arts in childhood which remained fairly stable beyond school. In addition, the rural constituency contained a higher than average percentage of interviewees who said they were, '*not interested in the arts at school and not interested now*' and they still felt the same. Again, this may indicate (at the margins) relatively fewer opportunities to stimulate participation after school. Throughout the report, much of the data suggests that rural respondents tended to polarise into two main constituencies: young people, largely middle class, with a history of arts involvement throughout their childhood; and others, whose biographies contained few significant arts experiences and who often expressed indifference to the arts.

Comparable results were produced by the gender breakdown (see Table 9.1), with males producing similar figures to urban respondents and females to rural respondents (though not quite as marked). With the probable exception of variable opportunities and facilities, very similar explanations could account for these differences (e.g. increases in 'media-arts: audience' activities account for much of the variation). Moreover, as with urban and rural interviews, males and females had different starting points in terms of their levels of participation while at school. Using data from Items 17 (i.e. current leisure involvement for the under-17s) and 30 (the full sample's recollection of their leisure-time interests while at secondary school) (it must be stressed that these are only rough indicators of pre-16 involvement), it seems that male involvement started off from a markedly lower baseline, so there was more scope for males to increase their participation, whereas females were perhaps more likely to be more extensively involved from an earlier age and therefore had less scope to increase. Additionally, there was anecdotal evidence that some young men, particularly in the 21 year old and above category, were willing to soften their macho image resistance to the arts.

With regard to ethnicity, four out of five (80 per cent) of ethnic minority respondents replied 'gone down' or 'stayed the same' compared with two-thirds (66 per cent) of white Europeans. Only one out of five of the former answered 'gone up'. Given that at school age, the ethnic minorities in their leisure time were comparatively high on 'media-arts: audience' but low on 'arts: participation', it suggests that for them there was less scope to expand consumption and, perhaps fewer opportunities (e.g. lower participation rate in higher education) or less receptivity to engage actively in the arts. There are obvious grounds for concern in these results.

The results disaggregated by age are particularly striking. As shown in Table 9.2, the 17-20 age group had a noticeably lower 'gone up' percentage and slightly higher than average 'gone down' and 'stayed the same' proportions. In the over-21 year old group nearly half had increased their involvement in the arts.

Table 9.2   Post-school arts involvement by age

Involvement since school	Total sample %	Age 17-20 %	21-24 %
Gone up	33	26	47
Gone down	32	35	30
Stayed the same	35	39	23
TOTALS	(377)	(246)	(131)

These figures are based on the weighted results (see Chapter 2).

Since Item 30 produced evidence that indicated that young people's recollections of their leisure-time pursuits while at secondary school displayed no significant age-related variation in their participation in the arts, the increased involvement for the over-21s is very significant and confirms findings of an upturn of interest in the arts in the older age group. It may also reflect the simple fact the older group had enjoyed more time for the changes to take effect.

Concerning social class, the skilled group (Social Class III) produced percentages close to those for the total sample. Whereas the group from a professional background (Social Class I and II) had 43 per cent answering 'gone up', only 21 per cent of the partly/unskilled group (Social Class IV and V) did so. The professional group also had the lowest proportion registering 'gone down': 26 per cent compared with 36 per cent for the partly/unskilled group. The latter class also produced the highest percentage replying 'stayed the same', many of whom were of the 'not interested before, not now' type. It appears that middle class interviewees were not only more likely to participate in the arts while of school age, but they were also twice as likely as working class young people (Social Class IV and V) to extend their levels of involvement after school. Qualitative and quantitative evidence from the interviews suggested that the experiences of higher education were a significant factor in extending this sub-samples' engagement in the arts (see Table 9.3). Again, this finding raises important questions for policy-makers.

Reasons for increased post-school involvement

Having discussed the frequency of responses given to the initial question, we now turn to consider the reasons given to explain the drift of their answers. The reasons given for those who felt that their involvement in the arts had 'gone up' are illustrated in Table 9.3.

Table 9.3   Reasons given for increased post-school involvement in the arts

Reasons (in rank order)	% of respondents who answered 'gone up'
More 'into' specific art form	29
Interests broadened	21
Part of work, profession	16
Part of HE course	10
More aware of arts	10
Other reasons	9
HE broadened interests	7
More autonomy since school	7
Some arts up, some down, but overall increase	7
Grew up; aged; matured	6
Social reasons	6
More time available	3
TOTAL	(126)

Interviewees could give more than one response, so percentages will not sum to 100 per cent. These figures are based on the weighted results (see Chapter 2).

As can be seen from the table, the most common response came from the 29 per cent who answered by referring to a specific art form in which they had increased their level of involvement. Typical answers in this category included '*with the steel band, I do more each year*' (not that the steel band was typical) from a 17 year old part-time employed female, or '*I started playing the guitar some years back*' from a 24 year old employed male. Another example was '*now I do poetry, I'm interested more than at school*'. This comment touches on a recurring theme which was mentioned earlier, namely, that many young people seem to come to the arts at a later age when they are able to do so of their own volition and choice, in their own way, and in their own time.

The second most frequent reason was that of widening horizons: 21 per cent of those answering 'gone up' gave this as an explanation. A typical reply within this category was '*especially appreciation of the arts* [I'm] *more prepared to listen to more types of music*' (a 24 year old female in part-time employment) or '*got involved in much more, changed to a different level of commitment*' (a 22 year old female in employment).

Perhaps unexpectedly, increased participation due to the activity being 'part of work or profession' proved to be a fairly common response (16 per cent). Such cases ranged from work influencing or leading to involvement in the arts, for example a 20 year old male from a professional background: '*work* [in a theatre box office] *... gone in different directions – insights into theatre, dance, ballet, opera ... experience broadened*', to a job that specifically entailed direct participation in the arts, such as an artist, '*because it's a way of life now*' or a 19 year old employed male who worked as a photographer.

Similarly, 'part of an HE course' accounted for 10 per cent of the 'gone up' responses. For example, '*gone up very much through foundation course in art and design ...*' (a partly/unskilled 22 year old female in 16+ full-time education) or '*we did art here as part of our course*' (a 19 year old in 16+ full time education).

Of a similar level of significance, 'more aware of arts' (which perhaps touches on similar ground to 'matured' and 'interests broadened') was mentioned by 10 per cent of those who answered 'gone up'. Among such responses were: '*more time and* [I have] *learnt to appreciate arts more*', '*more awareness ...*', '*more attentive to art surrounding me*' (23 year old in 16+ full time education), and '*appreciate things more and have more interest in them*' (male, 22 years in 16+ full time education). Another interesting example was '*travel has made me realise there is more to life – different ways of living*'.

At 9 per cent, 'other reasons' figured quite highly in the rank order. Not far below this came a set of answers grouped under the label of 'HE broadened interest' in the arts. This factor came out quite strongly in the qualitative data: '*University societies, more prolific opportunities*' (the reply of a 24 year old employed male from a working class background), '*see art in different ways through college – more grown up*', and '*I do a lot of back room work around the university for their productions – sit and watch the productions*' (the answer of a 22 year old unemployed male who had just left university). Another such example, was '*at school you didn't want to, it's not the done thing. Influence from college changes that*' (18 year old male from Social Class III in 16+ full time education). This response alluded to the importance of peer influence and the frequent tendency for young males, especially school age ones, to be influenced by what they consider to be the 'non-macho', or 'pansy' image of the arts. The prevalence of this attitudinal barrier may be seen as a salient factor in explaining the fact that male involvement and interest in the arts was less than that of females. Greater 'autonomy since school' was an explanation that was conspicuous in the qualitative data, despite only accounting for 7 per cent of the answers. For example:

> *It's gone up but it's changed. I was more arty because of school and you're doing it anyway because you're at school. Now it's more sort of choice.* (22 year old female, trainee)

> *Much more drama, painting and sculpture. I prefer doing it off my own bat rather than at school – I'm not sure I liked the compulsory element there.* (20 year old male in 16+ full time education)

> *I get more time to myself and can do my own art.*
> (20 year old male in employment)

> *More money, more freedom.*
> (20 year old female in 16+ full time education)

> *... it's opened up to me more, I can go and look without feeling stupid, no teachers watching, I can make my own decisions about it. In school you were told what to do, but since I've left school I can choose myself.*
> (17 year old male in 16+ full time education)

Finally a telling extract, which incorporates this dimension was offered by an art and design student who after a decrease in involvement after school had recently 'found the arts'. He explained:

> *Well, through leaving school and being kind of lost and not knowing what you wanted to do, and doing things that you didn't particularly want to do, but you just had to do because of .... just to learn about life .. in a way, and .. just kind of searching for the things you want to do, that you really want to do and then finding it .. and then really getting into it.*

'Some arts up, others down', which is numerically of equal importance at 7 per cent, referred to the perception that although some aspects had declined, others had developed, so there was still a net increase. Within this category, a frequent remark went along the lines of '*going to see things has increased, but participating has decreased – there is much more opportunity here – art gallery and theatre*'.

Fractionally less important (6 per cent), is 'grew up' or 'matured'. One example was, '*I'm involved in the musical society and go and see things, plays, films etc., I can't really say why, except you get mature ...*' (24 year old male in employment).

Social reasons for increased involvement in the arts were frequently volunteered (again 6 per cent), and can be illustrated by the following comments:

> *Art galleries, exhibitions – knowing artists in the area and people interested in the arts.* (24 year old employed male)

> *People I've met are more involved and interested.*
> (19 year old female in employment)

> *My friends here are more interested.* (23 year old female)

A 21 year old employed female gave an example of social reasons of a slightly different nature:

> *I go to the theatre more often ... it has 'pose value' – I want to appear cultured.*

In this case, status-seeking factors appear to have become the overriding motivation. For most of the other respondents, social reasons were seen as complementing other factors which affect levels of participation.

'More time' was an aspect that seemed quite prevalent in the qualitative data though it actually only achieved 3 per cent of those that answered 'gone up', (for example, '*I get more time to myself*' and '*I have more time*').

Having more money accounted for a significant portion of 'other reasons' (11 per cent). One respondent remarked: '*Because I go to the theatre, cinema and clubs – because I've got more money (a bigger overdraft actually!)*'.

Another interesting example coded under 'other reasons' pointed to an alleged failure of the education system to provide an effective introduction to the arts at school:

> *I've developed a personal interest in some things now. I appreciate things more.* [There was] *nothing to build on from school.*
> (Skilled 24 year old female in employment)

The responses of those whose post-school involvement in the arts had increased offer important insights into the processes of how participation in the arts develops for some young people, and by implication, how it may be nurtured and encouraged for others. The results, particularly the significant age-related variations, are consistent with the theory that in the immediate post-school years, many young people, especially those who do not continue in full-time education, experience a decline in their level of arts participation, which, for some, is followed by a significant increase in interest in their late teens and early twenties. Reasons proffered for an initial decline ranged from shortage of money, removal of compulsion, lack of encouragement and stimulus from teachers, a search for self-identities (e.g. '*I had to find myself*'), and a need to grow and develop through an anti-institutional rebellious stage. Reasons for a subsequent upturn in participation levels at a later age often included not only institutional influences (e.g. work, further and higher education), but also strong emphases on self-autonomy and independent motives. The latter often alluded to the freedom for young people to engage in 'what arts they wanted, in the way they wanted them' without compulsion and pressure. Such motives were seen as being especially important for artistic and creative enterprises which were deemed to require a high degree of volition, personal commitment and, at times, inspiration. It should be recognised, however, that the overall level of increased involvement had more to do with a rise in 'consumer/receiver' or audience roles rather than a substantial growth in active 'producer' engagements in the arts (e.g. a typical comment was '*going to see things has increased, but participating has decreased*').

This interpretation of the findings raises a number of interesting policy questions. The apparent increase in receptivity among the older age band may suggest, for example, that efforts to widen young people's access to the arts would find more fertile ground among the over-21 year olds than their younger peers in the immediate years beyond post-compulsory schooling. Similarly, it would appear that youth arts policies for the latter group, particularly those outside full-time education, could benefit from 'arm's-length' strategies which encourage freedom of action and permit the locus of control to remain with the individual participant. Furthermore, the evidence prompts the question of whether the arts in the school curriculum are prescribed and taught in such a way that they actually fuel resistance to them rather than minimise, if not pre-empt, negative attitudes to them beyond the school-leaving age. It is conceivable, for instance, that if the arts were taught through negotiated curricula, which offered plenty of scope for young people's own cultural preferences and tastes, post-school disaffection towards the arts could be reduced considerably.

An analysis of the effects of the different independent variables on the reasons given for increased post-school involvement in the arts produced the following main points. It must be remembered that whilst the differences in percentages may seem large, the total number of cases may be small; hence, results must be interpreted with caution.

Table 9.4   Selected reasons for increased post-school arts in involvement by gender

Reasons	% of respondents who answered 'gone up'		
	Total sample	Gender	
		Male	Female
More 'into' specific art form	29	41	15
Part of work	16	10	22
Part of HE course	10	4	18
More aware of arts	10	14	5
More autonomy since school	7	1	15
Social reasons	6	3	9
TOTALS	(126)	(71)	(55)

Interviewees could give more than one response, so percentages will not sum to 100 per cent. These figures are based on the weighted results (see Chapter 2).

From Table 9.4, it appears that females answering 'gone up' were more likely to be active in jobs and courses that involved the arts than males. To a similar extent, they were more likely to have experienced increased involvement because of greater autonomy since leaving school and because of participation in the arts for social reasons. In contrast, males were more likely to have increased their involvement due to the development of a specific interest – often music. They were also more likely to explain their 'gone up' response through reference to a general heightening of awareness of the arts. To some degree, the findings reflect the female bias towards arts and liberal arts subjects in further and higher education.

Table 9.5   Selected reasons for increased post-school arts involvement by age

Reasons	% of respondents who answered 'gone up'		
	Total sample	Age 17-20	21-24
Interests broadened	21	11	31
Part of work, profession	16	19	·11
Some arts up, others down; but overall increase	7	11	2
Grew up; matured	6	0	11
TOTALS	(125)	(63)	(62)

Interviewees could give more than one response, so percentages will not sum to 100 per cent. These figures are based on the weighted results (see Chapter 2).

A similar analysis for age-related variations confirms the trend and implications discussed above (see Table 9.5). Although the 17-20 year olds were more likely than the over-21 year olds to have experienced increased arts involvement due to work, the older group were more likely to report an extended level of participation due to general maturation and the widening of interests. Once again, for a significant group of the 21-24 year olds a picture emerges of greater engagement in the arts, albeit mainly in the mode of consumption, accompanying a process of personal and social development, which includes a general broadening of horizons.

Reasons for decreased post-school involvement

Turning to the reasons given for decreased involvement in the arts after leaving school, Table 9.6 presents the frequencies for the main reasons offered by those who answered 'gone down' to the opening question.

By a considerable margin, the most frequent reason given for decreased involvement on leaving school was having less time available. This was clearly related to the nature of their current status position. The employed, for example, appeared from the qualitative data to be generally those most commonly restricted by shortage of time. Several interviewees referred to this problem:

> *I'd like to have more involvement – more involvement now, if I had a bit more time.* (19 year old female, employed)

> *Probably gone down in terms of hours spent, but stayed the same in terms of commitment and feeling. Work taken up a lot of my time.* (19 year old female, employed)

> *Haven't got time really.* (20 year old female, employed)

Table 9.6   Reasons given for decreased post-school involvement in the arts

Reasons	% of respondents who answered 'gone down'
Less time than before	35
Drifted away post-school	26
Other reasons	14
Other things to do	10
No interest in arts	8
No longer compulsory	6
Earning money is more important	6
Lack of money	6
Some arts up, others down, but overall decrease	3
TOTAL	(125)

Interviewees could give more than one response, so percentages will not sum to 100 per cent. These figures are based on the weighted results (see Chapter 2).

Perhaps of greater concern, or a problem offering more scope for amelioration, is the 26 per cent who 'drifted away' from the arts after school. For example:

> *It went down, what I did at school ... never did do any more – it just stopped.*   (18 year old female in 16+ further education)

> *I haven't done anything since then.*   (19 year old female, employed)

> *When I was at school I was doing a lot of artistic things but when I left I didn't carry hardly any of them on.*   (21 year old female, employed)

Such comments often implied that, relative to when they were at school, they lacked the initiative to seek out arts participation for themselves. The following comment begins to make this point explicit:

> *At school a lot of things are organised for you to participate in, but during my year out I haven't had the time, energy, or inclination to get involved.*   (19 year old male from a professional background about to enter 16+ further education)

The third most common category of response given to account for decreased involvement comprised a general set of factors grouped under the term, 'other reasons'. These tended to focus on two main factors. Firstly, lack of information on, and availability of, arts activities were mentioned with some regularity:

> *Not much going on around here ... or I haven't been aware. I'd like to have more involvement.*   (19 year old female university student)

or

> *It decreased, I don't really know what's going on.*
>   (20 year old female in 16+ further education)

Secondly, there were accounts of the decline in arts involvement after leaving courses of further or higher education:

> *It stayed the same whilst I was at university but it has suddenly gone down since I came home ... ... there was a lot to do in Newcastle – my friends were involved in the arts.* (21 year old female)

> *Since I left college and couldn't get a job, I haven't done any of those things.* (19 year old female, employed)

Mentioned by 10 per cent of respondents, 'other thing to do' covered similar ground to 'drifted away' and, in some cases, overlapped with 'lack of time'. Examples included:

> *I probably listen to the radio but I've taken up more sport since I left school.* (20 year old female, employed)

> *I haven't made any time for it, I've been too busy working for qualifications –* [also] *boyfriend.* (18 year old female, trainee)

> *I have different hobbies now.* (18 year old female, employed)

Other significant categories included 'no interest in the arts', 'earning money is more important', and 'a lack of compulsion'. The latter was demonstrated by one 18 year old female trainee: '*at school you had to do it, now you don't*'. Similarly, '*don't have to go to lessons, that was the only reason I used to do most of it*' (17 year old female in 16+ further education). This was not an uncommon attitude, especially among 17-20 year olds.

Whilst, for some young people, more available money after leaving school was perceived to be a reason for an increase in arts participation, a shortage of it was more frequently a cause of reduced involvement, particularly for those who were not in employment. As an illustration, a 20 year old female in 16+ further education replied, '*I don't have the financial means to take part*' and a 17 year old pre-college female from a professional background responded, '*money situation, I was homeless for a time*'.

To summarise, the two main reasons given as explanations for a lower level of arts participation were a 'lack of time' and a sense of 'drifting away' from the arts after leaving school. It often seemed that the response categories with lower percentages were related to, or overlapped with one of these two main reasons. Factors which tended to cluster around the first issue focused on concrete or material obstacles, while those related to the second main reason tended to be more attitudinal or psychological in nature. In other words, lack of time, lack of money, lack of information on, availability of, and accessibility to arts activities, and the removal of opportunities to attend organised arts involvement at school (or 16+ further education) were perceived to be the main concrete reasons for decreased involvement, whilst the arts no longer being compulsory and requiring instead an element of initiative and self-motivation to continue, insufficient interest, having other interests or channels for energy were frequently seen as the key attitudinal barriers to account for declining enjoyment in post-school arts activities. The former set of perceived reasons and problems often appeared to exacerbate the effect or extent of the second type.

Analyses of the 'gone down' responses by the independent variables were again restricted to gender and age, due to insufficient numbers in the sub-sets for other variables.

Table 9.7   Selected reasons given for decreased post-school arts involvement by gender

| | % of respondents who answered 'gone down' | | |
| | Total | Gender | |
Reasons	sample	Male	Female
Less time than before	35	29	41
Other reasons	14	0	25
Other things to do	10	16	5
No interest in arts	8	15	2
TOTALS	(125)	(62)	(63)

Interviewees could give more than one response, so percentages will not sum to 100 per cent. These figures are based on the weighted results (see Chapter 2).

As displayed in Table 9.7, males were more likely than females to have experienced decreased involvement in the arts due to 'no interest' and also, having 'other things to do'. Compared to males, females were more likely to experience a decline in involvement because of 'less time' and 'other reasons' (see above discussion of Table 9.6 for examples of the two main 'other reasons'). These results are another indication of the general trend throughout the findings that male interest in the arts remains lower than females. The evidence is consistent with the general interpretation that females were more likely to engage in the arts if more time was available, while males were comparatively more likely to say they were not bothered about the arts, even if more time was available.

Respondents in the 17-20 year old age band (see Table 9.8), having more recently left school, were more likely than the over-21 year olds to attribute their decreased involvement to the two closely related factors of a removal of compulsory obligation and 'drifting away after school'. For the over-21 year old group, work, the priority given to earning money and lack of time, which was often related to occupational pressures, were more significant factors in their explanation of reduced participation in the arts. The qualitative data for Item 35, and the above statistics, lend weight to what has already been proposed concerning age-related variations.

Table 9.8   Selected reasons for decreased post-school arts involvement by age

Reasons	% of respondents who answered 'gone down'		
	Total sample	Age 17-20	21-24
Less time than before	35	28	51
Drifted away post-school	26	30	18
Other reasons	14	10	21
No longer compulsory	6	9	0
Earning is more important	6	1	13
TOTALS	(125)	(86)	(39)

Interviewees could give more than one response, so percentages will not sum to 100 per cent. These figures are based on the weighted results (see Chapter 2).

Reasons for a status quo post-school involvement

Finally, we move on to look at those who answered Item 35a by stating that their post-school level of involvement in the arts had 'stayed the same'. The results for this group are displayed in Table 9.9.

Table 9.9   Reasons given for unchanged post-school involvement in the arts

Reasons	% of respondents who answered 'stayed the same'
No interest any time now or when at school	40
Continued involvement	33
Some up, some down	10
Other reason	7
Lack of time	5
Other things to do	4
No longer compulsory	1
TOTAL	(136)

Interviewees could give more than one response, so percentages will not sum to 100 per cent. These figures are based on the weighted results (see Chapter 2).

The most common reason offered to explain unchanged involvement was 'not interested in the arts – now or when I was at school'. So whilst the attitudes associated with the 'drifting away after school' response from those who replied 'gone down' may be a cause for concern, 'no interest at any time' is a more challenging and deep-rooted problem. A very typical example was, '*I've never done anything in the arts and I still don't*' (17 year old male, trainee) and also, '*non-existent before, non-existent now*' (18 year old female, employed). A less extreme example was, '*I wasn't very arty at school, so leaving has not made much difference*' (male, employed).

The other major – and more positive – perceived reason for participation 'staying the same' was 'continued involvement'. The most typical kind of response in this category stressed that their participation in the arts had largely been out of school so their post-school level of involvement was not greatly affected by leaving. Illustrative comments included:

> *I have carried on doing what I have always done, I was never that involved at school anyhow.* (20 year old female, employed)

> *Same interests: working and music – not catered for by school.* (21 year old male, employed)

> *Interest has stayed the same and revolves around myself, not schools, colleges or work.* (20 year old female, employed)

> *I've always been very active.* (20 year old female, 16+ further education)

> *I still read and go to the cinema.* (18 year old female, unemployed)

Continued involvement was also reported by interviewees who were in further and higher education institutions where they found similar opportunities to those available at school; for example: '*Because I'm in a very similar situation to when I was at school*' (19 year old female, 16+ further education). Another dimension to this category of response was that even though involvement may continue in the same quantity or at the same level as before, the perceived importance or quality of experience may increase. The reply of a 20 year old employed female highlighted this point: '*Not really* [increased] *but I probably appreciate it more*'.

Among the less frequent responses, 10 per cent of those indicating unchanged levels of involvement suggested that their participation had risen in certain areas, while declining in others: 'some up, some down'. For example:

> *Not so involved in drama and painting, more involved in reading, music and degree work* [architecture]. (24 year old female, employed)

> *Change in emphasis – do more singing now and more generally involved in music and art – drawing.* (18 year old female, pre-university, unemployed)

Similarly, this category included young people who had experienced a period of higher involvement followed or preceded by one of lower involvement, e.g.:

> *It went up at university, then came down with my job ... ... opportunities at university.* (23 year old male, employed)

Examples of 'lack of time' answers included '*Not much time with being at work and playing sport*' (20 year old male, trainee), and '*always taken a keen interest in the arts – job ... lack of time prevents increased involvement*' (24 year old female, employed).

An additional point perhaps worth a mention is that the responses suggested that friends may act not only as an influence increasing arts involvement, but similarly in helping sustain involvement or averting a drift away. This was illustrated by such remarks as: '*drama group, joined with friends when left school*' (19 year old female, employed) and '*still have the same peer group and enjoy the same things ...*' (17 year old male, trainee).

Cross-tabulations by gender produced the only reliable and significant set of comparisons.

Table 9.10   Selected reasons given for unchanged post-school involvement in the arts by gender

| | % of respondents who answered 'stayed the same' | | |
| | Total | Gender | |
Reasons	sample	Male	Female
No interest now or when at school	40	48	34
Continued involvement	33	23	40
Some up, some down	10	5	14
TOTALS	(136)	(56)	(80)

Interviewees could give more than one response, so percentages will not sum to 100 per cent. These figures are based on the weighted results (see Chapter 2).

Males were more likely than females never to have had any interest in the arts at any stage (see Table 9.10). Females in comparison to males were correspondingly more likely to have continued involvement and also were more likely to have had a change in emphasis in their arts participation.

The results offered throughout this section suggest that the gender and social class differences in arts involvement after formal education are quite striking. The report now turns to another possible arena of arts opportunity beyond school, namely that of youth clubs. Whether this opportunity can redress the apparent non-association between males, working class young people and the arts will be among the issues looked at.

Youth Clubs and Arts Participation

In view of the contribution that the youth clubs movement has made to the advocacy of youth arts (Chamberlain, 1991; Feldberg, 1991;) and the potential of the youth service for widening young people's access to the arts, it was clearly important for the research to collect evidence on respondent's levels of participation in youth clubs, particularly in the arts domain. Accordingly, Item 34 in the interview schedule posed a series of questions which were progressively filtered to elicit young people's accounts of their general involvement in youth clubs and their particular engagement in the arts within them. Since this question focused specifically on youth clubs, it was expected that the responses would show a higher rate of attendance at youth clubs than the 3 per cent who mentioned it as one of their main leisure interests when replying to Item 17 (see Chapter 3).

All respondents were asked whether they currently (i.e. within the last year) attended a youth club or centre (Item 34a). The results for this opening question are displayed in Table 9.11. Two-thirds of those interviewed had not attended a youth club within the last year. While the majority of those who attended a club at least once a week were under the age of 17, the majority of non-attenders were over-17 years old. The latter were also more likely to be female than male. The findings suggest that, in considering the potential of youth clubs as a vehicle for broadening arts participation, the maximum constituency or target group reached through this means would be approximately one-third of the 14-24 year old population. Moreover, this target group seems heavily biased towards school-aged young people.

Table 9.11   Current attendance at youth clubs by age and gender

| | Total | Age | | | Gender | |
| | sample | Under-17 | 17-20 | 21-24 | Male | Female |
Level of attendance	%	%	%	%	%	%
More than once a week	17	27	8	16	22	12
Once a week	14	21	9	8	15	12
Once, twice a month	2	5	1	0	3	1
Less than once a month	1	1	1	1	2	1
Not at all	66	46	81	75	58	74
TOTALS	(667)	(259)	(281)	(127)	(327)	(340)

These figures are based on the weighted results (see Chapter 2).

The vast majority of attenders went to their clubs at least once a week. Most of the clubs mentioned were local authority youth centres, though church-affiliated clubs, sport clubs (e.g. boxing), project centres, and other specialist clubs (e.g. Young Farmers' clubs) were also cited. Special project centres, sporting and social clubs were more likely to be mentioned by the over-21 year olds, for whom there was, in contrast to the 17-20 year old group, an increased attendance rate at the more than once a week level.

Social class was found to have a definite and consistent association with current attendance at youth clubs. Whereas only 15 per cent of young people from professional backgrounds were in the habit of going to youth clubs at least once a week (i.e. once per week plus more than once per week), 25 per cent and 47 per cent of skilled and partly/unskilled respondents respectively were doing so. A similar relationship was apparent in the disaggregated results for educational attainment: e.g. while only 13 per cent of those with seven or more GCSEs attended at least once a week, 34 per cent of those without any GCSEs went to a youth club for a minimum weekly visit. Hence, although youth clubs may be restricted to a minority (in terms of current attendance) and a membership largely of school age, they clearly have the capacity to attract young people from less privileged backgrounds and with limited academic attainment.

Attendance showed no significant differences according to ethnicity and only very slight variations emerged for urban and rural residency. For the former, there were marginally higher proportions attending at least once a week (33 per cent compared to 25 per cent), though this was largely compensated for by a higher share of rural young people attending regularly but less frequently than once a week. Analyses of attendance by the respondents' current status positions revealed that those in employment were the least likely to go to youth clubs (e.g. 88 per cent said they had not been to a youth club during the last year), while those at school or unemployed were the most likely to attend youth clubs at least once a week – 47 per cent and 36 per cent respectively. The latter statistic – relative to those for respondents in other post-school positions – demonstrates the significance of youth clubs for the unemployed.

Another way to gauge the constituency of young people reached through youth clubs is to conceive of it as the sum of those who were currently in the habit of attending and those who had attended in the past but had ceased doing so at the time of the interview. Consequently, interviewees were asked whether or not they used to go to a youth club or centre (Item 34b). The results for respondents who replied 'not at all' to the initial question about current attendance are presented in Table 9.12.

Table 9.12 Previous attendance at youth clubs by gender

Level of attendance	Total sub- sample of current non-attenders %	Gender	
		Male %	Female %
Frequently	39	45	35
Now and then	20	22	18
Only once or twice or never	41	33	47
TOTALS	(442)	(191)	(251)

These figures are based on the weighted results (see Chapter 2).

From these results, it can be calculated that just over a quarter (27 per cent) of the interviewees who answered the youth club item (N = 668) were neither attending a youth club at the present time nor had attended one in the past. Conversely, almost three-quarters (73 per cent) of the sample said they were either current or past attenders. Moreover, 55 per cent of interviewees were or had been frequent attenders (i.e. at least once a week). From this perspective, the proportion of young people declaring themselves to be youth club members is significantly higher than the one-third who were current attenders. As Table 9.12 shows, the figures on past attendance patterns indicate a male bias similar to those of current attendance.

Although at different ages when interviewed, respondents who had attended youth clubs in the past (i.e. but not within the last year) were invited to specify the age at which they had stopped going. The results are set out in Table 9.13. The modal age for ceasing youth club attendance (for this particular group) was 14. Reinforcing the earlier finding that the majority of current attenders were of school age, 93 per cent of previous attenders had stopped going to a youth club before they were 17. Maintaining young people's interest beyond that age clearly poses a challenge for youth club leaders, and has obvious implications for the contribution the youth service can make to extending young people's access to the arts.

Table 9.13   Age when youth club attendance ceased

Age	% of sample who had attended youth clubs in the past
Up to and including 11	14
12	8
13	12
14	27
15	21
16	11
Over 16	7
TOTAL	(281)

These figures are based on the weighted results (see Chapter 2).

Non-attenders, both currently and previously, were requested to give reasons for their decision to withdraw from youth club attendance. Their replies to this question (Item 34c) are summarised in Table 9.14. The two most common reasons were that the respondents felt no need to continue attending the youth club because they had developed other fulfilling interests or they had exceeded the upper age limit imposed by the club. Approximately a third of the sub-sample were quite critical of the club they attended: some considered that it provided an inferior service, often including poor management, other respondents said they had become bored by the activities on offer. If the aim is to sustain involvement beyond 17, then the message from this sample of young people was that youth clubs will need to provide a well-organised service which meets the needs of young people and stimulates their interest.

Table 9.14   Reasons given for ceasing youth club attendance

Reasons	% of total answering the question
No need, other interests	25
Over age range	22
Got fed up, bored	19
Poor service, management	17
No accessible clubs	14
Club closed down	8
Other (e.g. moved house)	8
Friends gave up	6
TOTAL	(343)

These figures are based on the weighted results (see Chapter 2).
Interviewees could give more than one response, so percentages will not sum to 100 per cent.

All attenders – both frequent and infrequent, as well as past and present – were asked to identify the main activities they participated in at their youth club (Item 34d). As with Item 17 (see Chapter 3), this allowed the researchers to assess the extent to which respondents would volunteer references to the arts without being prompted for specific arts-related activities – although, by this stage in the interview (unlike Item 17), interviewees were undoubtedly aware of the focus on the arts. The responses to Item 34d were coded under the same 'detailed' and 'broad' activity categories used in Item 17 and outlined in Chapter 3.

By substantial margins, sporting activities were the most prevalent; over half (52 per cent) of all **responses** (N= 958) referred to a sport (see Table 9.15). By appreciable degrees, snooker, pool and table tennis were the most popular. Other sports mentioned with some frequency were football, badminton, squash, orienteering, outdoor pursuits, boxing, martial arts and aerobics. The next most important broad category was social interchange (16 per cent of all responses), with meeting friends and socialising cited as the principal activity. Miscellaneous activities (e.g. organising parties or discos, computers, travel and in-door games) accounted for 12 per cent of the responses.

Only 11 per cent of the activities mentioned could be categorised as 'arts: participation'. Of these, painting and drawing (36 references), drama and theatre (20 references) and music-making (12 references) were the only individual arts: participation categories to receive more than ten mentions. 'Media-arts: audience' activities, predominantly watching TV or videos and listening to music, amounted to 9 per cent of all responses.

Rural respondents were slightly more likely to use youth clubs for social and media consumption reasons (e.g. listening to music) than their urban peers, who were relatively more likely to attend clubs with specialist sports amenities (e.g. swimming, boxing) and engage in sports in general youth clubs (e.g. football, orienteering). 'Arts: participation' activities showed no significant variation between urban and rural interviewees. Similarly, disaggregation by social class produced no major differences for any of the broad categories of activities. There were, however, significant variations according to gender. While male respondents were much more involved in sports (61 per cent of the responses from males referred to sport, compared to 42 per cent of female ones), female interviewees were more involved in miscellaneous activities (especially travelling, trips, indoor games) and 'arts: participation' activities (especially singing, dancing, drama, sewing and textiles, but not painting and drawing).

Finally, analyses of the results by age revealed some interesting, if, at times, only slight, differences. As Table 9.15 shows, relative to younger respondents, the over-21 year olds were more likely to see social contact as a main activity. The middle band (17-20 year olds) had higher proportions of responses for sporting and 'media-arts: audience' categories, while the school-aged group had the highest percentages in 'miscellaneous' (especially, computers and going on trips) and 'arts participation' activities (especially, painting/drawing and music-making). With arts participation rates being particularly low for the 17-20 year olds, it appears that youth clubs, were either focusing on other activities or they were not succeeding in encouraging young people over-17 to see the arts as one of their main club activities.

Table 9.15   Broad categories of main youth club activities by age

	% of total number of responses		
Broad areas of activity	**Total sample**	**Age**	
		Under-17	**17-20**	**21-24**
Miscellaneous	12	15	11	8
Sport	52	50	55	51
Social	16	14	15	23
Arts: participation	11	15	8	11
Media-arts: audience	9	6	11	7
TOTALS	(958)	(394)	(407)	(157)

These figures are based on the weighted results (see Chapter 2).

Since this low level of participation may be a reflection of limited opportunities and provision rather than lack of interest on young people's part, interviewees were asked if their youth club offered facilities and opportunities in the arts. Over half (53 per cent) of those who felt able to answer this question (N = 478), believed that opportunities in the arts were on offer at the club or centre they attended; 47 per cent thought they were not. Interestingly, a very large discrepancy existed between the number of young people who stated that artistic opportunities were available and the relatively small proportion of respondents who volunteered arts participation as one of their main youth club activities. This suggests that it was the interviewee's lack of interest in involvement in the arts rather than a shortage of opportunities which constituted the main barrier to participation, though, of course, another interpretation could question whether the opportunities on offer were of an appropriate type and quality to stimulate young people. It could also be a matter of concern that approaching half of the respondents' clubs appeared not to present young people with opportunities to participate in the arts – though that again could be a reflection of leaders' perception of the limited interest in the arts among their clientele. While the evidence presented here suggests they may be right in that perception, it also underlines the need for arts provision in youth clubs to be extremely well-organised and skilfully presented if it is to overcome the apparent attitudinal barriers which seem to inhibit young people's involvement. Clearly, effective training for youth leaders and arts providers in this area is of paramount importance. It underlines the need for a wider application of the kind of training initiative piloted in two authorities as part of the 'GAP project' (see Garcia and Becket, 1993). Supported by the Calouste Gulbenkian Foundation and Youth Clubs UK, the GAP project aims to promote the use of the arts as a tool for working with young people, principally by offering training courses to youth workers.

Before leaving the question of whether or not respondents felt that their clubs had offered opportunities in the arts, it is worth noting that a larger share of urban interviewees answered in the affirmative than their rural peers: 56 per cent of the former compared to 47 per cent of the latter. It was also noticeable that the responses varied according to age: whereas 63 per cent of the under-17 year olds reported that their clubs provided artistic opportunities, only 49 and 44 per cent of 17-20 and over-21 year olds (respectively) did so. These differences were almost certainly due to the different type of clubs attended: while the younger group was more likely to go to local authority clubs which offered a range of activities, the older groups were more likely to join specialist sporting or social clubs.

Asked specifically whether they had participated in arts activities at youth clubs, 26 per cent of the sub-sample who answered the youth club item (N = 668) replied that they had. The fact that many more interviewees declared that they had joined in arts activities than, in response to the earlier item, had signalled arts participation as one of the main activities they engaged in at youth clubs, indicates the rather transitory and occasional nature of many young people's involvement in youth club arts events (e.g. one-off graffiti or drama workshops). The question elicited some familiar variations and trends: female respondents, urban ones and the under-17 year olds had relatively high rates of participation in arts activities.

Asked for reasons why they did not join in arts activities, non-participants frequently mentioned a lack of interest in either the particular opportunities on offer or the arts in general. A variant of the disinterested reply was '*my mates are not interested*'. The only other reason to be cited with some frequency referred to the activities not being available at the times when the respondent normally attended the club.

Finally, interviewees who had participated in arts activities at their youth clubs were asked if they had enjoyed the activities and whether they felt they had gained anything by participating in them. The vast majority of responses were positive about their experiences, though most found it difficult to describe their reactions and perceived benefit in any more specific terms than '*it was enjoyable*' or '*good fun*'. The most prevalent reason for this enjoyment revolved around a sense of group identity, collegiality and team work: '*I enjoyed everyone working together*' or '*working with my friends and others on the same thing was good*'. The second most common reason referred to improved skills, '*I learnt how to put make-up on for plays*' or '*I learnt to do graffiti art better*'. The next most frequent reason focused on gains in terms of self-esteem and a sense of achievement: '*I felt pride in what we did*', '*I felt good about myself and the mural we did together*' or, simply, '*we were successful*' and '*it was* [psychologically] *rewarding*'. Other perceived benefits included:

♦ a lack of competitiveness, pressure, criticism compared with school;

♦ autonomy (again, in contrast to school), e.g. '*you only do it because you want to*', '*doing things that appeal to me*' and '*doing it how you feel is right*';

♦ enjoying having more equipment than at home; and

♦ becoming more confident, less inhibited.

For the small minority who said they did not enjoy the activities, the most frequently mentioned criticism alluded to the superficial nature of the activities: '*I got nothing out of it because it was not done enough to be valuable*'. Such comments lend weight to the earlier interpretation that many of the artistic activities were experienced as one-offs and, as such, not afforded significance in young people's perceptions and priorities of what is meaningful and valuable to them.

To conclude, this chapter has surveyed the evidence relating to young people's perceptions of their participation in the arts since leaving school and their experience of the arts in youth clubs. In so doing, the analysis has begun to touch on the influences and opportunities which appear to affect the degree of participation rates beyond compulsory education, as well as the reported effects of involvement in the arts on offer in youth clubs. The following chapter takes up these themes in greater detail.

10. Effects, Opportunities, Influences and Needs

Using the vernacular, 'turned on' and 'turned off', this chapter first examines data on young people's views on who or what influenced any commitment to the arts, and conversely, any factors which contributed to an arts aversion. A third of the total sample were unable to suggest any direct or specific turn-on factor: for the rest, it appeared that the most significant influences were people with whom the respondent had on-going and sustained contact, such as parents (particularly mothers), secondary teachers and friends. These 'contagious' influences showed variation according to gender, social class, age, ethnicity, and educational attainment. Arts experiences *per se* were much less frequently mentioned. Teachers and friends were also often cited as 'turn-off' factors, but family members far more rarely. Similarly, arts experiences themselves rarely were felt to be the cause of any aversion.

The major area of young people's perceptions of the outcomes of any arts involvement is a further theme of this chapter. Here, it emerged that two-thirds of the total sample affirmed some positive effects of engaging with the arts. Some twenty different categories of response are exemplified (in such areas as personal development, social development, skill acquisition). The rank ordering and percentages of these responses are then outlined and key variations in responses – such as by social class and educational attainment are explained.

The chapter concludes with an account of young people's views on whether and what arts involvement they would have welcomed in their earlier years, and an overview of what involvement they felt to be a 'future' need.

Introduction This chapter relays the findings from a final series of questions in which the sample of young people were asked to offer views on:

♦ who or what had been influential factors in their arts participation and appreciation;

♦ the effects (such as personal or social development) accruing from their arts involvement to date;

♦ whether (and what) missed opportunities for arts involvement were evident retrospectively;

♦ whether (and what) specific types of arts activities might be welcomed in the future;

♦ the kinds of difficulties constraining future arts involvement; and

♦ the types of support most needed to ensure continued involvement in arts activities.

In this way, the concluding section of the interview requested respondents' accounts intended to be of direct relevance to practitioners, policy makers and funders (potential and existing) within the field of youth arts.

Inspiration and Aversion Factors

Some people say they got interested in the arts because somebody or some event turned them on to the arts, ... looking back over your life, can you remember anything or anybody turning you on to the arts?

All interviewees were asked to respond to the above question (Item 36a) – and its preamble (and, in so doing, were actually being encouraged to reflect and expand on Hargreaves' (1983) 'conversive trauma' theory). Once probed about any such nominated influences, the interviewee was then asked the complementary question (Item 36b): '*similarly, can you remember anything or anybody turning you off the arts?*'.

The results of this open pitch for accounts of influential factors in what might be termed arts inspiration and aversion, were collated and coded into a series of some forty categories.

Being 'turned on' to the arts

The rank order of categories arising from the sample's responses to the question on being 'turned on' to the arts is given in Table 10.1. This table contains all categories which received a minimum of ten mentions.

In this way, one-third of the total sample felt they could not nominate any direct, positive influence upon their appreciation or participation in the arts (though it must be stressed that non-nomination was not always synonymous with lack of arts interest). Of the two-thirds who did recall something or someone turning them on to the arts, it is noticeable that almost half of the top twenty categories referred to people with whom the respondent had first-hand and on-going contact – particularly secondary arts teachers, friends, mother and father.

Table 10.1 Factors affecting being 'turned on' to the arts by gender

| | Total sample | Gender | |
Category	%	Male %	Female %
No such effect recalled	33	33	32
Secondary arts teacher	14	17	12
Friends	12	11	13
Mother	7	4	10
Self-discovery	7	6	7
Father	5	3	7
Attending theatre	5	2	8
Participating in drama	5	7	3
Relative	5	2	7
Artistic role model	4	6	3
Sibling	4	5	3
Cajoled, encouragement	4	5	3
Both parents	4	3	5
Painting, drawing	4	3	4
Primary teacher	3	3	4
Encountering literature	3	3	3
Joining in music-making	3	3	3
Desire to emulate	2	1	4
Visit to gallery, museum	2	2	3
School	2	1	4
Boyfriend, girlfriend, spouse	2	2	2
Participating in dance	2	0	4
Hearing pop music, tapes	2	3	1
Family	2	1	3
Getting inspired	2	1	2
Youth worker	2	3	1
Atmosphere, arts around me	2	1	2
Taking part in writing	2	2	1
TOTALS	(681)	(338)	(343)

Interviewees could give more than one response, so percentages will not sum to 100 per cent. These figures are based on the weighted results (see Chapter 2).

Taking into account the high number of responses in some of these categories, the notion that arts appreciation is a largely 'contagious' phenomenon is endorsed by this evidence. Illustrations of this process surface in the following examples.

My drama teacher in the fourth year – she was really enthusiastic – it rubbed off on everybody, even those who didn't originally want to go to her lessons – she gave you confidence without putting you under pressure – there was the freedom to do it in your own way and your own time. (Female, 19, from a professional background)

I had a lot of friends interested in the arts side of things – there was a lot of interest there. Their interest inspired me because they were so passionate about it. It took me a long time – I searched and I looked and thought 'no way' but I've found something within the English side which is the most unobvious; you can read a book and not understand it and then you look deeper and then you do understand it, and then you think 'Yes, I've got it right'. There were people who painted and drew, they were naturally good artists, I'd never call myself that – they were recognised in the school as that. They encouraged me not to have a go but to look at, think about, which is probably more important. (Male, 18, from a professional background)

My mum ... she loved going to the theatre and listening to classical music. She encouraged me, e.g. took me to Stratford.
(Female, 19, Social Class III)

My dad, because he just used to draw pictures with me and when I went to school, I did it there. (Female, 16, Social Class IV and V)

I like classical music 'cos it was what I was listening to when I was a kid, 'cos of my grandma always listening to it.
(Male, 15, Social Class IV and V)

It is also evident that drama participation and theatre consumption were registered as significant arts experiences more often than any other art form. Indeed, in effect, only one in every hundred young people nominated attendance at a classical music concert or hearing classical music as a significant arts 'turn-on' experience, while only one in fifty mentioned a visit to galleries and museums. Encountering (or 'consuming' – see Chapter 6) literature and painting and drawing (which might be seen as more accessible art forms) were each referred to by about one in 25.

I have a specific memory of Pirates of Penzance when I was 15 from which my interest in theatre took off. It was the best thing ever – I went back three times. (Female, 23, Social Class I and II)

At primary school when I was doing the annual school play – that got me interested. It was Jack and the Beanstalk. I had the main part, it was a comedy. I was given responsibility to get the play right – I was to stall it to pass some time, it was ahead of schedule. I had to stop it: so I rested, sat down in the middle of the stage and just talked to the audience for 15 minutes. I made them laugh. That really got me going [in the arts]. (Male, 15, from an unskilled family background)

English Literature [turned me on]: *we did 'Wuthering Heights' and that started an interest. I've read the Bronte biographies and been to Haworth a few times.* (Female, 22, Social Class IV and V)

The ranking of factors causing arts 'turn-on' or inspiration shows some interesting differences when the usual independent variables were applied.

First, when gender differences in arts inspiration were looked at, it was noticeable that there was virtually an equivalent percentage of males and females recalling no specific influence or 'turn on'. Of those mentioning first hand inspirational contacts, males were more likely to nominate a secondary arts teacher – and also a youth worker, while girls referred more often to their parents – particularly their mothers – or a relative. Males were slightly more likely to mention an 'artistic role model', which is perhaps in keeping with this tendency for males to gain inspiration from beyond the immediate parental sphere of influence.

> *Guitar music turned me on! The first time I heard Chuck Berry, that's what got me into playing the guitar.* (Male, 15, skilled manual)

> *What really got me interested in art itself was Andy Warhol and his paintings – through the course we had to look at books, pick an artist and explain why we liked them, do work like the artist and make a speech (about the artist we'd chosen).*
> (Female, 21, skilled non-manual)

Of those who nominated arts experiences as an inspirational factor, it was noticeable that more girls mentioned theatre attendance, while more boys focused on drama participation. Participating in dance was apparently an almost uniquely female source of inspiration.

Turning to the breakdown by ethnicity, major differences occur in a number of areas. Firstly, the ethnic minorities sub-sample showed the highest percentage of young people suggesting they could recall no-one or nothing turning them on to the arts. Nearly half (46 per cent) responded in this way, compared to about a third (31 per cent) of white Europeans. It was noticeable that the ethnic minority sub-sample recorded the lowest percentage of nominations for secondary arts teacher, mother and theatre attendance but the highest percentage of nominations for siblings and participation in dance. This may suggest that, for this group, being turned on to the arts through the older generation is less common, while any family influence is rooted in the youth culture transmitted through brothers and sisters. Additionally, theatre was not the source of inspiration evident in the sample as a whole. Of course, shortage of role models may be a factor here.

When the different age groups were considered, significant variations arose in the nominations of categories of influential people (or 'contagion'). Thus, the youngest age band emerged as the group most likely to suggest being turned on to the arts by family: they recorded the highest percentage of references to a relative (e.g. grandmother or cousin), a sibling and mother. Similarly, the under-17s more often nominated a secondary arts teacher, and responses in the category 'youth worker' were almost exclusively among the under-17s. These results may reflect the fact that this age group was chronologically closer to daily familial involvement, secondary school and youth club attendance. In contrast, the over-21s showed the highest percentage of nominations for 'friends'. Equally, this oldest age band more often suggested that partners (e.g. boyfriend/girlfriend/spouse) were their source of arts inspiration. This finding may well reflect the important social function of arts in adulthood, and it therefore perhaps is not surprising that the over-21s were the group who consistently ranked the highest percentages in nominating encounters with consumer arts as a 'turn on' factor. Figures for the encountering of literature, visual arts (e.g. galleries etc.), and theatre attendance demonstrated this trend.

It was noticeable that the 17-20 age band ranked the highest percentage for 'no [turn on] effect recalled'. Similarly, among all three age bands, they consistently recorded the lowest percentage of response for the family categories ('mum', 'dad', 'sibling' and 'relative'), for youth workers as well as for secondary arts teachers. This may corroborate the findings elsewhere that this age band often appeared to register least positive responses to arts, set apart from the consistent institutional arts support available to young people of school age and yet without the financial independence or interest to participate in and consume an adult-oriented arts scene.

When urban and rural differences are examined, 'family osmosis' appeared more evident in the rural than urban sub-sample. The former registered slightly higher percentages for mother, father, both parents, siblings and family. However, the urban sample showed a higher rating for friends. 'Youth worker' as a source of arts inspiration was exclusively an urban nomination, which may suggest that young people in rural areas have the paucity of opportunities to 'catch' the arts from this potentially influential source.

Moving onto the breakdown by social class, Table 10.2 gives details of all categories which received ten or more responses.

First, there is a notable difference between those in professional classes suggesting no 'turn on' effect compared to young people from skilled or partly/unskilled backgrounds. The fact that only half as many (18 per cent) of the highest social class category are unable to nominate a source of arts inspiration in comparison to the other two categories (35 per cent or more) may be a very significant finding. There seems considerable evidence to suggest that there is a prevalence of parental arts osmosis among the professional classes. Reference to the table shows that mum, dad and both parents rank highly as sources of inspiration with this social class; whereas the sub-sample from partly/unskilled backgrounds rated their secondary arts teachers highly. It is also evident that friends and partners (spouse/boyfriend/girlfriend etc.) and artistic role model featured less often as sources of arts contagion among the partly/unskilled sub-sample. Thus, it is at least possible to conclude that the social norms of this category of social class are less likely to include a focus on arts involvement.

Table 10.2   Selected factors affecting being 'turned on' to the arts by social class

Category	Total sample %	Social Class I & II %	III (N & M) %	IV & V %
No such effect recalled	33	18	35	36
Secondary arts teacher	14	14	11	21
Friends	12	13	15	5
Mother	7	14	6	6
Self-discovery	7	8	5	8
Father	5	8	3	7
Attending theatre	5	6	6	4
Participating in drama	5	6	6	3
Relative	5	7	7	0
Artistic role model	4	5	7	1
Sibling	4	5	3	6
Cajoled, encouragement	4	3	2	8
Both parents	4	8	4	2
Painting, drawing	4	2	2	6
Primary teacher	3	4	4	2
Encountering literature	3	6	3	2
Joining in music-making	3	4	3	2
Desire to emulate	2	2	3	2
Visit to gallery, museum	2	3	2	2
School	2	4	2	2
Boyfriend, girlfriend, spouse	2	2	3	0
Participating in dance	2	3	2	1
Hearing pop music, tapes	2	3	3	0
Family	2	5	1	2
Getting inspired	2	2	2	2
Youth worker	2	2	1	3
Atmosphere, arts around me	2	3	1	2
Taking part in writing	2	0	2	2
Discovering artistic talent	2	2	2	0
TOTALS	(681)	(105)	(359)	(217)

Interviewees could give more than one response, so percentages will not sum to 100 per cent. These figures are based on the weighted results (see Chapter 2).

Finally, the breakdown by educational attainment shows some interesting continuations of trends in the 'contagious arts' hypothesis. Table 10.3 gives the percentages for the highest ranking twenty five responses to the sources of arts 'turn on' by the four categories of GCSE (equivalent) attainment.

Table 10.3 Selected factors affecting being 'turned on' to the arts by educational attainment

Category	Total sample %	GCSEs			
		None %	1-3 %	4-6 %	7+ %
No such effect recalled	35	44	47	24	32
Secondary arts teacher	13	11	9	16	13
Friends	14	16	7	16	14
Mother	6	1	8	5	10
Self discovery	6	3	10	5	7
Father	6	4	6	9	4
Attending theatre	6	6	5	3	9
Participating in drama	5	5	3	4	5
Artistic role model	4	3	6	4	5
Cajoled, encouragement	4	8	2	3	3
Both parents	4	3	1	1	8
Painting, drawing	4	4	0	5	5
Primary teacher	4	3	2	3	7
Encountering literature	4	3	4	9	2
Relative	3	0	9	3	1
Sibling	3	1	3	2	4
Joining in music-making	3	0	0	5	5
Hearing pop music, tape	3	1	3	1	5
Visit to gallery, museum	3	3	0	3	3
School	3	3	0	3	3
Boyfriend, spouse	3	0	4	7	3
Participating in dance	1	0	0	3	2
Family	1	0	0	3	2
Desire to emulate	1	1	0	1	3
TOTALS	(429)	(98)	(71)	(91)	(152)

Interviewees could give more than one response, so percentages will not sum to 100 per cent.
These figures are based on the weighted results (see Chapter 2).
Approximately 4 per cent of the relevant post-16 sub-sample (N=429) constituted missing cases for this analysis.

Here, highest educational attainers recorded the greatest percentage of nominations for their mother, both parents, and primary teacher as a source of inspiration – all very evidently early (as well as perhaps particularly sustained) first-hand influences. Thus, along with the prevalence of mother as an arts 'turn-on' factor for females and those with professional backgrounds, the interesting possibility that inspiration which secures long -term arts commitment is often a 'matrilineal' phenomenon begins to present itself. The high educational attainers also most frequently mention theatre attendance as a turn-on to the arts. In addition, hearing a classical record was only registered by high attainers (other interviewees giving this reply were below the relevant examination age).

In contrast, the lowest educational attainers least often mention mother (as well as spouse) and self-discovery. Equally, the two lowest categories of educational attainment do not register joining in music-making as a source of arts inspiration – perhaps corroborating the tendency (evident in Chapter 8) for music to often be closely associated with high educational attainers. It should be noted that over 40 per cent of both these lower attainment categories also could not recall any inspirational factors.

Being 'turned off' the arts

Moving on to look at the opposite phenomenon – namely recalling any event or person that was responsible for 'turning the respondent off the arts' (or having caused, in effect, 'aversion' to the arts), the rankings for the full sample are set out in Table 10.4. This table contains all the categories which received at least ten nominations.

Table 10.4 Factors affecting being 'turned off' the arts by gender

Category	Total sample %	Gender Male %	Female %
No such effect recalled	56	51	61
Secondary arts teacher	9	9	9
Pretentious artists	5	7	3
Friends	5	8	1
Others lack of interest	5	8	2
Lack of ability	4	3	5
Poor teacher	4	3	4
Joining in music-making	3	2	3
Little interest	3	3	2
Aggressive teacher	2	3	2
Both parents	2	2	2
Inadvisable career move	2	2	2
Lack of confidence	2	1	2
Individuals uncatered for	2	1	2
TOTALS	(681)	(338)	(343)

Interviewees could give more than one response, so percentages will not sum to 100 per cent. These figures are based on the weighted results (see Chapter 2).

The first noticeable aspect of the results for the total sample is the high percentage (over half) of young people who did not experience any such arts aversion. Also, secondary arts teachers and friends appear in the top two rankings of sources of arts aversion, just as they did in nominations for arts inspiration. In contrast, it is very striking that there was a complete absence of references to mother as a turn-off from the arts, as is the very low ranking of other family influences – father and sibling were each mentioned by less than five respondents in total; relative by less than ten; while both parents were nominated by only 2 per cent of the total sample. Thus, family members were apparently very rarely seen as a source of arts turn off, perhaps corroborating the significance of a sustained influence and role model for arts involvement. A 'family inheritance' of arts involvement thus re-emerges as an important factor to consider.

The most frequent nomination for an aversion effect is quite clearly young people's recollected encounters with a secondary arts teacher and teaching which was perceived to be ineffective.

> *We had this nun at school, this complete maniac and she really used to – we used to do choir and thinking back now, I probably would have enjoyed it if it hadn't been for her. I would have kept it up – but she was very competitive and we did all these competitions and she was very violent if anything went wrong, and she used to do the plays and if anything she turned us off. She took any enjoyment out of it 'cos she put so much pressure on us. She was a complete nutter – my sisters are still frightened of her.* (Female, 19, skilled manual)

> *Drama teacher* [turned me off] *– I didn't take it to A–level 'cos though they were enjoyable lessons, it didn't go the way I wanted it to go – I wanted to get into video things. I was put off 'cos I couldn't develop anything I wanted to do, even though he kept saying we could.*
> (Male, 17, professional)

> *My art teacher in the third year – she said 'you're not thinking of taking art – if you are, you can forget it'. She gave me negative vibes, but I was pretty useless at it.* (Female, 19, professional)

This critical perspective on teachers is obviously worrying, but it needs to be weighed carefully against evidence from the earlier section on conversive trauma (where secondary teachers were ranked highest as a source of arts inspiration), as well as looking carefully at which categories of young people cite this turn off effect and why.

Beyond that, the relatively high incidence of references to being turned off by pretentious artists, friends and others' lack of interest suggests arts aversion is quite often felt to be caught from peers; from direct encounters with arts personages within the arts world and from an environment where arts is little valued. In this way, again by implication, arts may require a careful induction or suffusion, and, without this, the 'by-pass' so notable in earlier chapters may be the inevitable result.

[My] mates (turned me off) music – they say you're a poofter [if you do it].　　　　　　　　　　　　　　　　　　　　(Male, 19, skilled manual)

Not so much an event turned me off, more the stigma associated with 'arts' at school – of being 'artistic', like posh people.
　　　　　　　　　　　　　　　　　　　　(Male, 17, professional)

Within the arts comes a lot of people who appear very pretentious. My experience with some is they tried to deflate your personality – they're never wrong but you are ... It limits your capacity to speak out: how do I as someone who can't paint etc. come up to their standard, talk seriously about the work to them if I'm not their standard. I can't criticise them but why should they talk down to me, discount me. There's a lot of snobbery.　　　　　　　　(Male, 18, professional)

Not exactly 'turned off' but our headteacher at first school scaled down arts involvement.　　　　　　　　　(Male, 15, professional)

Reference to Table 10.4 also shows how rare it is for actual arts encounters (or consumption) to be the cause of turn-off. Activities such as attending theatre, hearing pop or classical records and visits to galleries were registered as sources of arts aversion by only 1 per cent of the total sample. Indeed, the sample were more likely to nominate their own lack of ability and confidence as causes of turn-off, rather than the arts experiences themselves.

Looking at responses by the key independent variables, some significant differences are evident. First, in a breakdown of the categories of 'arts turn-off' by gender, Table 10.4 shows that a higher percentage of males in effect responded affirmatively to the notion of arts turn-off, rather than rejecting the concept: three-fifths of females, compared with half of the male sample, could think of nothing or no-one who had directly caused any arts aversion. It is noticeable that males were much more likely to mention friends (about one in 12 boys reported this, as opposed to one in a hundred girls). More males than females also registered others' lack of interest, as well as pretentious artists. This may raise again the idea of male youth culture being less sympathetic – or oriented – to the arts.

Additionally, although the percentage of nominations for secondary arts teacher as a source of arts 'turn off' was equivalent for both males and females (9 per cent), it was noticeable that females gave slightly more references to the calibre of their arts teachers – the epithets, 'poor teaching' and 'boring teacher' were used more by females than males. All this may suggest that an arts interest is a more acceptable norm for young females, and hence girls are more likely to nominate their own perceived inadequacies, or that of their teachers, as an explanation for any aversion feelings.

Major differences between urban and rural responses to the issue of arts 'turn off' were not evident except in a small number of categories. Young people from rural backgrounds were more likely to respond by referring to their own lack of interest or '*not getting much out of the arts*': 6 per cent of young people from rural locations stated this, compared to 1 per cent of urban young people.

When then ages of respondents were considered, several categories of arts turn-off showed notable differences. Table 10.5 shows the age band breakdown of all categories with more then ten responses.

Table 10.5   Selected factors affecting being 'turned off' the arts by age

Category	Total sample %	Age Under-17 %	Age 17-20 %	Age 21-24 %
No such effect recalled	56	56	61	46
Secondary arts teacher	9	10	9	7
Pretentious artists	5	3	2	12
Friends	5	7	4	1
Others' lack of interest	5	5	6	1
Lack of ability	4	4	2	6
Poor teacher	4	2	4	6
Joining in music-making	3	2	4	1
Little interest	3	2	4	1
Aggressive teacher	2	2	1	5
Inadvisable career move	2	2	3	1
Both parents	2	0	3	3
Lack of confidence	2	0	1	6
TOTALS	(681)	(261)	(288)	(132)

Interviewees could give more than one response, so percentages will not sum to 100 per cent. These figures are based on the weighted results (see Chapter 2).

Particularly noticeable here is the predominance of views among the over-21s about the off-putting characteristics of people associated with the arts world – in effect, seen by one in eight of this age group as a cause of arts turn-off. In comparison to the two younger age bands, the sample of over-21s hardly rated their friends or others' lack of interest as an adverse influence. The influence of friends as a source of arts aversion was slightly more important for the under-17s than for other age bands. Put together, this may suggest that it is the image and social culture surrounding the arts, rather than direct peer influence, which increasingly is felt to affect the appetite for arts involvement as young people mature. In keeping with this, it is worth noting that the oldest age-band make more frequent mention of their own lack of ability and confidence, as if, in appraising the qualities appropriate for arts involvement, they are more ready to find themselves 'lacking' in some capacity (rather than simply following peer norms).

Moving on to look at 'arts turn off' by social class, Table 10.6 again gives a breakdown of all categories with more than ten responses.

Table 10.6   Selected factors affecting being 'turned off' the arts by social class

Category	Total sample %	Social Class		
		I & II %	III (N & M) %	IV & V %
No such effect recalled	56	45	55	63
Secondary arts teacher	9	17	10	4
Pretentious artists	5	5	4	5
Friends	5	4	5	4
Others' lack of interest	5	3	8	2
Lack of ability	5	5	3	6
Poor teacher	4	7	4	2
Joining in music-making	3	6	2	2
Little interest	3	3	2	2
Aggressive teacher	2	1	2	3
Inadvisable career move	2	4	2	0
Both parents	2	0	3	0
Lack of confidence	2	2	2	2
TOTALS	(681)	(105)	(359)	(217)

Interviewees could give more than one response, so percentages will not sum to 100 per cent.
These figures are based on the weighted results (see Chapter 2).

A number of trends emerge from this breakdown. First, respondents in the professional sub-sample were most likely to affirm the notion of arts 'turn-off' as put to them by the interviewer. Indeed, nearly two-thirds of the partly/unskilled sample responded that they could think of nothing or no-one who had specifically turned them off the arts.

Turning to those who could identify causes of an arts aversion experience, it is striking that young people from professional backgrounds most often nominated their secondary arts teacher and voiced the specific criticism of poor teaching. Equally, this sub-sample were more likely to mention the arts as an inadvisable career move. Young people from skilled backgrounds ranked highly in attributing turn off to others' lack of interest and both parents. Thus, a slight but significant difference in emphasis may be apparent: with the higher social class, in effect, more often attributing any arts aversion to factors beyond self or, conversely, expressing the view that self was not well served by serious arts involvement or specialisation.

The Effects of Arts Involvement

Being involved in the arts has made me realise who I really am. I know what I can do. I can be somebody else, and still be myself. It's like I can't believe that people really like me – it's a sort of image thing, but it is really me there. Also, it gives confidence and lets out stress ... (Male, 15)

The interview question (Item 37), *'do you think that what you do now in the arts, or what you've done in the past has had any effects on you?'* which required first either an affirmative or negative response, opened up the major area of young people's perceptions of the outcomes of their arts involvement to date. Following the initial closed response, the interviewees were then offered probes as to whether they could identify any personal or social development accruing from their arts experiences; whether there had been any acquisition of specific skills; and whether 'motivation' and a further interest in the arts had also resulted.

Looking first at the closed responses, Table 10.7 shows almost two-thirds of the total sample affirming some effects of arts involvement.

Table 10.7   Whether arts involvement had any effects by social class

Category	Total sample %	Social Class I & II %	III (N & M) %	IV & V %
Affirmative	64	83	60	59
Negative	36	17	40	41
TOTALS	(681)	(105)	(359)	(217)

These figures are based on the weighted results (see Chapter 2).

Breakdown by the key independent variables showed certain sub-samples registering other than this two-third majority. With male and female samples' affirmation being 60 per cent and 67 per cent respectively, other major variations from the two-thirds majority were: urban and rural 66 and 57 per cent respectively; and white Europeans and ethnic minorities 65 and 50 per cent respectively. The latter proportion for the ethnic minorities is particularly significant.

Moreover, when the social class was considered, the variation was even more marked (see Table 10.7). While some four-fifths of the professional class acknowledged arts involvement had definite effects on them, this was about three-fifths of the respondents in other social class categories.

At the analysis stage, when looking in detail at the descriptions of arts effects as identified by the sample in response to the open question, *'what were the(se) effects?'* and its subsequent probes, each interviewee's replies could be allocated up to ten codes. This high number of coding options was deliberately planned in order to provide the maximum opportunity for capturing the subtle variations in young people's nomination of arts effects: it was felt that the issue of impact and consequences of arts involvement was vital information for all policy-makers and practitioners in youth arts. Some 27 distinct categories of effect emerged. Table 10.8 offers the full range of the sample's nominations, in rank order (with percentages for each). However, before this, the following chart provides examples of verbatim responses for all the categories - again in rank order. This is to provide maximum information on the key issue of effects.

Has your arts involvement in the past and what you do now had any effect?

Category of response	Example of comments *[...the effects which my involvement in the arts has had is ...]*
Specific skill	*For music, I've learned to make songs, by myself, not out of key, that sound right.* (Male, 15, professional) *I now have qualifications in the theory of music as far as I'll need them, and practically, I'm two-thirds there. It also helps to do performances and I know now what to do to put a performance on.* (Female, 14, professional) *I improved in Art A-level – it shows what you can do when you put your mind to it. You build up quite an impressive amount of work you might not think you could've done before.* (Female, 18, skilled)
Increase in self-esteem, confidence	*I suppose drama made me more confident because we're actually made to talk and stuff, act out things.* (Female, 14, professional) *The acting and performing made me more able to go in front of people, to cope with 'nerves'.* (Male, 17, professional) *It enabled [me] to speak [my] mind, not scared to say what you think.* (Female, 16, skilled manual)
More interest in arts	*Made me more interested and I want to do it more than anything.* (Female, 14, professional)
Started specialism	*I never used to be interested in drama, but now I want to do more of it.* (Male, 14, Skilled non-manual) *In the past year, I've had to think about what I want to do. Everything I do is to do with music, and I'd like to be a music teacher.* (Female, 14, professional)
Get on with others	*It does help you relate easier to other people.* (Male, 20, Skilled non-manual) *I think people in dance/drama are forward anyway – they're easy to get on with.* (Male, 18, professional)
Communicating with others	*Yes – able to get out and communicate better – from the drama.* (Male, 19, professional) *Ability to overcome problems in training and communication, therefore able to train others.* (Male, 20, skilled manual,) *Friends like the same music and films – something to talk about.* (Male, 17, skilled non-manual) *... it made me come out of my shell, I can communicate now a lot more to people.* (Male, 19, skilled manual)

Category of response	Example of comments *[...the effects which my involvement in the arts has had is ...]*
Make friends, meet people	*The theatre is a good way of getting to know people without it being too obvious. I got to know a lot of people – I get two tickets and say 'I've got tickets for the theatre, do you want to go?'* (Female, 19, skilled manual) *Yes, because I've got into music and going to 'gigs' and stuff, I've met a lot of people, I find – because you meet people who are into the same music as you, you find it really easy to get on with them.* (Male, 18) *The arts subjects here* [at school] *are a friendlier way of learning. You can't really avoid becoming more friendly with people and you're certainly not encouraged to work by yourself so that helps.* (Male, 17, skilled)
More insight, awareness, understanding	*I've learnt* [through the arts] *how to be diplomatic and cope with different situations.* (Female, 16, partly-skilled) *.. enables you to get a different perspective on what you see.* (Male, 18, professional) *Yes, broad involvement in differing areas, widens understanding of different types of people whose interests may be more limited.* (Male, 17, professional) *Going to plays has made me think, I suppose.* (Female, 20, partly-skilled)
Broaden interests, mind	*I've got better skills, more knowledge and so more to talk about. I don't only read the Sun!* (Female, 22, partly-skilled) *Yes – different styles convey different people's ideas – it broadens the scope of your interests.* (Male, 15, professional)
More open- minded, questioning	*... more open mind to things.* (Female, 21, professional) *... increases sensibility to some things, a step further in appreciation.* (Male, 23, professional) *I'm more critical now – I don't just let it wash all over me – I'm not just prepared to accept it because it's there – I question.* (Female, 19, skilled manual) *Arts, and design for me ... it makes you more analytical, as does English. It teaches you a way of thinking rather than sticking to the rules.* (Male, 17, skilled manual)
Able to express myself	*In drama we stand up and say what we want and so I do it out of school as well.* (Female, 15, skilled non-manual) *The arts (especially drama) is very valuable – it gets all your feelings out ... you can't do that in maths, and you can learn about yourself.* (Female, 17, professional)
Ability to work with others	*It's good working with other people, learning how to get on with people.* (Male, 20, skilled non-manual) *Yes – helps you work with others which is a benefit when you go for a job.* (Male, 14, professional)

Category of response	Example of comments *[...the effects which my involvement in the arts has had is ...]*
Helped generally, just enjoy	*No, it hasn't had any effects, it's just my own enjoyment.* (Female, 21, skilled non-manual)
Better at drawing and painting	*Arts taught me a lot: it's taught me not to be so heavy with a pencil.* (Female 16, professional)
Wanting to know more about the arts	*I'm happy to take drama further – to be an artist or a drama teacher – or a zoologist.* (Male, 15, professional) *Yes – definitely – next year, when I go to university, I'll be wanting – and able – to get involved in drama. I have the confidence to do that.* (Female, 19, professional)
Stress, anger relief	*Music relaxes me.* (Male, 15, professional) *Music cools me down a lot. It stops me getting angry. If I get angry I go and play music and then I feel better.* (Female, 18, professional) *If something annoys me, I'll go and paint my models or read – (it calms me down).* (Male, 20, skilled non-manual)
More creative, imaginative	*Yes – art has changed me from doing stupid things like painting a wall to putting it on paper – I'm more creative.* (Male, 23, skilled manual) *Helped me look at things in a more creative way.* (Female, 24, professional)
More knowledge of the arts	*Knowledge of music, knowledge of painting and artists and general knowledge which is nice to have. They're all areas which I would like to one day go into more deeply.* (Female, 24, professional)
Organise life better	*[Because of my ballet training] I understand what hard work really is – people don't realise how hard the work is – they see a performance and think it looks easy.* (Female, 20, professional)
More visual awareness	*I appreciate things more – I can look at a piece of art and because I've done it [art] too, I can see how much hard work's gone into it.* (Male, 15, professional) *Practice with drawing affects the way you look at things.* (Female, 20, partly-skilled) *My video making ... makes you look at different things that you wouldn't look at normally.* (Male, 16, skilled)
Become more lively	*It's changed me into a person who likes to be silly. I don't mind that ... after the play I get really very excited.* (Male, 14, skilled manual)

Having given examples of verbatim comments for all those categories recording ten or more responses, Table 10.8 shows the rank order and percentages of these categorised responses.

Table 10.8 Perceived effects of arts involvement

Responses	Total sample %	I & II %	Social Class III (N & M) %	IV & V %
Specific skill	27	38	28	21
Increase self-esteem, confidence	27	39	25	25
More interest in arts	17	23	16	16
Started specialism	16	22	13	19
Get on better with others	13	18	12	14
Communication with others	12	20	10	12
Make friends, meet more people	11	20	15	2
Insight, awareness	9	16	6	12
Broader interests, broadened mind	9	19	8	6
More open-minded	8	13	8	6
Express myself more	7	11	5	8
Ability to work with others	6	13	6	2
Helped generally, just enjoyment	6	6	6	5
Better drawing, painting	6	7	4	7
Wanting to know more about arts	5	11	5	4
Stress/anger relief	5	6	3	6
Other	4	7	3	4
Creative, imaginative	4	7	5	0
More knowledge of arts	3	5	4	1
Organise life better	3	7	1	4
More visual awareness	2	2	2	3
Became more lively	2	3	2	1
TOTALS	(681)	(105)	(359)	(217)

Interviewees could give more than one response, so percentages will not sum to 100 per cent.
These figures are based on the weighted results (see Chapter 2).
As shown in Table 10.7, 36 per cent registered no perceived effect of previous arts involvement.

Of course, this full categorisation could have been elided into several broader sets of response. For instance, the categories: 'getting on with others', 'communicating with others', 'making friends easily' and 'working with others' all fall readily into a broad 'social development' category. Equally, within the range of responses focusing on personal development, the positive effect on young people's sense – or projection – of self ('more self-esteem', 'express myself more') could be viewed as a distinct category, somewhat different from the 'cognisance/discriminatory intellect' outcomes such as 'insights and awareness' or 'more open-minded and questioning'. Other responses referred – more literally if not tautologically – to arts involvement leading to a sustained interest or increased knowledge in the arts.

Despite these possible alternative categorisations, the presentation of the fullest possible range of responses (as outlined in Table 10.8) should provide the most useful detail in a form which remains closest to young people's own constructs.

In the rural and urban samples, the urban respondents showed a higher percentage of references to effects such as 'acquired a specific skill' (29 per cent to 21 per cent) and 'more interest in the arts' (19 per cent to 11 per cent). Equally, they outranked the rural respondents in the area of cognisance/discriminatory intellect with 10 per cent claiming 'more insights and awareness', compared with 6 per cent of the rural sample. Beyond that, young people in urban locations consistently ranked a slightly higher percentage of responses in the areas of social development as an outcome of arts involvement with, for instance, 12 per cent mentioning 'making friends/meeting more people' compared with 8 per cent of the rural sample, and 'ability to work with others' referred to by 7 per cent of the urban sample compared with 3 per cent of those in rural locations. In contrast, the rural sample showed a higher response rate in the category 'started specialism'. Put together, these results appear to suggest that young people in urban settings more readily see arts as offering social benefits and sustained stimulus, perhaps given the likely proximity and greater profusion of arts opportunities. These findings on differences in arts effects nominations are also consistent with the evidence in Chapter 3. Here, leisure pursuits among young people in urban locations were noticeably stronger in arts consumption (such as cinema, video, music, reading) which may account for the higher nomination of social outcome and increased awareness/broadened mind. The rural sample's greater reference to 'started specialism' and particularly better at painting and drawing also links back to Chapter 3's findings, and may suggest a location has some connection with a focus on the art form itself and solo participation.

Gender differences were also apparent in the category of 'making friends' (male 8 per cent; female 14 per cent) and yet most evident in the categories alluding to an enhanced sense of self (e.g. self-esteem recorded: male 24 per cent, female 30 per cent and self-expression: male 3 per cent, female 11 per cent).

The most marked areas of differences in the responses by age are that the youngest age band perceived the effects of their arts involvement much more in terms of definable arts skills ('specific skill' and 'started specialism'), while the older respondents (21-24) most certainly rank the highest responses in those categories which are descriptors of a more generalised intellectual development: 'insights and awareness', 'breadth of interest', 'enjoyment' and 'communication'. This finding may reflect an inevitable perspicacity and maturity of outlook which comes with adulthood (and a greater accumulated experience of arts), suggest that the value of young people's arts education and involvement was increasingly recognised in retrospect, or indicate that the arts experiences of the older group were qualitatively different to those of the younger respondents.

Very little comment need be added on the inexorable pattern of highest responses coming from young people in the professional social class category as exemplified by Table 10.8. However, particularly marked differences are apparent in the categories of 'increase in self esteem', with well over a third of Social Class I & II respondents suggesting this effect, in comparison to only a quarter of those from the skilled or partly/unskilled categories. Additional analyses established that the highest percentage responses were often evident in the sub-sample of females from professional backgrounds, most notably in the personal development categories of 'increase in self-esteem', 'more confidence' and 'making friends'. The lack of responses by males from Social Class IV and V is particularly evident in the areas of sociability, 'getting on with others' and 'making friends'. However, the relatively small sample sizes need to be taken into account when considering these sub-categories.

Table 10.9   Perceived effects of arts involvement by educational attainment

Responses	Total sample %	None %	GCSEs 1-3 %	4-6 %	7+ %
Specific skill	22	11	20	23	27
Increase self-esteem, confidence	26	14	27	18	36
More interest in arts	16	13	5	18	22
Communication with others	13	5	9	17	15
Started specialism	12	10	4	13	16
Insight, awareness	12	16	1	13	12
Get on better with others	11	6	6	10	15
Make friends, meet more people	11	4	4	7	20
Broader interests, broadened mind	11	8	6	18	13
More open-minded	11	10	1	11	12
Helped generally, just enjoyment	7	7	8	10	5
Express myself more	6	1	4	6	12
Ability to work with others	6	1	3	5	11
Better drawing, painting	6	11	5	3	6
Wanting to know more about arts	5	0	2	3	9
Stress, anger relief	5	6	0	4	8
Creative, imaginative	4	5	6	3	4
Organise life better	4	2	2	4	6
More knowledge of arts	3	1	0	0	7
TOTALS	(437)	(101)	(74)	(93)	(152)

Interviewees could give more than one response, so percentages will not sum to 100 per cent.
These figures are based on the weighted results (see Chapter 2).
Approximately 40 per cent of the relevant post-16 sub-sample (N=437) constituted missing cases for this analysis.

With regard to educational attainment variables (Table 10.9), a high proportion of respondents (over a third) nominating increase in 'confidence and self-esteem' surfaced among the most successful educational attainers. This sub-sample also show a particularly high rating on 'express myself more'. 'Making friends' is also a category where high educational attainers' responses are very much more frequent than in the other groups. It is noteworthy that respondents with 1-3 16+ subject passes often recorded fewer effects: they had the highest non-response rate (56 per cent) and registered the lowest percentages referring to such effects as 'more interest in the arts', 'started specialism', 'insights and awareness', 'more open-minded' and 'stress and anger relief'. This is consistent with earlier findings: it appears that the lower educational attainers, as well as valuing arts less, are also less likely to perceive the positive effects of the arts.

Views on Past Involvement and Future Needs

Past involvement

The initial closed response to the question, '*looking back, would you have liked more involvement in the arts?*' (Item 38a) produced the distribution displayed in Table 10.10.

Table 10.10 More (past) arts involvement wanted by age

| | Total sample | Age | | |
| | | Under-17 | 17-20 | 21-24 |
Responses	%	%	%	%
Yes, more wanted	66	65	61	78
No, not wanted	34	35	39	22
TOTALS	(678)	(258)	(288)	(132)

These figures are based on the weighted results (see Chapter 2).

Thus, two-thirds of the total sample felt more arts involvement would have been welcomed. Variation from this two-third majority was evident between the urban and rural samples: while 69 per cent of the former would have welcomed more involvement in the arts in the past, only 56 per cent of rural respondents did so. Confirming earlier results, the 21-24 age band contained a particularly high proportion of interviewees (see Table 10.10) who would have liked more arts involvement than they had experienced. In this way, ethnic minorities, social class and gender appeared to make very little difference to young people's majority view that more arts involvement would have been welcomed. These results amount to a powerful request which clearly poses important challenges for future policy-making in the arts and educational areas.

To the 34 per cent of interviewees who responded that they did not particularly want to have had more arts involvement, the interview schedule had posed the question, '*why not?*'. The following eight major reasons surfaced from the 227 respondents who replied to the question (see Table 10.11).

Table 10.11   Why more (past) arts involvement not wanted

Reasons	%
No interest in arts	48
Done enough already	36
Prefer other subject(s)	12
Lack arts ability	8
Shy, dislike participation	4
Dislike teachers, school	4
Not enough time	4
Other	3
TOTAL	(227)

These figures are based on the weighted results (see Chapter 2). Interviewees could give more than one response, so percentages will not sum to 100 per cent.

The different sub-samples showed a number of significant variations. Particularly striking was the virtual equivalence between male and female responses, except that the former were more likely to suggest they had preferred other subjects, and to nominate their own dislike of school and teachers. Again, it is interesting that those from professional backgrounds and high educational attainers were more likely to say that they felt they had 'done enough' arts. Over-21s and high educational attainers were more likely to express directly a preference for other subjects, while 17-20 year olds and the partly/unskilled were the groups nominating most references to 'no interest in the arts'.

Young people interviewed in the sample were then asked to outline which particular arts or creative activities they would have most welcomed when younger (Item 38b). Table 10.12 shows the ranking of each category where six or more responses emerged. It should be stressed that respondents were able to register up to three responses.

Table 10.12   Examples of (past) arts opportunities welcomed by gender

Responses	Total sample %	Gender Male %	Gender Female %
Drama	20	17	23
Musical instrument skill	14	12	15
Painting, drawing	12	15	10
Arts at an earlier age	7	5	10
Opportunities to try other art forms	5	3	7
Ballet, dance	4	1	8
Acting	4	5	2
Sculpture, modelling	4	5	3
Design	3	4	2
More time spent on arts	3	3	3
More opportunities to see performances	3	2	4
Opportunity to take arts interests further	3	2	3
Anything	3	3	2
More performing opportunities	3	3	2
Writing, scripts, etc.	2	2	3
Photography	2	3	2
More interest in you, encouragement	2	1	2
Media studies	2	2	2
More specialist teaching	2	2	1
Guitar instrumental skill	1	3	0
More facilities	1	1	1
More theory	1	0	2
More on techniques taught	1	1	1
TOTALS	(681)	(338)	(343)

Interviewees could give more than one response, so percentages will not sum to 100 per cent.
These figures are based on the weighted results (see Chapter 2).
As shown in Table 10.10, 34 per cent registered that they would not have welcomed more (past) arts opportunities.

Thus, drama stands out as the arts activity which would have been most welcomed – in effect, one fifth of the total sample said this. Acting as a separate category also figured highly. This result is particularly significant in view of what observers may consider to be the low profile given to drama within the National Curriculum.

Musical instrument skill ranked second and a further 1 per cent (9 young people, all males) actually nominated guitar skills.

Variations from the total sample responses were evident in the rural sample, where 'arts at an earlier age' was mentioned by almost one sixth (13 per cent) of respondents, compared with only one in twenty (5 per cent) of young people from urban locations. The urban sample registered a higher response rate in 'drawing and painting' (14 per cent compared with 8 per cent).

Notable gender differences are displayed in Table 10.12. Here again, responses show somewhat predictable trends – more males nominating 'doing and making' arts activities (e.g. acting, design), while females clearly outrank males in welcoming earlier opportunities for expressive arts such as drama, dance, as well as 'seeing more performances'.

The different age bands showed variations in the areas of 'musical instrument skill' and 'arts done earlier' where the youngest age band showed highest nominations. The over-21s registered highest responses in the areas of 'seeing more performances', 'trying other art forms', and the rather plaintive 'anything'!

Most notable in the disaggregation by social class was the predominance of responses from professional backgrounds in the areas of 'opportunities to try other arts forms' and 'seeing more performances'. This emphasis was also apparent in the breakdown by educational attainment, where the high attainers registered significantly higher percentages. However, more fundamental participatory arts skills – musical instrument playing and drawing and painting were mentioned by those who had no GCSEs or four to six and by all social classes – respondents for Social Class IV and V were particularly oriented towards welcoming more opportunities in painting and drawing.

Future Needs and Interests

Having discussed the kinds of activities which would have been welcomed at earlier stages of young people's 'arts career', each interviewee was then asked (Item 39): '*are there any arts activities you'd like to take further and do more of in the future?*'. To this closed question, again, two thirds suggested they would (see Table 10.13).

Table 10.13 Whether future arts activities wanted by age?

	Total sample	Under-17	Age 17-20	21-24
Responses	%	%	%	%
Yes, more wanted	66	68	61	71
No, not wanted	34	32	39	29
TOTALS	(669)	(255)	(284)	(130)

These figures are based on the weighted results (see Chapter 2).

No significant differences emerged in responses by gender but variation from the two-third/one-third division occurred in:

♦ **the 21-24 age band** (71 per cent affirmed they would like future arts involvement – see Table 10.13 for corresponding figures for other age bands);

♦ **ethnic minorities** (58 per cent affirmed they would like future arts involvement, compared with 66 per cent of white Europeans);

♦ **interviewees from professional backgrounds** (82 per cent affirmed they would like future arts involvement, compared with 64 per cent skilled and 61 per cent partly/unskilled social class categories);

♦ **young people in higher bands of educational attainment** (72 per cent of those with four to six GCSEs/GCEs and 69 per cent of those with more than seven GCSEs/GCEs affirmed they would like more arts involvement, compared with only 46 per cent of those with three to six GCSEs and 52 per cent of those with none).

Looking again at the kinds of activities which were then identified by the respondents, Table 10.14 shows the following breakdown.

Table 10.14 Future arts activities wanted

Category	%
Drawing, painting	14
Drama	13
Music - unspecified	8
Design, computer graphics	7
Learning instrument	6
Other	6
Dancing	5
Writing	4
Fashion	4
More theatre visits	4
Playing in a band	3
Photography	3
Singing	2
Media, film, TV	2
Pottery	2
Crafts: unspecified	2
Reading	1
Sculpture	1
Visit art galleries	1
Spray painting, graffiti	1
TOTAL	(681)

Interviewees could give more than one response, so percentages will not sum to 100 per cent.
These figures are based on the weighted results (see Chapter 2).
As shown in Table 10.13, 34 per cent registered that there were no arts activities they wanted to take further in the future.

Differences between the sub-samples' responses again show fairly predictable trends. Thus, while the urban and rural sample showed no outstanding differences, analyses by gender revealed that design and computer graphics, playing in a band and photography were mentioned more by males, while drama, drawing/painting, dance, writing and fashion were nominations cited more by females.

With respect to age, the younger age bands also significantly mentioned fashion, design and computing as an arts area of interest, while the older age band rated drawing and painting, learning an instrument, writing and theatre visits.

Within the variable of social class, a number of trends emerged. First, in only three areas – design and computer graphics, dance and fashion did the professional sub-sample not present the highest and equal highest percentage rates. In these three areas the highest percentage rate was for young people from skilled (Social Class III) backgrounds. It was also noticeable that females from skilled backgrounds more often suggested fashion and indeed were the only sub-sample who nominated visits to art galleries.

Obstacles to future arts involvement

A further question, designed to identify factors which were felt to prohibit young people's future arts involvement, asked 'is there anything which is making it difficult to take these [arts] activities further and develop them?'.

Eight distinct types of response emerged and the rank order of these identified obstacles to future arts activities are set out in Table 10.15.

Table 10.15 Obstacles to future arts activities

Obstacles	%
Lack of spare time, time	16
Need for money, equipment	12
No local opportunities, arts group etc.	10
Personal aptitude, attitude (e.g. lazy)	8
Work commitments	7
Distances to travel	3
Lack of encouragement at school	2
Need for arts qualifications	2
TOTAL	(681)

Interviewees could give more than one response, so percentages will not sum to 100 per cent.
These figures are based on the weighted results (see Chapter 2).
As shown in Table 10.13, 34 per cent registered that there were no arts activities they wanted to take further in the future.

These categories cover perhaps three distinct types of difficulty:

(i) those who saw their arts involvement as constrained by other competing commitments or alternative interests ('lack of spare time' or 'work/exams'):

The time I get at school isn't enough [to develop my interest in video]. *We have a Wednesday afternoon recreational side to do it in but it isn't enough: you have to squeeze it into free periods then – and that's difficult with A-levels.* (Male, 17)

(ii) those who directly pinpointed being disadvantaged by the lack of funds, resources or, more fundamentally, a deficit of opportunities/facilities for arts involvement ('no local opportunities' or 'distances to travel'):

It means having to find out information about it, find spare money, and find a friend who'll go to the theatre with you who'd be interested. (Male, 24)

It's hard to say. You have to take in your geographical situation – the place I live there isn't anything like this – there's got to be somebody to start something to give people the opportunities. (Female, 18)

I'd love to see more plays but travelling, and the distances are a problem. Here, it's quite remote, and the things at [the nearest city] *are not too good.* (Female, 16, at school)

(iii) those who firmly located any difficulty as a personal issue of 'attitude or aptitude': in effect, a kind of arts deficiency. For some, the deficit is viewed as the consequence of non-compatibility or success in earlier phases of their arts career (e.g. 'lack of encouragement at school').

Taking PE and business studies meant I had to drop art and that has stopped me from developing my drawing and painting skills – it makes it hard to pick it up again. (Male, 16)

Close scrutiny of the statistics produced by comparing the responses for the different sub-samples revealed that alternative interests and competing commitments were consistently mentioned more by the female, urban, professional and higher educational attainers sub-samples. Being disadvantaged by arts opportunities and facilities deficit was consistently mentioned by those with lower educational attainment and females. The over-21s displayed the highest percentage rate in lack of local opportunities, while the younger age bands rated more responses in 'distances to travel'. The travel issue was mentioned more by the female and rural samples particularly. Significantly, 'money and equipment' was nominated by those sub-samples it might be presumed were the most likely to be able to finance their own arts interests - those from professional backgrounds, the over-21s and high educational attainers. No such pattern readily emerges in the area of personal deficit (and indeed, overall, this is the least mentioned obstacle to arts involvement). However, it may be interesting to note that low educational attainers, males and the oldest sub-sample more often defined the difficulty as their own arts deficiency, while the youngest, the most successful educational attainers and females were more likely to implicate their school arts experiences.

Kinds of Assistance Needed for Future Arts Involvement

The young people who did suggest they would like to have future arts activities were finally asked to outline the kinds of assistance or support most needed. A number of broad categories emerged, and Table 10.16 shows the ranking of all those responses which totalled at least 1 per cent. Examples of verbatim responses in each of these categories precedes the table showing the ranking of the total sample.

Types of assistance or support envisaged

Category of response	Examples of comments *[... the types of assistance/support I need is ...]*
Tuition, e.g. night classes	*The LEA should invest in lessons so more are available.* (Male, 15, professional) *Training to get on to the course and overcome the problem of not having the A-level. I have a definite ambition to do the further design course and am frustrated at not having done A-level at school.* (Male, 20, skilled manual)
Venue, workshops	*If there was a place round here to do arts I'd go anyway. I wouldn't need any egging on really.* (Female, 18, partly-skilled) *I think maybe there should be more clubs to do with the arts, so people could go to these clubs and develop their art skills.* (Female, 16, professional)
Money, a grant	*It would be good if there was a subsidised local theatre group. I'd rather have local authority funding than having individuals bid directly to somebody – this would cause favouritism and also be stifling to creativity if groups have to plan and budget in advance.* (Male, 24, professional) *... money to get to venues – it's difficult to get to some places as a lone female. Also finance for violin lessons – also lack of transport is a problem.* (Female, 21, professional)
Support (encouragement, appreciation)	*I need the support – from people I know, my friends and from my Mum, but she gives it anyway.* (Female, 14, skilled non-manual) *Yes – more help from the teacher. There's nothing wrong with the teacher, it's just a big group and different people come in for second day of drama and that spoils our play – there for one lesson, but not for the next.* (Male, 15, partly-skilled) *... someone constantly there to say 'go on, try, you can do it'. Without this [I] wouldn't take it any further.* (Male, 15, professional)
Materials, equipment	*What I'd really like to do is to have the equipment and experiment with it myself – I don't like people telling me what to do. If you're really being creative with it, someone telling you what to do isn't a good idea.* (Male, 17, professional)
Books, information	*I need someone to come along who had already done it, to tell me where to go* [to do arts]. (Female, 19, unskilled) *I'd like to see magazines, where you could get information like that, also I think it would encourage more people into acting and art.* (Female, 16, professional)

Category of response	Examples of comments *[... the types of assistance/support I need is ...]*
Showing how to do particular skills, teaching in method	*People showing you how to do stuff.* (Male, 16, skilled manual) *I need help to get ideas and how to design. I need to know what different ages of people like to wear.* (Female, 15, partly-skilled)
Good grades, reference	*May be a good reference from the teacher at the Tuesday art group.* (Male, 16, skilled non-manual) *I've been told by my design teacher it helps to have a degree first, so I'm taking an architecture degree and at the end of that I'll decide whether I want to carry on.* (Male, 17, skilled non-manual)
Cheaper rates	*Student cards, stand-bys etc. are a great boost.* (Female, 19, professional) *Offering discount rates.* (Female, 22, skilled manual)
Local organised trips	*It'd be easier if there were more organised visits, e.g. through church to get to see those things – it's easier to get round to going if there's a group of you.* (Female, 17, skilled non-manual) *If trips were organised, I would go on it.* (Female, 17, professional)
Childminder	*It would be great if there were special opportunities and even bursaries for young mums – myself – I have found so much inspiration through the feelings I've had from motherhood. – especially early on but I wasn't able to record them in the way I wanted at the time and I think a retrospective view isn't quite the same.* (Female, 23, partly-skilled)

In terms of percentages of responses, Table 10.16 shows the ranking of the total sample.

Looking at the totals of the top two answers, along with 'showing how to do particular skills', suggests a considerable advocation of continued supervision and direction within the arts, whether informal or formal. Interestingly, the breakdown by the usual variables showed little differences by gender, ethnicity or location, but some slight variations were evident by age band.

Thus, while tuition and workshops show a considerable response from over-21s (as does 'money/grant'), it was the under-17s and 17-20 year olds who responded more often in terms of directly being supplied with equipment. Also, the 17-20 year olds emerged as the sub-sample most often mentioning the need for 'information'. This may confirm the findings elsewhere, that as a target age-group, they feel least informed about arts opportunities available to them. It is perhaps also significant that in this category of needing 'information', skilled and partly/unskilled respondents equalled the percentage rate of the professional sample, whereas in almost all other categories of support needed the professional sample gave the highest percentage of responses. Interestingly, it was the under-17 group – the sub-sample still at school – which felt most in need of moral support, encouragement and appreciation in the arts.

Table 10.16 Types of assistance or support envisaged

| | Total | | Age | |
| Category | sample | Under-17 | 17-20 | 21-24 |
	%	%	%	%
Tuition e.g. night classes	9	10	5	13
Venue, workshops	8	7	7	13
Money, a grant	8	5	9	14
Moral support (encouragement/appreciation)	6	10	3	4
Materials, facilities, equipment	5	7	5	3
Books, information	4	3	5	3
Showing how to do particular skills, teaching methods	3	4	3	3
Good grades, reference	1	2	1	0
Cheaper rates	1	0	1	3
Local trip organisation	1	0	1	0
Childminder	1	0	0	3
TOTALS	(681)	(261)	(288)	(132)

Interviewees could give more than one response, so percentages will not sum to 100 per cent.
These figures are based on the weighted results (see Chapter 2).
As shown in Table 10.13, 34 per cent registered that there were no arts activities they wanted to take further in the future.

Final Comment

This chapter, like all the others in Part 2 of the report, has presented a range of findings which suggest that demographic variables such as gender, age, social class and educational attainment have consistent associations with arts involvement.

In the third and final part of the report we turn from this quantitative demographic analysis and present a different way of interpreting the data set. This is done by analysing how arts involvement is associated with certain attitudes and by giving examples of how significant encounters with arts which may affect attitudes can happen at different phases of an individual's leisure life, formal education and beyond.

The following two chapters, therefore, do not focus on demographic patterns, but seek to gain insight from scrutiny of the language used by the young people themselves in their accounts and views of the arts.

PART THREE

FURTHER ANALYSES
AND SUMMARIES

11. Attitudes to the Arts: Towards an Overall Typology

Based on qualitative analysis of the sample's verbatim responses, Chapter 11 attempts a classification of attitudes towards the arts as expressed by young people. These are listed as a set of twelve positive attitudes (or motivations) associated with arts involvement, followed by a set of eight negative attitudes which emerge as barriers to participation. The accompanying textual commentary tentatively offers a ranking of the most significant attitudes for young people's sustained commitment to the arts. It is suggested that a self-identity or self-expression motive (*'I participate in the arts because it's how I define myself, it's a means of self-expression'*) and a physiological motive (*'I participate in the arts because of feeling a real buzz'*) are particularly evident among arts enthusiasts.

In this chapter, the study moves away from reporting and commenting on quantitative findings, and seeks to provide an interpretative overview of the attitudes which accord most with young people's participation in the arts. In this way, the study acknowledges that while results based on demographic variables can provide detailed correlation with arts involvement, these variables themselves cannot entirely explain – nor predetermine – an individual's disposition towards or, participation in, the arts. Correlation and causality are not synonymous. Hence, in trying to account for the different degrees of arts participation, attitude types (or psychographic factors) must also be taken into account.

Different attitude types have been quoted incidentally throughout the report, and also already discussed in Chapter 7. These qualitative and illustrative data have demonstrated the wide variety of descriptors used by the young people when outlining their views, attitudes and experiences of the arts. It became apparent that certain of these attitude-descriptors consistently accompanied arts affiliation, while others generally accompanied non-engagement. For example, terms like '*a real buzz*', '*a feeling of adrenaline*' (i.e. an excitement vernacular), or the language of self-expression and self-realisation (e.g. '*a sense of achievement*', '*self-esteem*') were often used by those who showed a particular commitment to the arts, and were noticeably absent from those who had more low key involvement. (The arts biographies of Chapter 12 provide more detailed illustration of these vocabularies).

It was thus possible to categorise the different 'vocabularies of motive' evident in the sample's accounts of their arts experiences into twelve main types of positive attitude and eight types of negative attitude. These collations of key attitudes, or typologies, are outlined below, with a brief commentary on their significance for arts involvement.

A Typology of Positive Attitudes

1. A general or unspecified motive

[I participate in the arts because] *...I get enjoyment, fun out of them*

Qualitative evidence would suggest that respondents who conveyed this attitude to arts involvement and could not develop their answers with some of the other vocabularies of motive within the typology, tended to also record qualified enthusiasm or lightweight commitment to arts. This was particularly evident in descriptions of participation in school arts, where if '*fun*' ... '*enjoyable*' were the only descriptors, self-sustained arts involvement appeared less likely to occur. Additional stimuli or support for skill-transference seemed to be necessary in order to ensure continued motivation.

2. An ability– or achievement–oriented motive

[I participate in the arts because] *...I want to be the best, to win*

The notion that arts participation was motivated by a (norm-referenced) desire to win or be competitive was very rarely evident in the sample. Some respondents did record the pleasure of, say, competing in musical competitions or being successful at an audition or being the central focus in a performance. However, for most interviewees, it was more likely that such enjoyment was registered as deriving from the intrinsic satisfaction of performing well and from extrinsic audience appreciation and attention rather than the feeling of being better than, or superior to, fellow performers.

3. A task-oriented motive

[I participate in the arts because] *...I want to improve, acquire new skills*

Where young people referred to their interests in self-improvement in arts skills as a motive for involvement, commitment to the arts tended to be very high. Vocabularies often included reference to the rigour and effort required to obtain new skills. It was noticeable how some art forms (e.g. music, dance) offered development opportunities – or 'routes' – for specialising or improving much more clearly than other forms. They also were on offer to younger children. Frustration for those young people (often male) who were interested in acquiring skills in a range of art forms was also manifest, particularly computer and graphic art and music-making.

4. A socialising motive

[I participate in the arts because] *... of its social benefits, meeting and making friends*

Participation in certain art forms (e.g. drama, music) was often registered as having social benefits, and certainly social aspects appeared to contribute to drama's high ranking popularity as a school-based activity. Arts activities at youth clubs also were often mentioned as having particular social and collaborative benefits.

Consumption of traditional performance arts (e.g. theatre) registered as a significant social benefit for only certain categories of young people, particularly those over-21, and the prohibitive cost was often noted. Specific or sub-categories of social benefits were occasionally noted.

5. A status-seeking motive

[I participate in the arts because] *... it helps my image*

This was very rarely evident in the sample's responses, although mention of a 'pose value' did surface as a motivating reason in a very few instances of traditional arts consumption, again largely among older interviewees. Indeed, there was more evidence to suggest that young people – especially young males – believed arts involvement incurs a loss of status and image among their own peer groups.

6. A social pressure motive

[I participate in the arts because] *... I am pleasing* [significant others]

Again very little explicit mention of this motive occurred among this sample of young people. However, those respondents who dredged up memories of, say, occasional theatre attendance with parents or school or a short-lived attempt at music lessons in earlier stages of their arts biography hinted at this source of motivation. If so, it would suggest that such an attitude does not ensure sustained and committed arts involvement.

7. A physiological or therapeutic motive

[I participate in the arts because] *... it's about relaxation ... feeling a buzz*

In many instances, the vocabulary of motive used by young people made reference to physiological effects and therapeutic responses accruing from arts involvement. '*The buzz*' (or perhaps what the nineteenth century aesthete Pater once called '*burning with a hard gemlike flame*') was very significantly associated with an on-going commitment to arts – whether it occurred from watching theatre, playing music, dancing or doing graffiti art. At the opposite end of the physiological continuum, references to the arts as assuagement (*soothing, relaxing, calming*) were also very evident. Identification and acknowledgement of physiological factors seem crucially connected to arts involvement.

8. A self-identity motive

[I participate in the arts because] *... it's how I define myself, helps my identity; it's an important means of self-expression*

This vocabulary of motive was also particularly associated with an on-going commitment to arts involvement: respondents often volunteered that they defined themselves as creative, artistic and, hence, gravitated to other like-minded people socially. It was very noticeable that those who defined the arts in terms of self-expression and communication were more likely to have higher rates of participation in the arts.

9. A relevance or comfortability motive

[I participate in the arts because] *... of feeling at home with* [form and content] *of an art form, and its conventions. It's something I can relate to*

Examples here might include the alternative musical experiences of young people (clubbing), the popularity of film in Asian communities, and the interviewee who described how her love of literature was transferable to theatre. Discomfort and lack of familiarity with an art form's conventions and content not only is likely to be a strong disincentive to involvement, but also might be closely associated with pejorative views about typical audiences and enthusiasts. ('*All theatre-goers are snobs*' etc.)

10. An intrinsic or aesthetic motive

[I participate in the arts because] *... of an appreciation of the qualities of art form ...*

References by young people to '*the buzz*' might well be vernacular for this positive aesthetic response and, as already noted, the vocabulary of excitement was certainly closely associated with high motivation and positive attitudes to arts involvement. However, it might also be significant that questions on definitions of the arts rarely received responses appertaining to appreciation of aesthetics, while artistic role models and different types of arts consumption (attending concerts, theatre) ranked with only 5 per cent or less as inspiration factors. It might also be the case that artistic role models appeared to be rarely encountered through the context of school.

11. A situation-specific motive

[I participate in the arts because] ... *I have a high regard for working with my drama teacher or youth worker*

As the most obvious example of situation-specific motivation, the significance of teachers in inculcating positive attitudes towards arts is very evident from the data (and also how often young people attribute 'turn off' to their secondary teachers). However, close examination of qualitative responses suggests that references to situation-specific motivation are usually accompanied by accounts of a sense of receiving particular (and personalised) attention and support. Young people's accounts of 'turn off' by situation-specific factors often referred to a lack of attention, support and encouragement. Situation-specific motivation may also need to be offered on a sustained basis in order to ensure continued interest, unless (or until) other positive attitudes result (e.g. task-oriented, intrinsic, physiological motivation).

12. A material or monetary motive

[I participate in the arts because] ... *of financial reward*

This motivation was not generally associated with positive attitudes towards the arts. Indeed, it was far more likely that arts involvement was viewed as a disadvantage in terms of career and remuneration. Certainly, a number of respondents felt that they had been advised against pursuing arts seriously by parents and teachers precisely for this reason. One rock musician noted how the music scene was being supplanted by computers as a major leisure and consumer interest for young people, and this in turn adversely affected opportunities for commercial success.

Having outlined twelve types of attitude associated with arts involvement, it is clear that some are more likely to correlate with a sustained commitment and interest, while others appear to accompany more limited and less consistent levels of engagement and some hardly figure as relevant sources of motivation. In other words, a tentative ranking can be suggested:

RARELY/ NON RELEVANT	LOW MOTIVATION	MID-LEVEL MOTIVATION	HIGH MOTIVATION
achievement-oriented	general/enjoyment	socialising	task-oriented
monetary benefits	social pressure	relevance/ comfortability	physiological/ therapeutic
status-seeking		situation-specific	self-identity/ expression
			intrinsic

Moving on to the opposite phenomena, namely the factors which inhibit participation in the arts, it should be noted that the data included non-attitudinal barriers such as locale, insufficient time, as well as important attitudes or points of view which seemed to be particularly influential in limiting young people's engagement in the arts. After a brief word on the non-attitudinal barriers, a very tentative typology of negative attitudes to arts participation is offered.

Non-Attitudinal Barriers

1. Lack of provision and opportunities

[for me, arts involvement]   *... is hindered by lack of opportunities*

As the report has indicated, lack of local opportunities was most mentioned by those with low educational attainment, over-21s and females. Defining the problem of provision as the more pragmatic 'travel difficulties' (i.e. *it's probably there but I can't reach it*) was mentioned more by rural respondents, under-17s and again females. However, with respect to rural interviewees, when positive attitudes towards the arts were exhibited, travel difficulties did not appear to be an overriding barrier.

2. Lack of time

[for me, arts involvement] *... is hindered by lack of* [spare] *time/other commitments*

This category of response was particularly offered by female, urban, Social Class I and II and high achieving respondents. These sub-samples might be seen as those who have consistently registered themselves as the most likely candidates for arts involvement.

3. Lack of money

[for me, arts involvement] *... is hindered by insufficient money and lack of equipment*

The evidence suggested this obstacle to involvement was particularly mentioned by those categories of young people who might be seen to be able to finance their own arts interests – Social Class I and II, over-21s, high educational attainers. This may reflect the strength of desire among such respondents to pursue and develop their artistic endeavours. It might also indicate the relative exclusivity of arts involvement beyond institutional provision.

Attitudinal Barriers

While the previous three categories in effect are commentary on how an individual appraises arts provision in relation to their personal circumstances, the following attitudinal types (or vocabularies of non-motivation) refer more fundamentally to how an individual adjudges arts involvement and provision in relation to their sense of self or personal identity. In this way, the barriers relate not to shortcomings in provision (e.g. *'it's not there', 'it's unreachable', 'it's too expensive'*), but to more fundamental deficiencies within the arts themselves as sources of satisfaction of psychic reward. Alternatively, the deficiency is expressed as a lack of artistic or aesthetic capability within self (the talent barrier).

1. A general or non-specific attitudinal barrier

[for me, arts involvement] *... is hindered by my view that it's boring, rubbish*

As with the equivalent general response in the typology of positive attitudes (e.g. *'it's fun/enjoyable'*), this vocabulary of non-motivation could usually be expanded to include other explanations within the barrier categories below. Equally, as the cameos showed, if pressed, respondents could often volunteer specific examples of positive responses to arts beyond this initial rhetoric of rejection.

2. A talent barrier

[for me, arts involvement] *... is hindered by my perceived lack of ability*

If this vocabulary of non-motivation was used, the person's perceived deficiency was usually defined in terms of having an inability to *participate* successfully in arts (e.g. *I can't draw; can't play an instrument – I'm tone deaf*): a deficit often recognised during formal years of arts education. Perhaps inappropriately, the self-construct of a lack of artistic ability can then be used as the reason for non-motivation as a consumer. The talent barrier may raise issues about the nature of arts education – its capacity to offer a differentiated curriculum; whether current secondary school specialisation penalises late developers in the arts, how much the focus is or should be on arts consumption and appreciation. For arts educators, policy-makers and researchers, it also raises the fundamental question of whether the extent to which the problem is based on real or perceived variations in ability.

3. An irrelevance or discomfortability barrier

[for me, arts involvement] *... is hindered by my lack of comfort with the art form's content and context*

Again, a counterpart to the positive attitude noted in the previous typology, namely that the conventions and content of an art form are, for some reason, deemed unfamiliar or irrelevant and hence a (likely) source of discomfort. Very often this vocabulary of non-motivation is accompanied by stereotypical views about social class or gender variances (e.g. *theatre is for snobs; dance is for girls*). The report's qualitative and quantitative evidence would suggest that many young people do not greatly deviate from these classic assumptions, which suggests that the equal opportunity debate and teaching could usefully focus on these pivotal issues.

4. A non-stimulus barrier (or lack of physiological or therapeutic value)

[for me, arts involvement] *... is hindered by my failure to be engaged/ excited*

While 'irrelevance' might well be a barrier category associated with assumptions which prohibit even attempting an art form, non-stimulus refers to the response of those who have tried and found themselves to be ungalvanised by, or in some way non-congruent with, an arts activity once attempted. In sum, for these young people arts do not deliver *'the buzz'*. It is at least possible that these failures to engage successfully with one art form then contaminate or prohibit attempting others.

5. Negative affective barrier

[for me, arts involvement] *... is hindered by my sense of unease while attempting it*

Examples here might be young people who find drama 'embarrassing' due to being the focus of attention, or who are discomforted by the compulsion to dance expressively. This may relate to lack of 'developmental synchronisation' or bad timing – being introduced to art forms at highly delicate stages of emotional and physical growth such as puberty and adolescence.

6. Situation-specific barriers

[for me, arts involvement] *... is hindered by my dislike of teacher x/ context*

The direct counterpart to a motive for involvement, in effect, situation-specific barriers are likely to involve other negative attitudes (e.g. in situation x I feel affective discomfort, non-stimulus etc.). It was evident from earlier findings that many young people attributed their non-motivation in arts to teachers (indeed, arts teacher was the highest ranking cause of arts aversion). However, this may need considerable extrapolation, given that teachers also received highest percentages of nominations for arts inspiration. The attributes of positive situation-specific factors are worth re-scrutinising.

7. Group image barrier

[for me, arts involvement] *... is hindered by my peers/family norms*

This attitudinal barrier relates to the non-motivation category of relevance but also appears as a generic view on arts. In particular, it seems evident that certain male youth cultures can exercise a powerful restraint on arts involvement. Several male respondents explained their lack of participation in the arts in terms of the arts 'not being the done thing with my mates'. However, examples of ways of overcoming this anti-arts group norm did emerge, e.g. youth workers, role models, a sense of personalised support broke down norms and values inherent in the group image.

8. A self-image barrier

[for me, arts involvement] *...is hindered by my sense of myself as not an 'arty' person/I'm more into sports*

Apart from their identification with groups, and therefore the norms of their groups, respondents also referred to perceptions and images of their 'selves' which appeared to have an important bearing on their degree of participation in the arts. Clearly, this particular attitudinal barrier has close affinities with what was described earlier as a 'talent barrier', in that perceptions of ability can be closely aligned with perceptions of 'self'. Comments relating to self-image, however, extended beyond 'ability' to suggest that their broader persona and make-up was not commensurate with their image of an 'arty person'.

Having identified and illustrated provisional typologies of positive and negative attitudes towards participation in the arts, it is tentatively suggested from the evidence of this study that the mere absence of negative attitudes was generally insufficient to precipitate significant engagement in the arts. Instead, sustained involvement was almost always accompanied by reference to 'high motivating' attitudinal types depicted in the first section of this chapter. Clearly, this conclusion, if substantiated by other research, has important implications for arts education and arts provision. In view of this it seems appropriate to explore, in greater detail, the empirical basis of the relationship between attitudes to arts participation and young person's 'arts biographies' or careers. This is attempted in the next chapter.

12. Arts Biographies

In this chapter, analysis of 14 individual young people's accounts of their arts involvement is presented. It offers a picture of the wide variation in opportunities for arts engagement available (or utilised) at different phases of school and leisure time; and also examines the differing vocabularies used by the young people to describe their arts experiences. From these individual arts-biography accounts, conclusions about the significant and recurring factors in successful arts engagement are evident, and corroborate many of the trends and findings from the quantitative analysis presented in previous chapters. Among these, peer culture, home background, sustained and personalised support emerged as critical influences.

To burn always with this hard gemlike flame ... we may well grasp at any exquisite passion or any contribution to knowledge that seems by a lifted horizon to set the spirit free for a moment or any stirring of the senses ... art comes to you, proposing frankly to give nothing but the highest quality moments as they pass, and simply for those moments' sake. Walter Pater 'The Renaissance'

Introduction This chapter uses a different – and essentially qualitative – approach to examine the interview data from the sample of 704 young people. It seeks to look in depth at a number of individuals, or cases, who represent contrasting attitudes and commitment to the arts, and to trace the 'story' of their arts involvement. Careful examination of the language, as well as the substance, of these young people's accounts of their arts experiences was a significant part of the analysis in order to further illuminate what influences arts 'affiliation' or 'abstention'.

As Appendix I shows, the standard schedule used with all interviewees first posed a substantial number of questions on present interests and attitudes to the arts (using both open and closed techniques). Having fully established the nature and degree of current involvement with arts (and also generally heightened 'arts' as a topic for discussion), interviewees were then asked to recall any art involvement – participation and consumption – undertaken in their leisure time at both primary and secondary school age. Experiences of arts offered during primary and secondary school, as well as at youth club, also figured in the schedule.

In this way, although not consecutive in the interview structure, an individual's arts opportunities could be retraced chronologically, and their accounts of likely future arts interests also added to the sequence.

In effect, a number of *arenas of opportunity* can be depicted and will be diagrammised as follows:

Primary Age	Secondary Age	Youth Club	Stated Current Interests	Stated Future Arts Interest
LEISURE Arts participation	**LEISURE** Arts participation			
LEISURE Arts consumption	**LEISURE** Arts consumption			
SCHOOL	**SCHOOL**	**WORK/ COLLEGE**		

*Within each arena of opportunity, if any **positive reference or recall** was made about undertaking arts, these are **highlighted** on each individual biography diagram as shaded areas.*

Other areas of questioning often added further detail and insight into the unique arts biography of a young person. In particular the qualitative analysis took close account of the nominated effects of any arts experiences; views on whether their previous opportunities for arts involvement were satisfactory; and nominations for specific influences – or disincentives – in connection with arts involvement.

These were added to the biographical picture and in this way, trends and types of arts biography did emerge. For example, some young people appeared to never affiliate to the arts, perhaps identifying with sport exclusively; other young people from an early age were surrounded and nurtured by arts-oriented family cultures; some 'found' arts at later phases in their lives, through encounters with influential 'others' – teachers, peers etc., or through a process of personal exploration and experimentation. The following cameos hope to capture some of this rich variation.

In the 14 cameos or case studies which follow, a diagrammatic overview of the arts biography of each chosen case is offered with accompanying analytical interpretation. The cameos are clustered to show a continuum of arts engagement, from those who represent apparently entirely negative attitudes, followed by examples of conversion to the arts, and two cases illustrating the distinctive contribution of youth clubs. Three enthusiastic arts-consumers are then presented and, finally, the arts biographies of four young people who have a particular commitment to participating in their chosen art form are examined.

Each cameo concludes with an analysis of the attitudes to arts expressed in the interview, using the typology of Chapter 11. This listing or accounting of attitudes has been given the nomenclature 'Attitude Quota'.

It should be emphasised that there is no sense in which the biographical case studies can be taken as in any way representative, or even typical, of the sample as a whole. Indeed, it is more the case that the cameos demonstrate the more 'successful' examples of young people who have, through various means, incorporated arts experiences into their lives. Hence, in order to meet one of the aims of the project, they represent a deliberately biased selection, which is oriented towards positive engagement in the arts. The statistical results presented throughout the report repeatedly pointed to the fact that arts participation was a minority undertaking – often the preserve of certain privileged sections of society. Thus, the following cameos could convey a very misleading and over-optimistic impression of young people's involvement in the arts if the wider picture established by the rest of the data was ignored.

Notwithstanding this, the biographical case studies provide ample testimony to the value and potential of the arts to enrich the lives of young people, as well as serve to underline the unique individuality of the respondents interviewed in the study. To this extent, the cameos offer a salutary caution when constructing stereotypes, and even generalisations, about young people and their participation in the arts.

Elizabeth and George: Non-involvement

... I think most people my age find arts stuffy and boring – all that stuff is too hard and you can't have fun.   (Elizabeth)

... arts are not like sport, sport is fast and exciting, but arts are slow ...   (George)

The first cameos are of two school age young people, Elizabeth and George, who unreservedly express anti-arts sentiments and foresee no likelihood of future interest. Both arts biography diagrams show no recall of on-going arts commitment at primary age, nor in secondary age leisure time and youth club. Peer and (in one case) family culture appears to figure strongly in their rhetoric of arts rejection.

Nevertheless, when pressed, these two young people can outline some positive interest in the arts opportunities offered by their respective secondary schools: the language they both use (*'making up'*) registers their pleasure in inventiveness.

Cameo One: Elizabeth

Background

Elizabeth is 14 and lives in a village in the Oxford area. Her father is a painter and decorator, her mother a cleaner. Elizabeth wishes to be a hairdresser.

Arts Biography Diagram

Elizabeth's diagram reveals that few of the possible arenas of opportunity are taken up with arts. Primary school and leisure-time pursuits at primary and particularly secondary age are strikingly not arts focused. Youth club also does not offer arts activities. Two arenas of arts opportunity are recorded: secondary school arts and some current interest in creating dance for a social context.

	Primary Age	Secondary Age	Youth Club	Stated Current Interests	Stated Future Arts Interests
L E I S U R E	Arts Participation NONE (playing out) *'We once made up a play'* Arts Consumption NONE	Arts Participation NONE (Going ot with friends) Arts Consumption NONE	NO ARTS AVAILABLE rounders table tennis snooker pool outings	(Going to town with mates) Ice-skating	NONE
S C H O O L / W O R K	NONE *'We didn't do much and I was never very bothered'*	**DRAMA –** *'we had to do one art in Y10'* **POTTERY** *'I really liked making things'* *'I don't think much of arts at secondary school'*		**DANCE - rave and disco** *'making up our own routines'*	

STATED EFFECTS: None

Comment

Elizabeth's arts biography shows a lack of involvement which is mirrored by her numerous assertions throughout the interview on the non-relevance of the arts. She states she is '*not interested*' in either traditional or youth arts; was '*never very bothered*' about arts at primary school, and also commented that she '*did not think much*' of secondary school arts experiences. Significantly, she volunteered that '*arts just was never something my family and friends were interested in*'. Perhaps not surprisingly, she could not suggest any arts activities she might have welcomed; nor any effects of the arts; nor any future arts interest. Her final comments reveal just how her peer culture might influence that stance and also how her lack of engagement appears to relate to the non-acceptability of anything with challenge or rigour as a leisure pursuit.

> *... I think most people of my age find all that* [arts] *sort of thing stuffy and boring. If anybody says they like it, everybody else makes fun of them, it's better to just do things with your mates, go around together, hang about. Even when I'm older I won't be interested, it's not any fun and it's fun I like. All that stuff is too hard really so you can't have fun.*

Despite this viewpoint, Elizabeth does reveal some positive engagement with arts. She mentions '*making up*' and rehearsing a play with '*just my friends at each other's houses*' as a leisure pursuit in her primary years, and similarly refers to her current enjoyment of dance as '*making up our own steps ... practising dancing in each others' houses*'. She stressed she enjoyed this dance activity because it was '*... something we like to do together ... it's having fun with friends, sharing something we all enjoy and having a laugh*'. Beyond that, Elizabeth spoke about enjoyment of pottery and here, significantly, used a vocabulary of achievement and described the self-esteem achieved through imaginative and creative activity '*... I liked making things – I used to imagine what I could make and was really pleased when it turned out as I had planned, it felt good to have made something*'. This interest was curtailed when Elizabeth made a choice to do drama in Year 10, though she did regret this decision: '*I wish I'd done pottery instead – I'd have got more out of making things*'. In this way, it is pottery which stands out as a significant aesthetic achievement in school. Drama, she claimed, was proving '*embarrassing*' due to the high number of boys in the class who made fun and inhibited the girls – '*so we can't really get into it*'. This again may intimate how Elizabeth is diverted from serious arts engagement by her peer culture. The repeated use of the term '*making up*' and '*making things*' is evident: perhaps hairdressing is to be the outlet for Elizabeth's obvious pleasure in creativity.

Elizabeth's Attitude Quota

POSITIVE ATTITUDES	COMMENT
general/non-specific (low)	'*it's having fun, having a laugh*'
socialising (mid)	'*sharing something with friends we all enjoy*'
physiological (high)	'*it felt good to have made something*'
NEGATIVE ATTITUDES	
general/non-specific	'*arts are stuffy and boring*'
negative affective	'*drama is embarrassing*'
situation specific	'*... the boys make fun of us, we can't get into it*'
group image	'*arts is something my friends and family are not interested in*'

Elizabeth's cluster of negative attitudes appear to derive from external factors (e.g. her male classmates' behaviour in drama), or from inherited views (those of her family and peers). Apart from negative general/non-specific rhetoric, she does not mention any barriers to involvement which could be seen as an intrinsic antipathy to arts. Significantly, general/non-specific positive attitudes are also described. Thus, a culturally imposed negativity (or misrecognition) might explain the apparent contradiction in Elizabeth's attitude quota: her rejection rhetoric co-exists with a high motivating attitude (evident in the descriptions of her creative pleasure and personal pride from pottery work). Equally, there seems irony in her acknowledgement of a positive attitude associated with socialising (in her collaborative invention of dance routines), while also suggesting all her friends are not into arts.

The possibility of a co-existence of negative and positive attitudes seems clear.

Cameo Two: George

Background

George is a 14 year old, who lives in a North Yorkshire village and is bussed to the high school in the local market town. His father is a mechanic and his mother does not work. He wishes to be an accountant.

		Primary Age	Secondary Age	Youth Club	Stated Current Interests	Stated Future Arts Interests
L E I S U R E		Arts Participation NONE (Football) Arts Consumption NONE	Arts Participation NONE (Cycling) Arts Consumption **Listening to rave music Going to cinema**	NO ARTS AVAILABLE Darts Table tennis Pool	(Cycling)	NONE
S C H O O L / W O R K		*We didn't do that much of it... we didn't do music'*	**DRAMA – 'I liked the thought-tracking in drama'**		**Computer graphics 'I've got a programme where you can devise your own games and invent your own backdrops ...'**	
STATED EFFECTS: None						

Arts Biography Diagram

This diagram registers how arts engagement occurs first only in George's secondary-age arenas of opportunity: a qualified acknowledgement of secondary school arts and leisure-time consumption of (typical adolescent) arts activities are evident. The arenas of opportunity at primary-age and at youth club were void of arts. Current interests include a minor interest in computer graphics.

Comment

George's rejection of arts and strong focus on physical activity is captured in his assertion that '*... arts are not like sport, sport is fast and exciting, but arts are slow*'. He acknowledged that arts were not important to him and volunteered he '*only really comes across them at school, not outside*'. He could not nominate any effects of his arts experiences, nor suggest any inspirational factors, nor conceive of any future arts interest. The biography diagram demonstrates this lack of engagement and continuity, with a particularly 'barren' arts life apparent in his primary years.

Nevertheless, some positive reaction to the arts was evident (such as to the notion of youth arts like graffiti, or his enjoyment of school drama and even customising his computer games). In these instances, George consistently used phrases such as '*making it up yourself* [it's more personal to yourself then] ... *making it what you want*'. His pleasure in drama derived from '*making up and improvising what would happen next rather than just watching. It is getting involved*'. Thus, by inference, George may perceive much of the rest his arts experiences to be passive, predetermined, prescriptive, unengaging. As he put it '*... the arts I've done so far, I've only done because we had to do it*'. Despite the glimmer of enthusiasm for drama, George also asserted that '*drama and dance are definitely more for girls. Most girls tend to like dance, but only a few boys do*'. In other words, the art forms perhaps most obviously offering the physicality, speed and spontaneity which he enjoys in sport are denied by peer pressure. It is noticeable that even though his youth club offers dancing, George stated he did not get involved, preferring pool, table tennis and darts. Equally, he stresses he only listens to rave music (rather than dancing to it). One final factor which George volunteered was his locale '*... there's not much art where I live ... if I lived somewhere else, I might experience more, I wouldn't have to travel such a long way*'. It is noticeable that the experience of performance does not feature in his own arts-biography account, though, when specifically questioned, he acknowledged being taken by his mother to the theatre in York on one occasion within the last year.

George's Attitude Quota

POSITIVE ATTITUDES	COMMENT
general/non-specific (low)	*'enjoy school drama'*
social pressure (low)	*'only done arts 'cos I had to'*
situation specific (mid)	*'drama is making it up and not just watching ... it's getting involved'*
NEGATIVE ATTITUDES	
non attitudinal:lack of opportunity	*'there's not much arts where I live'*
general/non-specific ⎤	
⎬	*'arts are slow, not like sport'*
non-stimulus ⎦	
group image	*'drama and dance are more for girls'*
self-image	*'arts are not important to me, sport is fast and exciting'*

George's rejection of arts is expressed by negative attitudes which include intrinsic barriers (e.g. self-image, non-stimulus). Physiological and self-identity motivations are not connected to arts but instead strongly invested in sports. Positive attitudes to arts register as those of only low or mid level motivation, hence, the contradictions apparent in the attitude quota of the previous cameo do not really surface here. This particular combination of positive attitudes does not infiltrate or influence an overall negative perspective.

Tim, Imran and Jim: Converting to the Arts

... writing is a very personal satisfaction, it can be anything you want it to be. (Tim)

... in writing, I'm expressing feelings which I wouldn't if I just talked about them. (Imran)

... writing gets me feelings onto paper and sorts me head out. (Jim)

The three cameos that follow are all, coincidentally, sports enthusiasts (or ex-sports enthusiasts), who have experienced some conversion to arts – and again, perhaps coincidentally, it is creative writing which figures in all three arts–biography accounts.

All three are older than the first two case studies, and it is easy to envisage how they might well have responded to questions on arts involvement in much the same way as George and Elizabeth if interviewed in their mid-teens. Peer influence as a barrier to involvement emerges again, while Imran offers new insights into cultural factors which are associated with non-involvement.

In their later years, it is noticeable that the impetus to arts engagement comes from personal encounters and encouragement outside secondary school and family. It would seem that Tim and Jim have both used and benefited from writing in a period of personal uncertainty. The problem of finding support and opportunities by which to develop late-emerging arts interests is apparent.

Whilst it must be stressed that these accounts are subjective, another common thread, particularly in the arts biographies of Imran and Tim, is a critical view of secondary school arts, and the sense of a lack of differentiation in arts teaching.

Cameo Three: Tim

Background

Tim is an 18 year old white male living in a rural location. Currently he is working full-time as a waiter in a local pub with a restaurant, having left Tertiary College (before taking his A-levels). He had made a deliberate choice to '*leave the education system for a while*' and '*develop*' himself. He lives with his parents: his mother is a department head in a secondary school and his father a lecturer. He does not know what career he wishes to pursue. Tim acknowledged that a defective eye, due to an accident when he was six years old, had affected his reading ability and this '*caught up*' with him particularly with regard to his aptitude in English literature at secondary school.

Arts Biography Diagram

This diagram shows how arts engagement was little evident in primary and secondary age, with only a fleeting interest in musicianship being recalled in Tim's early secondary years. College became the first arena of opportunity to propel a serious interest in the arts. Nevertheless, current and future interests are strongly arts oriented.

Comment

Tim has been successful as a sports person in both the primary and secondary school phases of his career, and thought this had contributed to his sense of '*a quiet confidence*'. He was unable to nominate any specific effects of the arts. His school arts 'career', particularly in music and drama, was consistently described as being on the level of '*fun ... a giggle*', and an acknowledged lack of engagement and sustained interest resulted. He nevertheless described as a '*thrill*' the opportunity to '*play with*' and '*pick up*' an array of instruments at secondary school compared to his minimal experiences of music during his primary education. Notwithstanding this, such light-weight descriptors of his arts involvement are perhaps telling: Tim quickly gave up private flute lessons begun at secondary school, investing all leisure time in football and tennis. (He also stated he had no time for youth club due to sporting commitments.)

Throughout Tim's account, there is evidence of a somewhat wistful appetance for the visual arts and a regret that he had not applied rigour to

	Primary Age	Secondary Age	Youth Club	Stated Current Interests	Stated Future Arts Interests
L E I S U R E	Arts Participation NONE (Football Tennis) Arts Consumption NONE	Arts Participation (Football Tennis) **FLUTE LESSONS** Arts Consumption NONE		**WRITING** **READING**	**WRITING** **READING**
S C H O O L / W O R K	*'At that time it was basically all good fun, nothing serious – it was a giggle, that's what it was there for – nothing more, nothing less'*	*'It wasn't the learning you valued in arts it was the fun'* **MUSIC**	**College** **WRITING and READING** *'inspired by English Literature course'*		
STATED EFFECTS: None					

this. He recognised he was '*not a naturally good artist ... but had developed and satisfied myself with it later*'. At one point in the interview, he reflected that '*I never really tried to paint or draw, I didn't like it at the time, I regretted it later, I realise I might have been able to if I'd tried hard enough – it's something I'd like to have been able to do*'. Tim saw teacher support and opportunity in the arts at secondary school as being available but '*...* [only] *there – if you knew you wanted them*', and felt '*penalised as a late developer ... arts subjects cease to exist in the fourth year*'. He also mentioned regretting that he had '*never been shown, taught or discovered drawing and painting techniques*'.

Despite nominating the '*pretentiousness and snobbery*' of the arts world as a turn-off, Tim identified his propulsion to literature and then writing as being '*inspired*' by girlfriends and friends who were interested and '*passionate*' about the arts. Peer pressure is, in effect, operating as a positive force in this instance. '*They encouraged me not to have a go but to look at and think about* [the arts].'

> *... it took me a long time, I searched and I looked and I thought no way, but I've found something* [for myself] *within the English side, which is the most unobvious ... you can read a book and not understand it and then you look deep in and then you do understand it, and think 'oh yes, I got it right'.*

His own writing provided '*a very personal satisfaction*' deriving from a control and ownership (very telling perhaps given Tim's admission of uncertainty about his future direction in life):

> ... *when you're writing it can be anything you want it to be, so long as you get the words right and it feels right to you ... as long as it makes sense to you, it can be anything in the whole world, you can be what you want to be.*

This writing interest was also inspired by reading Dylan Thomas poetry and assignments in English literature at college. Nevertheless, Tim saw the need for support in developing skills in writing. He felt untrained in the skills of personal expression, suggesting that '*98 per cent of writing at school is not personal writing – that's where the practice should be. Personal writing is more powerful than anything, but that's one that has least opportunity*'.

Finally, Tim suggested that gender might be a significant factor in the lateness of his commitment to arts. Identifying school as '*the time you're most influenced by any art, unless your family are artistic*', he added:

> ... *it's a general thing that girls mature more quickly than boys – does that maturity involve understanding of arts? Am I two years backward to the girls now? Are all males behind in their understanding of art, failing to understand as we go through secondary school? Though I don't mean to stereotype, most males are quite butch and sporty ...*

The lack of continuity and absence of any early commitment to arts is evident in Tim's arts biography diagram.

Tim's Attitude Quota

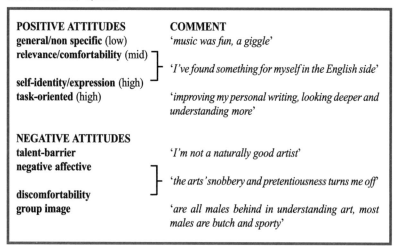

Tim's complex array of negative and positive attitudes still results in a final and committed engagement with the arts. The presence of two high-level motivating factors (self-identity/expression and task-orientation) in this attitude quota are no doubt highly significant. There is no self-image barrier to participation. Tim's account suggests that low-level motivation (general/non-specific enjoyment) was the limit of any earlier inducement to arts engagement, with gender-assumptions (group image) also a possible barrier to more serious involvement. However, peers have recently operated as a stimulus to arts involvement. Tim's quota seems to show that such negative attitudes as group image, negative affective and even the talent barrier can be overcome by the introduction of high level positive attitudes.

Cameo Four: Imran

Background

Imran is a 23 year old Asian male, currently undertaking a computer programming course at an adult training centre. He is also taking a GCSE in English at evening class and a sports coaching qualification. He already has a degree in information systems for business. His father is a retired weaver and his mother a housewife. His chosen career is to be a systems analyst or management consultant in computers, and then move into professional sports coaching.

Arts Biography Diagram

This diagram shows how neither Imran's primary nor secondary school registered as arenas of opportunity for serious arts engagement. Youth club also does not feature arts activities. Some arts consumption in primary age is evident and also dance as a leisure-time pursuit during secondary years. Current and future interests appear more fully arts oriented, but, given the prior low-key involvement, a need for basic provision and information is acknowledged.

Comment

Imran's commitment to sport (and latterly to coaching young children) is a clear and common thread throughout his leisure life. Indeed, Imran nominated his sports-coaching as a creative activity. He reported '*just not getting into*' arts, but some recent interest in writing songs with his friends emerged (though he acknowledged he could not play an instrument). Perhaps not surprisingly, Imran could not nominate any positive effects of the arts, and suggested that his arts involvement had declined since leaving school because '*the subjects I chose to study are totally different*'. At one point in the interview, Imran referred to the fact that '*most kids at school don't enjoy the arts*'. Imran could not nominate anyone or anything turning him onto the arts, though he suggested that '*seeing arts on TV*', was a turn-off '*...they seem to make out that arts are boring, you get the impression from TV that arts are not very interesting*'. Future interests are to participate in drama and music, two areas in which Imran has acknowledged he has only a rudimentary or non-existent experience. Hence, the basics of '*how to start*' and '*where to go to start*' are areas of support needed.

Notwithstanding this, careful study of Imran's arts-biography account appears to show a continuing refrain of interest in dance – he recalls '*enjoying watching ballet on TV*' as a child of primary age.; undertook

	Primary Age	Secondary Age	Youth Club	Stated Current Interests	Stated Future Arts Interests
L E I S U R E	**Arts Participation** NONE (Football) **Arts Consumption** **READING** **LISTENING TO** **MUSIC** **WATCHING ARTS** **ON TV**	**Arts Participation** **BREAKDANCING** (Football Martial Arts) **Arts Consumption** NONE	*'Discussion'* *'Talking about problems'*	Football Thai Boxing Sports-coaching	**MUSIC** **DRAMA** *'I need basic information about how to start'*
S C H O O L / W O R K	*'Can't remember, it was just school, I'm not very positive about it - never saw it as arts'*	*'Teachers didn't tell you enough about arts - except it decreased chances of a job ... we weren't given much practice or guidance'* **MUSIC — *'it was practical not writing'***		**WRITING for** **GCSE** *'Helping friends write music (but I can't play)'*	

STATED EFFECTS: None

break-dancing as a teenager, and chose to select as the prime example of the lack of Asian role models in the arts the fact that there were no Asian ballet dancers. Imran suggested not only that his cultural background was a barrier to arts involvement, but that gender also militated against his experience in the arts, as the following comments show:

> *there is Asian art , but Asians don't get into the arts – there are no role models at school or in the media. You don't see Asian ballet dancers – or in theatre or in music either. That's a disincentive, it might make you more interested if there were more role models.*

> *it was only girls and women who used to go to drama and dance. Men didn't. At our school, boys weren't allowed. I think those things should be open to boys.*

Currently, the opportunity to write '*descriptions and diaries*' for his GCSE has allowed Imran to enjoy '*expressing feelings which I wouldn't express if I just talked about them*' and to be '*using my imagination*'. It is significant that Imran volunteered the fact that while at secondary school, he did not enjoy English literature or writing, '*the teachers should've been more patient with those who couldn't do it very well*'. He also referred to his enjoyment of school music because '*it was practical instead of writing*'. These two arts interests appear to re-surface and converge in Imran's current (low-key) involvement in song writing with his friends.

Imran's Attitude Quota

POSITIVE ATTITUDES	COMMENT
general/non specific (low)	'*I quite liked music*'
situation specific (mid)	'*music was practical, not writing like the rest*'
socialising (mid)	'*I enjoy making music with friends*'
NEGATIVE ATTITUDES	
general/non-specific	'*you get the impression arts aren't very interesting*'
irrelevance	'*Asians don't get into arts; boys don't do drama and dance*'
negative afffective	'*the teachers should've been more patient*'
situation specific	'*the subjects I chose are different, sports is my*
self image	*creative activity*'

Imran's comments would appear to reveal quite a range of negative attitudes or barriers to participation, though this quota may well relate to a high level of articulateness as well as the obvious cultural and gender factors underpinning his arts rejection. Positive attitudes remained at mid-level motivation. Nevertheless, the socialising motive seems to act as a spur to developing future arts interests.

Cameo Five: Jim

Background

Jim is 21, unemployed and living with an aunt in a northern city. His mother works as an assistant in a fish and chip shop and he is presently looking for labouring work.

Arts Biography Diagram

This diagram registers Jim's fairly positive recall of primary school arts (in the form of literature and music), as well as his leisure-time arts consumption at primary age. There is then very much no take up in the secondary-age arenas of opportunity. A 'Pauline' conversion occurs and current and future interests are very strongly arts focused indeed.

Comment

Jim's biography diagram bears witness to an a somewhat chequered engagement with the arts in his younger years. Apart from singing, and particularly reading (which elicited the only real burst of enthusiasm from him when he recounted owning a Hans Anderson story book which was his

	Primary Age	Secondary Age	Youth Club	Stated Current Interests	Stated Future Arts Interests
L E I S U R E	**Arts Participation** NONE (Pinching bikes Boxing) **Arts Consumption** READING	**Arts Participation** NONE (Boxing) **Arts Consumption** NONE	Disco Boxing	**WRITING SHORT STORIES and POETRY** **LISTENING TO MUSIC**	**MORE WRITING** *More writing - in particular to write a book* *Want to do a writing course but cannot afford it*
S C H O O L / W O R K	*'All right, used to like them. I learnt a little bit'* **READING** *'used to like reading'* **SINGING** *'had a good voice'*	NONE *'I had no time for school. I thought school was pointless. I had no interest in the arts'*			

STATED EFFECTS: *Putting feelings on paper, gets it off my chest, what I'd like to say to politicians ...*
Understanding and insight
It makes me find out more about the things I write about ...

'*pride and joy*'), he admits that by the time he reached secondary school, the arts held no appeal for him. He began boxing at the age of 10, an activity which seems to have taken up all his time and energy, he acknowledged he '*used to live, sleep and eat boxing*'. He was expelled from school at the age of 15 because he '*hoyked a teacher out of the window*', turned professional as a boxer at the age of 18 and then drifted into drinking and taking drugs. A relationship turned sour when he hit the woman involved.

Jim traced his present significant interest in writing (illustrated by the biography diagram) to an encounter with a '*woman at a community centre*'. She gave him a list of five words – love, misery, peace, hate and friendship and from this he began writing short stories and poems. Looking at the arts biography, it may also be significant that Jim was so appreciative of reading and literature during his primary school years. His current writing appears to have led to a period of personal exploration during which he has been able to assess his situation, to dispense with drink and drugs and to take positive measures to control his temper. Writing allows him to '*get if off me chest ... gets me feelings onto paper*' and he affirms that it '*sorts me head out*'. Jim recounted how he now writes about '*living in the system, drugs, love, peace, everything that goes on in the world today – what goes on in this community, how hard it is*'. Among the effects of his arts experiences he included '*learning how to be more peaceful within myself*'. He is currently concerned with trying to write a book about living in a community like his and believes '*there should be more to help the likes of me ... more classes when you're trying to get straight*'. He recounted his attempt to enrol for a correspondence course in writing, which proved prohibitively expensive. He also helps out at the local youth club.

Jim's Attitude Quota

POSITIVE ATTITUDES	COMMENT
general/non specific (low)	'*I used to like the arts (at primary school)*'
relevance/comfortability (mid)	'*[the book] was my pride and joy*'
self-identity/expression (high)	'*it gives me understanding and insight*'
task-oriented (high)	'*I want to do a writing course/write a book*'
physiological (high)	'*it gets it off my chest*'
NEGATIVE ATTITUDES	
general unspecific	
non-stimulus	'*no interest in the arts, school was pointless*'
irrelevance	

This attitude quota again shows very vividly how fairly entrenched negative attitudes can be superseded by high level motivations. Equally, the barriers to involvement evident in Jim's secondary years appeared to suppress (or put on hold) low and mid level motivations associated with his primary school arts and particularly reading and literature. The resurfacing of a literature interest appears to reconnect Jim to these earlier positive attitudes.

Wayne and Davy: The Contribution of Youth Clubs

... if I wasn't here [doing arts]*, I'd be out doing drugs and stealing cars.*   (Wayne)

I would have liked to be a professional graffiti artist and learnt graphics and design.   (Davy)

The two following cameos illustrate the significance of youth clubs as a forum for arts engagement. Here are two perhaps archetypally 'difficult' young males, finding opportunities for undertaking arts in community centres which offer support and facilities for young people on a sustained (more-than-once-a-week) basis.

In keeping with the previous cameos, both these boys' arts biographies show a minimal interest in (and even a degree of hostility towards) secondary school arts. Nevertheless, their accounts do reveal an underlying and consistent thread of commitment to leisure-time art or craft, which youth club facilities have been able to nurture and encourage. Both boys also pinpoint collaboration and sociability as a significant aspect of the youth club arts facilities. In one case, the significance of the youth arts workers as role models is very evident.

Major differences in accounts of future interest are apparent in the two cameos, perhaps explained by Davy's evident sense of his own innate ability and an accompanying self-motivated interest in visual art. Perhaps Wayne, in contrast, exemplifies the need to offer sustained support and stimulus to those who are less able to be 'psychically rewarded' by their artistic ability. Clear differences in the boys' descriptors of their arts experiences also emerge: the vocabulary of excitement and self-realisation are only really present in the one case.

Cameo Six: Wayne

Background

Wayne is 16 and lives on a large housing estate on the outskirts of a northern city. He has no father and his mother is a laundry worker. He wishes to work in the travel business.

Arts Biography Diagram

Wayne's arenas of opportunity at primary and secondary age register particularly low-level involvement and then a dramatic increase through youth club attendance. However, arts remain a secondary interest currently, and no future interest is professed.

Comment

Wayne affirmed that arts had not had much significance for him at either primary or secondary school, commenting that '*if you have to do it, you don't really enjoy it the same*'. Despite acknowledging an interest in drama at secondary school, he could not identify any effects of his arts experiences nor any future arts interests. Perhaps this relates to the fact that he viewed drama as '*just fun*' and something he enjoyed because he was '*no good at paper work*'. He had no regrets about dropping drama after Year 9 '*... there were other things I wanted to do – it's not that important* [to me]'. Wayne's most sustained interest appears to be cooking. He also refers to '*making things*' – peg bags and teddy bears and this craft orientation seems to resurface in his selection of 'collage' as a valued primary school experience, and in his choices of arts activities at youth club (which significantly, he attends more than once a week).

	Primary Age	Secondary Age	Youth Club	Stated Current Interests	Stated Future Arts Interests
L E I S U R E	Arts Participation NONE (Cooking Making things) Arts Consumption NONE	Arts Participation NONE (Cooking) Arts Consumption **READING**	**ART WORK:** **Printing** **Painting** **Collage** **Murals** **Video-making**	Sport	NONE
S C H O O L / W O R K	'*I can't remember... we just had to do it*' **COLLAGE WORK**	'*not good ... the teachers only like the ones who are really good at arts and didn't give attention to those who weren't*' **DRAMA**		**VIDEO-MAKING MURAL**	
STATED EFFECTS: None					

It is through his involvement with a local youth club that Wayne has experienced his most positive reaction to the arts. He spoke enthusiastically about the painting, collage work, murals and video-making he did there. He stressed it is '*the only arts that means anything to me*' and that without it he would be '*out doing drugs and stealing cars*'. He nominates the youth workers at the club as the inspirational factors for this interest: also mentioning their 'skills' as sign-writers and graphic artists '*they've learnt us how to do things*'. Conversely, at school, teachers would '*put you down and make you feel like trash if you were not very able*'. It is noticeable that in spite of his obvious enthusiasm for the arts activities at the youth club, Wayne continues to use descriptors such as '*it's fun*', '*I enjoy it a lot*'. He added that '*everyone joins in and does a piece ...*', perhaps suggesting it is the collaborative aspect of the experience that has particular significance for him. There is a sense of corporate achievement evident in the language ('*everybody took a part in it – you feel proud when it looks so good*'), but no real sense of any powerful emotion which might self-sustain his enthusiasm. This apparent discontinuity is demonstrated by the biography diagram.

Wayne's Attitude Quota

POSITIVE ATTITUDES	COMMENT
general/non specific (low)	'*drama/youth club arts is just fun*'
situation specific (mid)	'*enjoy drama 'cos I'm not good at paper work.* [Youth club arts] *is the only arts that means anything to me ... the youth workers learn us to do things*'
socialising (mid)	'*everyone joins in ... took part*'
NEGATIVE ATTITUDES	
general/non-specific	'*not good ... can't remember*'
situation specific	'*the teachers only like the ones who are good at art*'
negative affective	'*they put you down and make you feel like trash*'

Wayne has strong negative attitudes to school arts, but it is noticeable that he does not voice the group image barriers which can be common among young people of his age, gender and social class. The influence of youth club arts – from which virtually all his mid-level positive attitudes derive – may be very significant here. There is a possibility that high level motivational attitudes could have been nurtured and developed from Wayne's early craft interest, but he himself does not apply such vocabularies of motive to this activity.

Cameo Seven: Davy

Background

Davy is a 17 year old living in a North East inner city area. His father is an electrician and his mother works in the catering industry. Davy is presently working towards an NVQ in bricklaying at FE college and would like to become a foreman.

Arts Biography Diagram

Davy's arenas of opportunity for his visual arts interest are confined to secondary age leisure-pursuits and youth club. (Primary and secondary school arts do not register.) Nevertheless, a sustained involvement in visual arts remains, continuing in training and as a current and future interest.

	Primary Age	Secondary Age	Youth Club	Stated Current Interests	Stated Future Arts Interests
L E I S U R E	Arts Participation NONE *(Writing on garage walls* *Walking around)* Arts Consumption NONE	Arts Participation **'Drawing on sub-way walls'** Arts Consumption **READING BOOKS ON ART**	**GRAFFITI DRAWING** Pool Basketball Baseball	**GRAFFITI DRAWING MYTHICAL CREATURES**	**GRAPHIC ART–** *'no assistance needed – but should've had help earlier on'*
S C H O O L / W O R K	NONE VALUED *'they were not very good'*	*'Too boring – not very good– you were set things to do'*	**Training scheme:** **DRAWING TO SCALE** **VIEWING BRICK-WORK ARTS**	Football Rugby	

STATED EFFECTS: *More imaginative.   Learning how to get on with people.*

Comment

The arts appeared to have little value for Davy while he was at school – he acknowledged that he found them boring, limiting and prescriptive. '*You were set things to do – I think you should just draw or paint what you want.*' The biography diagram demonstrates clearly his complete lack of engagement with arts offered throughout his school years.

However, in his leisure time and through the training scheme, the biography diagram shows significant involvement in the visual arts. Davy does a lot of graffiti art in his spare time and draws mythical creatures. It is worth noting that some of these arts activities might be interpreted as vandalism – spray painting swastikas on construction site huts. He suggested that one of the effects of this involvement has been his becoming more imaginative and this is perhaps borne out by his assertion that, for him, the arts mean '*you draw what you feel*'. His interest in drawing seems to stem from an early age though, as already noted, his arts experiences at school would appear to have acted as a disincentive. In retrospect, he regretted not having the opportunity to do '*modern arts, graphics and design*'. Youth club arts had provided materials for developing his graffiti art and Davy also mentioned '*learning to get on with people*' as an outcome here. Perhaps significantly, he could not nominate any one or anything as inspirational factors in connection with his present involvement in visual art which suggests that he has reached this stage through a process of personal experimentation. It is noticeable that Davy read art books – on graphics illustration and modern art in his own leisure time during earlier adolescence. He would like to pursue an interest in graphic art and felt now that earlier assistance and support would have been of great benefit ('*they could have improved our drawing skills, shown us different ways of mixing colours – a whole different way of looking at things*'). He registers his engagement with graffiti art through the language of excitement and self-esteem with phrases such as '*a little buzz*', '*feeling really good inside when people say it's really good*'. It is worth noting however, that to some extent this 'buzz' may well be derived from the illicit nature of the activity itself: '*looking over your shoulder in case you get caught is a little buzz too*'. Significantly, Davy pointed out this activity had 'gone down' as he had matured a lot and it was initiated by friends as there was '*nowt else to do*'.

Also, Davy's conviction about the validity of his art form [*'I think that most modern artists have copied off street art'*] – is not always matched by his peers. '*Kids at college who think that anyone who draws on a wall or paper is stupid*' were nominated as a turn-off, suggesting that to struggle against prevailing peer culture can happen to visual artists as much as to dancers or actors.

Davy's Attitude Quota

POSITIVE ATTITUDES	COMMENT
task oriented (high)	'*I was able to develop my graffiti art at youth club ... read books on illustration*'
physiological (high)	'*feeling a buzz and feeling good inside when people say it's really good*'
self-identity (high)	'*to me, arts means drawing what you feel*'
socialising (mid)	'*doing graffiti art on buildings was started with friends*'
NEGATIVE ATTITUDES	
general/non-specific	'*arts at school were boring, not good*'
non relevance	'*you were [just] set things to do in art*'
non stimulus	

This quota shows a cluster of high level motivation attitudes which corroborate the long-term commitment to alternative visual art evident in Davy's biography. In contrast, the formal school arts curriculum has engendered only negative attitudes and has failed to connect with, or harness, this enthusiasm. Davy pinpoints how school has not provided the stimulus for establishing high-level motivation attitudes, by explicit reference to, for instance, the absence of task-orientation ('*they could have improved our skills*') and self-identity. Davy's independent acquisition of high-level motivation attitudes appears to nullify the possible barrier of group image ('*kids at college think it's stupid*') which can limit some young people's arts engagement, as Elizabeth (Cameo One) showed.

Susan, Marie and Christina: Consuming the Arts

the arts have given me inspiration, insights and, through them, I can talk to a broad group of people. (Susan)

... arts have definitely broadened my mind, I'm a lot more literate, more critical and probably more confident. (Marie)

the arts have made me more broadminded, more aware and more confident, I've more conversation skills. (Christina)

The next three cameos depict dedicated arts consumers (particularly of theatre), whose arts biographies share a number of common features. They are all young women whose training – if not always home background – would suggest entry to Social Class I and II.

It is notable how a reading-literature/drama-theatre interface emerges in all three: reading particularly surfaces as a common interest from primary age leisure time onwards. (It is interesting to compare their developments in the arts with Jim's – Cameo Five – who registered a similar reading enthusiasm at primary age.)

Significantly, sustained and supported arts consumption features in all three's accounts, though the sources of these consumer-opportunities differ (sibling, primary and secondary teachers are variously mentioned and indeed nominated as inspiration factors).

Finally, remarkable similarity in the outcomes of their literary/performance arts appreciation are registered: the young women show a considerable consensus about the social value of arts consumption and the kinds of personal qualities it inculcates.

Cameo Eight: Susan

Background
Susan is a 24 year old, undertaking a social policy degree at a new university in the north of England. Her father is a retired building estimator, her mother a housewife. She wants to work in local government social services.

Arts Biography Diagram
This diagram suggests take-up in most arenas of opportunity, although some qualification in primary school is evident and no youth club arts were available. Susan's nomination of drawing as a current and future interest suggests the strong influence of secondary school arts experiences. The opportunities for arts consumption at secondary school also show continuity. Theatre registers as a leisure pursuit in adulthood.

Comment
Susan's arts biography shows a consistent leisure interest in visual art from primary age onwards, which was particularly heightened by her secondary

art teacher. Susan nominated him as an inspirational influence: '... *he encouraged experimentation, but* [also offered] *structure*'. She felt this teacher had '*brought out*' and '*nurtured*' an interest which '*... outlasted my education*', and hence accounted for her continuing to do some drawing and sketching in her leisure time as a way of '*relaxing*'. Also, Susan pinpointed secondary school as offering opportunities in arts consumption – theatre trips (referred to as '*different and enjoyable*') and to art galleries (referred to as '*inspirational*'). Reading as an enjoyable arts activity is also iterated throughout Susan's biography. Indeed, '*listening to stories*' is all that Susan can suggest as a valuable arts experience at primary school.

	Primary Age	Secondary Age	Youth Club	Stated Current Interests	Stated Future Arts Interests
L E I S U R E	Arts Participation NONE (Playing out) **DRAWING** Arts Consumption **READING**	Arts Participation CYCLING **DRAWING** Arts Consumption **READING**	NONE *'We talked and played games'*	CYCLING AEROBATICS	**DRAWING AND PAINTING**
S C H O O L / W O R K	*'We weren't pushed much – we didn't do much and not made aware of arts'* **LISTENING TO STORIES**	**ART** **ART GALLERIES** **THEATRE TRIPS** *'we had plenty of opportunities'*	**HE** Social Policy Degree	**READING** **DRAWING/ PAINTING** **OPERA** **THEATRE TRIPS**	**OPERA/ THEATRE**

STATED EFFECTS:	*insights* [from art galleries] *communication skills*	*challenges* *social skills and social opportunities*

Susan suggested her friends and college colleagues were a second source of arts influence. With them, her interests as an arts consumer could be '*shared and developed*' and now included opera ('*a truly wonderful experience*'). For this reason, it may be significant that Susan chose to pinpoint the opportunity to appreciate music as an omission from her school arts biography. She also nominated '*pretentious people*' as a source of turn off from theatre/opera attendance, which may result from her recent arrival on the mainstream arts consumption scene, and a lack of knowledge of these two art forms.

Arts consumption was becoming a significant social as well as aesthetic experience now for Susan. She referred to this sociability aspect in her account of the effects of arts as well as gaining insights. However, she also chose to mention the arts association with '*white middle classness*' and also pointed out the prohibitive expense of being a committed arts consumer '*... there should be discount for ballet and opera for students and young people ... more should be available to everybody. Unless you are a certain type of person, basically wealthy, you just don't get the chance to experience these things*'.

Susan's Attitude Quota

POSITIVE ATTITUDES	COMMENT
task oriented (high)	'*teacher nurtured interest, provided structure and experimentation*'
therapeutic (high)	'*drawing is now a way of relaxing in leisure time*'
intrinsic/aesthetic (high)	'*inspirational art galleries, wonderful experience of opera*'
socialising (mid)	'*with friends, sharing and developing arts interest*'
general/non-specific (low)	'*theatre trips were enjoyable at school*'
NEGATIVE ATTITUDES	
lack of money	
(negative-affective)	'*pretentious people are a turn off from the arts*'

This attitude quota registers a range of high-level arts motivations, clearly linked to a well received and influential secondary arts education. It is also possible that the mid-level socialising motive verges on the task-oriented, with Susan's notion of *developing* her interest in opera with friends.

The major barrier to Susan's arts engagement is financial. No negative attitudes *per se* emerge in her account, though there is a possible discomfort associated with the general ambience of her new interest in high arts consumption (such as opera). This does not appear to affect interest: no doubt there is some bolstering or protection from discomfort by her friends' shared interest. Negative attitudes such as irrelevance, group image/self image barriers are not in anyway evident. This is not surprising: Susan's age, gender, class and educational attainment would suggest she exemplifies the demographic variables most often associated with arts engagement.

Cameo Nine: Marie

Background

Marie is a 19 year old undertaking a BA in communications and public media. Her father is a carpenter, her mother a housewife. She lived in Ireland during her primary school years. She is partially sighted in one eye and deaf in one ear.

Arts Biography Diagram

Marie's biography diagram shows how arenas of arts opportunity are almost entirely confined to leisure-time (and also by encountering arts through therapy and medical treatment). Quite starkly, both primary and secondary schools are seen to contribute very little indeed. College becomes the first institutional arena of opportunity to offer Marie the arts stimulus she required, and from there interest and commitment flourishes.

	Primary Age	Secondary Age	Youth Club	Stated Current Interests	Stated Future Arts Interests
L E I S U R E	Arts Participation **'SPEECH and DRAMA'** **(therapy for medical reasons)** Arts Consumption **READING**	Arts Participation NONE Arts Consumption **READING** **ARTS EVENTS**		**STUDENT RADIO:** news editor reviewer of films and theatre **READING**	**DRAMA**
S C H O O L / W O R K	*'Very little done...'* *'it was very poor – we concentrated on the work side'*	*'Not much done or provided'*	**HE** **BA in Communication and Public Media**		

STATED EFFECTS:	*broadened my mind ...* *made me more questioning*	*made me more confident* *has provided social contact*

Comment

Marie's arts biography shows a direct linkage between her current interests and her long-standing leisure commitment to reading (perhaps also along with the remedial treatment – in speech and drama – for her speech and hearing disability). Arts at both primary and secondary school were described in quite negative terms, though Marie did have the opportunity to take a GCSE in drama. She suggested it was the personal reading commitment which propelled her intense interest in drama. *'... I've always been interested in reading and I've got quite a broad imagination. I think theatre is a natural progression: it's like seeing books and plays come to life.'* Marie's descriptors of theatre attendance show all the hallmarks of the vocabulary of intensity, *'I love getting lost in the mystery of it all, theatre is very magical. I get a great buzz out of it'*. Marie's interest has led her to be a very strong and active 'consumer' who has flourished in her specialism within an HE environment.

Marie indicated that it was her family/home background which was a source of inspiration: *'we are all arty to some degree – we were always encouraged to read a lot ... my sister dragged me along to* [arts events] *when I was younger – I think she probably also instilled an interest in me'*.

Significantly, Marie saw herself as disadvantaged in a school and peer culture which had actively promoted sports. Secondary school only provided *'things like netball clubs'* and Marie noted that *'I need more confidence – very often if you don't shine at sports you're not seen as valid, if you're not out there winning games, you don't count'*. She regretted the lack of opportunities for arts consumption, theatre visits and arts events during her school career, rather than pinpointing specific art forms she would have liked to participate in.

Notwithstanding this, Marie saw her arts experiences as having the effect of giving confidence; adding significantly to her perceptiveness and providing valuable social contact.

Maria's Attitude Quota

POSITIVE ATTITUDES	COMMENT
physiological (high)	*'I get a real buzz out of* [theatre]*'*
intrinsic (high)	*'I love getting lost in the mystery of it all, theatre's magical'*
relevance (mid)	*'I've always been interested in reading ... theatre is a natural progression'*
socialising (mid)	*'it's provided social contact'*
NEGATIVE ATTITUDES	
lack of opportunity	

This quota shows high level motivational attitudes associated with being a consumer of the arts. No negative attitudes are apparent, beyond a recognition of the limited opportunities offered by primary and secondary school. Unlike Susan in the previous cameo, there is no evidence of a possible negative affective barrier regarding the general ambience of theatre attendance: Marie's early induction to arts events by her sibling may be a significant factor here.

Cameo Ten: Christina

Background

Christina is a 24 year old history teacher from London. Her father is a clerk and her mother a housewife. She is from a Mediterranean background. She intends to make a career of teaching.

Arts Biography Diagram

This diagram shows the continuity in arts consumption throughout Christina's leisure-time arenas of opportunity. The progression to theatre from this literary consumer experience is also closely linked to her highly acclaimed arts education at primary school. Nevertheless, future interests specifically did not include participation.

	Primary Age	Secondary Age	Youth Club	Stated Current Interests	Stated Future Arts Interests
L E I S U R E	**Arts Participation** NONE (visiting family playing out) **Arts Consumption** **LISTENING TO MUSIC** **READING**	**Arts Participation** **DANCING IN CLUBS** **Arts Consumption** **THEATRE** **CINEMA** **MUSIC** **READING** **ART GALLERIES**	(*'Not aware - my parents would have forbidden it'*)	**CINEMA** **THEATRE** **READING** **DANCING** Socialising Pubs and Clubs Eating Out	NONE
S C H O O L / W O R K	**DRAMA** *'I loved everything to do with it'*	*'Not as developed as it could have been, teachers didn't put themselves out enough'* **DRAMA** **LITERATURE**	**UNIVERSITY** History Degree		

STATED EFFECTS:	*... confidence*	*... better vocabulary; language and written expression*
	... more aware of people's make-up – emotions and reactions to different situations	
		... helped me express myself
	... more broadminded	*... more discussion points/conversation skills*

Comment

Christina's arts biography shows a particularly significant and influential encounter with high calibre arts teaching offered during her primary school. She enthused about her love of drama at that age (*'I loved everything to do with it'*), describing how she was involved in every school play *'I loved acting, pretending to be someone else, I liked being the centre of attention ... it was ego-boosting'.* This enthusiasm was seen to result from the quality of teaching '*It was well presented at our school, we had a teacher who was a real drama freak'*. Moreover, it was her primary school teachers whom Christina nominated as her main source of inspiration in the arts '*all the way through primary school, the teachers were really into theatre and plays and encouraged us to go'.* This commitment, especially to participating in drama, continued in secondary school where Christina described again the pleasure of '*getting on stage, being someone else, it makes you feel someone special and confident'.* Equally, Christina herself directly connected her drama experiences in primary school to her interest in literature '*drama got me interested in literature and story writing'*, and in turn literature emerged as a valuable arts activity for Christina at secondary school, '*loved reading – I got into the stories and the war poetry – I found it beautiful and moving'*. Some caveats about the quality of arts opportunities did surface in Christina's overview of her secondary school, where she felt they '*were not as developed as they could have been, not enough opportunity'*. Christina was not able to take drama after Year 9 and regretted this, also suggesting, when asked to reflect on earlier arts opportunities, that she would have appreciated '*more drama and amateur dramatics'*.

The lack of opportunity to fully develop drama after primary school appears to have contributed to Christina diverting into becoming a consumer rather than participant. She volunteered theatre as something very important to her, something she went to frequently and increasingly so since leaving college. Christina saw theatre-going as a '*grown up thing to do'*: adding '*it also has a pose-value, I want to appear cultured'* and '*as a leisure pursuit I can't get enough...'*. She stated she had no arts activities which she might want to develop in the future. Participation – and the '*ego-boost'* which drama had provided is now something she can get from dancing and clubbing: '*it's great to strut your stuff'*.

In terms of effects of the arts, Christina was clear in the amount of '*confidence'* that drama had given her and that it had enhanced her social capacities '*... I've got more to say, I'm more interesting to talk to because I've read a lot and seen a lot of plays ...'* as well as the empathy and perceptiveness, writing and language skills accruing from her commitment to language-oriented art forms.

Christina's Attitude Quota

POSITIVE ATTITUDES	COMMENT
therapeutic (high)	'*on stage, you feel someone special, an ego-boost'*
aesthetic/intrinsic (high)	'*I found reading* [war poetry] *beautiful and moving'*
relevance (mid)	'*drama got me into reading and story writing'*
status seeking (rare)	'*theatre-going has a pose value, I want to appear cultured'*
NEGATIVE ATTITUDES	
lack of opportunity	

Showing a very similar attitude quota to that of the previous cameo, there is nevertheless a significant variation in Christina's classic acknowledgement of arts providing her with 'cultural capital' (status seeking is categorised as a very low level motivational factor in the typology). This may perhaps explain why she has no nominations for future arts involvement: the high level motivational factors all in fact relate to previous arts experiences offered by school. An apparent high level of enthusiasm for arts ends up appearing a little lightweight when attitudes are carefully analysed. The absence of task-oriented attitudes may also be significant.

Jackie and Peter: Arts as Creative Expression

... I think arts means a skill where you have to do something that's creative: it puts somebody in a position when they know what you mean but it's not like you're talking to them [they know what you mean] *by what you are doing.* (Jackie)

... To me, arts means anything that's the creative side of life, it's not sitting at a desk all day ... it's expressing yourself. (Peter)

The following two cameos are of young people whose (very different) home backgrounds have clearly influenced and encouraged a serious engagement with music and dance. As such, they stand in notable contrast to the previous cameos, where family influence was very evidently not mentioned as influential on participation.

Both have had sporting interests and prowess within their biographies, and the physicality of dance features in their accounts. (Indeed, it is even implied in each of their arts definitions outlined above.) It is equally noticeable how, in both these definitions, concepts of expression and creativity are clearly articulated. This contrasts sharply with, for example, George and Elizabeth in Cameos One and Two (who after considerable probing, could summon the phrase '*making up*' but were unable to volunteer any arts definition).

Both Peter and Jackie readily use the vocabulary of excitement and self-esteem/ realisation in describing their arts involvement, and significantly, both are currently engaged in rigorous study of the art forms which they enjoy. The absence of opportunity in primary school arts is another notable commonality. However, this has not ultimately affected their arts commitment, given the sustained support, success – and hence self-motivation – evident in other arenas of their arts biographies.

Cameo Eleven: Jackie

Background

Jackie is a 15 year old Afro-Caribbean living in an inner city area in the north of England. Her father is a bouncer and her mother is a shop assistant in a bakery. Jackie wishes to be a chef.

Arts Biography Diagram

This diagram shows Jackie's leisure-time arenas of opportunity suffused with a rich contemporary arts culture, and quite distinctively so at primary age. Equally, her secondary school (which actually specialised in performing arts) features strongly as a further arena offering wide arts experience, while Jackie herself seems to have exploited the more limited opportunities of her primary education. The biography diagram thus shows a continuity in performing arts engagement, evidenced by her stated current and future interests.

	Primary Age	Secondary Age	Youth Club	Stated Current Interests	Stated Future Arts Interests
L E I S U R E	Arts Participation (Football and climbing trees) *'Paint and make up poems to go with them'* **SINGING WITH BAND** Arts Consumption **WATCHING & LISTENING TO FATHER'S BAND**	Arts Participation **DANCE** Swimming Shot putt Javelin Arts Consumption **READ DANCE MAGAZINES from America**	Sports: discus weight training badminton basketball	Sports: shot putt discus javelin Cooking (making up recipes)	**DRAMA**
S C H O O L / W O R K	**POETRY** **'I loved everything to do with rhyme'** *'My primary school didn't have no dance or anything'*	**DANCE** **DRAMA** **MUSIC-MAKING** **VISITS TO THEATRE/ WATCHING DANCE**		**MUSIC-MAKING** **READING** **MAKING UP SONGS** **SINGING & DANCING**	

STATED EFFECTS: *Realised I can get somewhere*
Quietened down, can work out any anger in my dancing
Made me realise I could get somewhere ... changed me

Comment

Arts would appear to have featured quite significantly in Jackie's life from an early age, as the biography diagram demonstrates. Her early home life seems to have been particularly music-oriented (her father played in a band)

and she was able to accompany him and join in practice sessions. Jackie herself acknowledged '*I do not think the world would be anywhere without music ... music is the best art anybody could've made up*'. This involvement in music has been sustained in her secondary years and encouraged by a school environment which gives her '*a lot of opportunity*' (e.g. creative music-making on the keyboard during lunch hour). Her commitment to music is exemplified through her assertion (in the vocabulary of intensity and self-esteem/self-realisation) that '*it's just the feel ... it gives me a hype ... it makes me feel it's really me doing it and I'm proud because I did it myself*'.

This suffusion of music led on to a dance interest – Jackie significantly commented on what had inspired her arts interest:

> ... *with me liking music and liking to dance and watching when I was little ... the boys I used to hang around with always used to be into the latest dancing and body-popping – I wanted to be like them.*

Equally she connected the music influence and her pleasure in poetry as a primary school pupil:

> ... *when the teachers used to say 'what do you want to do?' I used to say poetry ... I think it was mainly because I loved everything I could do with rhyme ... poetry helped me to write songs because once you can rhyme a poem you can put words into places where you want them.*

It is notable that Jackie commented on how primary school had not offered her '*dance or anything else*'.

Within secondary school, Jackie's earlier predilection for dance gave way to a preference for drama because she felt she could already do what was being taught in dance. She readily admitted that she had had an attitude problem and acknowledged a history of violence towards teachers in her primary years. Among the effects of her involvement in arts she nominated the realisation that she could '*do something with myself*' through it, that it had helped her to '*quieten down*' and control her temper. She noted that '*arts have changed me a lot*'. She then was able to return to dance and learn the techniques she had previously dismissed. Her aggression can be controlled because '*I can take it out in my dance*'. She would like to extend her involvement with drama.

The biography diagram illustrates a barren patch in Jackie's leisure arts involvement after her earlier interest, followed by her gradual reintegration after 'finding' arts again in the context of school. As she noted '*at the end of the day you need school, but then you also need* [the motivation] *in yourself*'.

Jackie's Attitude Quota

POSITIVE ATTITUDES	COMMENT
self-identity (high)	*'arts have changed me'*
task-oriented (high)	*'I'm learning techniques, you need the school but also the motivation in yourself'*
therapeutic/physiological (high)	*'I can take my aggression out in dance ... music: it's the feel – it gives me a hype'*
ability-oriented (low)	*'through arts, I realise I can get somewhere'*
status-seeking (low)	*'wanted to be like the boys who were into the latest dancing'*
NEGATIVE ATTITUDES	
lack of opportunity	*'at primary school ... no dance'*

This attitude quota shows considerable high level motivation: the intensity of interest perhaps confirmed by the lack of mention for mid- or low-level positive attitudes such as socialising and general/unspecific. There is some possible seeking of alternative arts cultural capital in Jackie's professed desire to emulate black male dancing, but high personal investment is also part of her motivation make-up. Similarly, the ability-oriented attitude operates in the context of a well established sense of psychic reward from dance and music. No negative barriers surface beyond the limited provision of primary school.

Cameo Twelve: Peter

Background
Peter is an 18 year old full-time dance student at a private dance school. His mother is a primary school teacher and his father a baker. He intends to be a professional dancer or involved in arts. Peter was particularly articulate on his sense of injustice at the lack of state financial support for those in training to be professional artists, pointing out that he receives considerably less money than someone his age who is unemployed.

Arts Biography Diagram
Peter's biography diagram shows leisure-time as the only arenas of opportunity in his earlier years. However, this engagement with formal arts training from an early age suffices to sustain involvement and indeed leads to specialisation.

Comment
Peter's biography shows a personal commitment to dance (and music) which was not connected to primary or secondary school, nor to arts activities offered through the school's youth club. His comments on these arenas of opportunity are almost entirely negative and indicate how, as a specialist, he perceives both an absence of skills acquisition and also a peer culture particularly antipathetic to his chosen art form. Indeed, he identified '*school peers attitude to dancing*' as a demotivator, ('*... these other people's attitudes*

meant there was always pressure to give up'). However, he added *'... but it didn't stop me, I had karate and a temper! – I once got suspended for two weeks'.* Of primary school, he commented *'primary school wouldn't have got me dancing even if offered'.*

<table>
<tr><th></th><th></th><th>Primary Age</th><th>Secondary Age</th><th>Youth Club</th><th>Stated Current Interests</th><th>Stated Future Arts Interests</th></tr>
<tr>
<td rowspan="2">L E I S U R E</td>
<td></td>
<td>Arts Participation
Karate
Judo

PLAYING CLARINET, PLAYING SAX

Arts Consumption
LISTENING TO MUSIC</td>
<td>Arts Participation
Karate
Judo

DANCE WRITING MUSIC

Arts Consumption
THEATRE MUSICALS</td>
<td>Darts
Kung Fu
Play pool
'the arts on offer didn't seem interesting'</td>
<td>DANCE
WRITING MUSIC
LISTENING TO MUSIC</td>
<td>DANCE CAREER</td>
</tr>
<tr>
<td rowspan="2">S C H O O L / W O R K</td>
<td>'Nothing sticks in my memory as to what they were offering me'</td>
<td>'Inadequate - I didn't learn anything technical ... the opportunities were there, but not specialist'</td>
<td>DANCE SCHOOL

'I'm here from 8.30 in the morning till 10 at night'</td>
<td></td>
<td></td>
</tr>
<tr>
<td></td>
<td></td>
<td></td>
<td>Karate</td>
<td></td>
</tr>
<tr>
<td colspan="2">STATED EFFECTS:</td>
<td colspan="5">The freedom to express myself   My strength - mental and physical
Socialising with other arts people
My physique and skills (e.g. co-ordination)</td>
</tr>
</table>

Arts influences and support were identified as coming entirely through his home background and culture: *'arts run in the family, my mum's an actress – they let me find and choose dance for myself'.* Peter explained how he had taken private dance lessons because it was initially a supplement to his martial arts, and, it seems, also an outcome of sibling rivalry *'... I started dancing because I couldn't stand not to do anything my sister could do and also with karate, I thought dance would loosen me up'.*

Peter's account of his involvement with dance reveals the degree of stamina (*'including mental strength to cope with kids taking the mick'*) and discipline it requires. The opportunity for self-expression and the intense pleasure of performing were conveyed: the psychic reward attached to displaying excellence was also evident *'I enjoy dance because of the freedom to express yourself – I'm an extrovert, I love showing off'*, [the arts have given me] *... my physical strength and physique'.*

Peter suggested the kinds of prejudice he himself had surmounted in order to persist in his chosen art form may not be so prevalent in the future, he cited the fact that '... *there are now some wonderful male dancers to be role models, it's getting more acceptable for males to dance. It's the influence of the drugs-related music – techno, rave etc. In modern dance, the best dancers are usually male and black*'.

Peter's Attitude Quota

POSITIVE ATTITUDES	COMMENT
task-oriented (high)	'[you need] *stamina and discipline*'
self-identity (high)	'*arts and dance is the freedom to express yourself*'
therapeutic (high)	'*it's the pleasure of performing, I love showing off*'
ability-oriented (low)	'*I couldn't stand to do anything my sister couldn't do*'
NEGATIVE ATTITUDES	
group image	'*school peers' attitude to dance meant there was always a pressure to give up*'

Again, an attitude quota showing much high-level motivation, and a particularly powerful example of how these intense positive attitudes can cancel out barriers such as peer pressure or group image. Without these high-level motivations, Peter's ability-oriented attitude was unlikely to secure a sustained involvement.

Anna and Sam: An Arts Education

... at the end of composing music, if you get a good piece, you get pleasure – it's really very pleasing ... there's a sense of achievement that it's worked. (Anna)

I like playing a song I've written, it gives me a good buzz, I just love it when it sounds good. (Sam)

The final cameos are of two school-aged young people, both with a long-term musical education and an interest in musical composition. It may be significant that sport is noticeably absent from their accounts.

Both of these young people have begun their interest via specialist teaching offered through primary school (although each has criticisms of arts education at primary level generally). It is also noticeable that each account makes reference to a parent facilitating and fostering consumption of music (concerts etc). In this way, every arena of opportunity (home, leisure, social life and school, consumption as well as participation) has provided further scope for involvement and improvement. A very powerful seamless and continuous reinforcement results. Whether – and how – music seems uniquely able to provide this total life-style for young people is an interesting issue.

The vocabularies of intensity and self-esteem are, inevitably, very pervasive in both accounts.

Another common feature of these arts biographies is the references which Sam and Anna make to the rigour involved in developing their music skills. Sam perceptively noted how he had been lucky with the opportunities available to him: but it is also evident that these opportunities were seized with commitment and dedication. (At this point, it is worth contrasting the views of Elizabeth in Cameo One, '*all that arts stuff is too hard and you can't have fun*'). A unique excitement and fulfilment, i.e. '*the buzz*', may be the rewards of arts, but effort may well be a vital ingredient to achieve it.

Cameo Thirteen: Anna

Background
Anna is a 14 year old who lives in a northern rural location: her father is a retired storekeeper and her mother a laboratory assistant. She wishes to be a music teacher. She has only 20 per cent hearing in one ear, which meant she '*... didn't really pick things up in detail, I really had to learn how to – it stopped me from learning music at first*'.

Arts Biography Diagram
This biography diagram shows every arena of opportunity exclusively filled with both arts participation and consumption, and particularly features music. Only primary school arts are given a more qualified approval.

Comment
Anna exemplifies a commitment to the arts which she felt was initially derived entirely from opportunities available through her primary school: progressing from recorder playing to flute lessons with a peripatetic music teacher. Primary school arts were '*the things you looked forward to in the week*', and, significantly, where she acquired '*the skills to read and play music*'. This strong interest in playing music continued in her leisure time on a wide array of wind instruments. A particular feature of leisure arts activity is her account of composing and creating music (now with tapes and keyboards and subsequently scoring it on manuscript paper). Anna refers to the '*sense of achievement*', '*... real pleasure and enjoyment*' of her music creation.

For leisure-time art consumption, at both primary and secondary age, Anna mentioned listening to music and going to the theatre with her father. This suggests that some general and sustained encouragement, if not direct skills transmission, were endemic to her home background. It is noticeable that Anna refers to teachers – music and dance – and also '*seeing musicals*' as her significant inspirational factors, and music composition as something she found and continued with by herself.

	Primary Age	Secondary Age	Youth Club	Stated Current Interests	Stated Future Arts Interests
L E I S U R E	Arts Participation PLAYING MUSIC PAINTING Arts Consumption THEATRE LISTENING TO MUSIC	Arts Participation MUSIC – playing in orchestras Arts Consumption THEATRE TRIPS MORE LISTENING TO MUSIC MORE	*'Too rough'*	PLAYING MUSIC COMPOSING LISTENING TO MUSIC DRAMA READING	MUSIC TEACHING
S C H O O L / W O R K	MUSIC – with peripatetic teacher *'arts was the things which weren't boring, you could have a good laugh ... there wasn't much painting they do more now I think'*	DANCE MUSIC TAKING PART IN SCHOOL MUSICALS *'good ... they've got the idea that things don't have to just be written work to be valuable'*			

STATED EFFECTS: *Everything I can I link to music, [acquiring] qualifications in music and skills*

During secondary school, Anna had joined two orchestras, was taking part in theatre productions and identified that the school's music teaching had the effect of '*making me listen to music more carefully*'. She felt the school conveyed not only that arts were fun, but also '*hard work*'. She referred to the pleasure of school offering '*a whole hour a week just devoted to music*'. School dance teaching '*... and the learning of new skills there*' also featured as a recently acquired pleasure in arts.

Anna's account resonates with comments that would seem to suggest her personal and social identity are now strongly associated with her music: she explains '*... everything I do is to do with music ...*', '*everything I can do, I link to music – even maths – I can learn circles by linking it to music...*', '*music has determined who my friends are*', '*... if I didn't do music, I'd have no hobby or past-time*'. She also refers to dance as enjoyable because '*it involved music ... [what I've got out of it] is helping [my music] because you have to listen so carefully to where you are*'.

One other notable feature in Anna's account is her emphasis on acquiring skills and the self-motivation and rigour involved. She mentioned '*Practice takes a lot of time*', that school conveys music as '*hard work*'. On her leisure-time composition, she indicates a perseverance '*I keep fiddling about with different styles of music, different types of composition until I find something I like – at the end of it, if you play it to somebody, there is a sense of achievement it's worked*'.

By inference, Anna's comment on her primary school arts does suggest an awareness of a lack of variety and depth in comparison to her secondary experiences.

Anna's Attitude Quota

POSITIVE ATTITUDES	COMMENT
task-oriented (high)	'*a sense of achievement, arts are hard work*'
therapeutic (high)	'[composing] *offers a feeling of real pleasure, enjoyment*'
self-identity (high)	'*everything I do is to do with music, without it I wouldn't have a hobby*'

Anna has an attitude quota entirely filled with high-level motivation. Other attitudes may also be present (such as socialising), but do not feature directly in Anna's account. No negative attitudes are registered, apart from a minor caveat of the lack of art forms available at primary school.

Cameo Fourteen: Sam

Background
Sam is a 16 year old living in the suburbs of a northern city. His father is a head of department in a secondary school and his mother is a university librarian. On career prospects, Sam suggested he wished to have something to do with music or architecture.

Arts Biography Diagram
Sam's biography diagram shows again the virtually exclusive arts investment in all arenas of arts opportunities which occurs through a musical education, coupled with interest and ability. Primary school – while offering the initial stimulus – does receive some retrospective criticism.

Comment
Sam's account shows a continuity in arts: he himself clearly recognised the value of a traditional music training for his current musical versatility and commitment to playing rock bass guitar in various bands. This, he felt, developed from the opportunity to learn violin through his primary school '*... it taught me all the notes, the technical terms, time signatures and dynamics. If I hadn't learnt the violin, I wouldn't be able to apply that to all the other instruments I now play*'. After being a member of junior string orchestras, at 14, Sam progressed to rock bands, having been inspired by a friend '*I used to just watch him, he was so good, and I used to think 'I*

want to be able to play a guitar like that' so he taught me a few basic things, and I just followed on from there – I found it really easy to pick up, having played violin – the chords and so on'. He acknowledges he cannot as yet read music for bass and so plays by ear. Learning bass techniques (and about jazz) is a future interest. He also valued the *'really good music department and really good teachers'* at his secondary school – *'... you learn a lot of composing and about different periods of music'.*

	Primary Age	Secondary Age	Youth Club	Stated Current Interests	Stated Future Arts Interests
L E I S U R E	Arts Participation **DRAWING** **VIOLIN PLAYING** Arts Consumption **ATTENDING MUSICALS AND CONCERTS**	Arts Participation **JUNIOR STRING ORCHESTRA** **IN A ROCK BAND** Arts Consumption **CONCERTS** **THEATRE**	Snooker Table-tennis Bowling **MAKING T-SHIRTS** **MUSIC:** *someone's dad once brought in some guitars'*	**MUSIC** – bass player in a band – writing music for songs **CONCERTS** Jazz Rock Opera	**MUSIC** *'learn about jazz in more depth, how they form jazz technique for bass guitar .. a career in music.* *There should be lessons, videos, more information on how to get into careers in the arts'*
S C H O O L / W O R K	**VIOLIN LESSONS** *'the only arts I was interested in'* *'I don't think there was enough variety not a wide enough angle on the arts'*	**MUSIC** **ART** *'my school is a very good school for arts, good teachers, a wide variety'*			

STATED EFFECTS:

... I appreciate things more – art, I can see how much hard work went into a painting, and listening to music – I can really appreciate it

... Confidence - from feeling you can play your guitar, you've done concerts

... techniques of music

I can talk to anyone about music - the places I go and people I meet are all based round music

Also evident is the ongoing musical impetus from Sam's home background – with his dad, from primary age, Sam went to musicals and concerts. He mentioned currently going to jazz concerts and festivals, and opera. Here, Sam described – in the vocabulary of intensity – *'shutting my eyes and really getting into it – my dad's like that too. A really good jazz pianist, it just makes you high listening to it'.* Not surprisingly, the pleasure of writing and playing music is again in this register '... *I like playing a song I've written, it gives me a really good buzz, I just love it when it sounds good'*.

Sam's arts biography also shows a sustained and consistent thread of interest in visual art, and he defines himself as a '*creative person, I prefer creative things'*. On effects of arts involvement, Sam includes confidence, sociability as well as musical and art skills and appreciation.

Perseverance and rigour also emerge in the arts-biography: on his current music-making, Sam noted '... *I think I'm always trying to improve my music, and that makes me happy, I just want to learn and get good at my instruments'*. Equally, he volunteered that at primary age, he had '*practised very hard on my violin, I was really interested'*.

Sam acknowledged, at various points in the interview, the privileged opportunities he had had compared to other young people, also suggesting the commitment his level of arts involvement required.

> *it's where you live, it's the way you are, your background, your parents and I think it's within yourself though as well if you want to do it. But some schools don't have the opportunities that my* [schools] *have offered ... people might have talents in all sorts of areas, but never have a chance to do it. ... There's a lot of wasted talent – without money, facilities or teaching: a lot of people could be really good musicians or painters but just 'cos of their situation, they can't expand and develop.*

His only criticism was to pinpoint the lack of a broad arts education in his primary school.

> *You should have more experience of different things – different instruments to be learnt and artists coming in – for dance, sculpture drama – so people at a younger age can see what they like and have a chance to do it.*

Sam's Attitude Quota

POSITIVE ATTITUDES	COMMENT
task-oriented (high)	'*I'm always trying to improve my music*'
therapeutic (high)	'*playing a song I've written, it gives a real good buzz*'
self-identity (high)	'*I'm a creative person, I prefer creative things*'
socialising (mid)	'*the places I go and people I meet are all based on music*'

This quota again registers key high-level motivational attitudes. The absence of barriers to participation in Sam's account might also suggest the acceptability of male musicianship, especially when linked to rock music. This stands in notable contrast to Davy and Peter (Cameos 7 and 12), whose chosen art forms – graffiti and ballet/dance – were somewhat at odds with their peer culture.

The Cameos – a Summary   Once again, it is important to stress that most of the cameos were intended to reflect 'successful' engagements in the arts (rather than being representative of the general patterns of young people's participation in the arts). However, they do give rise to some salient issues relating to the problem of sustained involvement in the arts. Key issues associated with an on-going arts involvement which emerged from the cameos included:

- the pervasive influence of peer culture – particularly the stereotyping of male involvement. However, some older interviewees (post-school) could pinpoint their peers as a positive influence;

- the importance of family, home and cultural background in developing an overt identification with the arts, or, at least, ensuring support and encouragement to the young person's arts involvement;

- the significance of 'others' – in effect, offering surrogate support not evident from family. A sense of a young people's arts engagement receiving personalised attention and support from a teacher, youth worker, friend and so on;

- the fundamental need for support and opportunities in arts engagement to be sustained;

- the prevalence of the view that art offers a unique feeling of excitement and exhilaration, '*the buzz*', and/or a sense of self-esteem which it is worth experiencing an on-going basis;

- the awareness of the concept of 'arts' as a forum for creativity; and, finally,

- evidence of the capacity to learn about, and invest in developing arts skills, and a commitment to the rigours and discipline of an art form.

13. Summary

This chapter seeks to summarise and extrapolate the key findings from the research, and includes sections on young people's main leisure interests, their definitions of the arts, arts as experienced at school, post-school involvement and youth clubs. It also summarises findings on effects, influences and needs. It concludes with summaries of the qualitative data analysis, the typology and the arts biographies.

Background of the Research

It has been stressed throughout the report that the research design went to considerable lengths to sketch and gauge the extent of arts involvement against a wider backdrop of young people's leisure pursuits and day-time commitments.

On a macro level, the research opted for an extensive interview programme undertaken by a team of trained researchers who were familiar with the locale and local communities in which they interviewed, in order to minimise any barriers associated with literacy and culture that a written questionnaire might encounter.

On a micro level, the standard interview schedule, used with all 704 interviewees, was constructed to ensure a multiple approach about the degree of involvement in the arts, using open and closed questions. The first open question aimed to provide an overview of young people's main leisure-time activities and interests. Asked prior to mentioning the arts, the question afforded a genuine indication of those activities uppermost in the young people's minds, instead of predicating thinking towards artistic, creative, or imaginative pursuits. Later questions sought to gauge involvement by asking closed and scaled questions on some 17 arts activities. These initial, volunteered rather than prompted, findings were likely to show a lower participation rate than in subsequent questions, but the placing of arts in the context of a wide range of activities engaged in by young people was seen to provide vital information for planners and policy-makers.

In these ways, the research collected three main measures of young people's current involvement in the arts:

(i)   an open-ended item on their main leisure interests and activities;

(ii)   a similar open-ended item on leisure-time and day-time activities they would describe as creative or imaginative; and

(iii)   a closed item on young people's degree of leisure-time and day-time participation in 17 specified art forms.

The major findings elicited through each of these items are summarised below.

(i) Open-ended item on main leisure interests

◆ 'Media-arts: audience' activities, principally watching television and videos, reading and going to the cinema, emerged as the category with the highest proportion (57 per cent) of respondents mentioning at least one activity within it.

◆ This was closely followed by sport, with 55 per cent of the sample mentioning at least one sporting activity - football, swimming, cycling and tennis/squash were the most popular.

◆ Less than a quarter (23 per cent) mentioned at least one 'arts: participation' activity as a main leisure interest: painting and drawing, and playing a musical instrument were the two most frequently mentioned activities.

A stark contrast is thus evident between leisure-time sports (where less than half of the sample were non-participants) and leisure-time arts (where over three-quarters did not refer to a single participating arts activity). In this way, it is possible to conclude that arts participation is, in effect, a minority undertaking as a leisure pursuit.

(ii) Open-ended item on imaginative or creative activities

On the issue of young people's perceptions as to whether they were engaged in imaginative or creative activities during the day and in their leisure time, it was found that:

◆ 61 per cent felt they were so engaged during the day, while 49 per cent responded in the affirmative for their leisure activity. Less than a third (30 per cent) felt they were involved in imaginative and creative activity in both spheres of their lives. Almost a quarter of the sample (23 per cent) said they were not ever thus engaged.

◆ Less than half (48 per cent) of the young people taking music as an option in Years 10-11 at secondary school saw this subject as creative or imaginative, and English was deemed so by 27 per cent . In contrast, 70 per cent of those taking (visual) art in Years 10-11 felt that this subject was creative or imaginative. Music-making or playing a musical instrument; painting and drawing; and writing were the most popular creative or imaginative 'arts: participation' leisure pursuits and were all thought to be more creative or imaginative in leisure time rather than in school activities.

◆ Almost a third (32 per cent) of the interviewees indicated that they did an 'arts: participation' leisure activity which they deemed creative or imaginative (in comparison with the 23 per cent who said such activities were their main leisure interests from (i) above).

♦ While a small minority of young people - with a slight bias to those with working class backgrounds - perceived imaginative and creative potential in everyday and sporting activities (mainly cooking but also football and aerobics), the majority in all three social class groups – especially Social Class I and II – saw 'arts: participation' pursuits as their main creative or imaginative outlet.

Overall, these findings suggest that young people still appear to be quite traditional in their perception of activities which they count as imaginative and creative – (i.e. activities in the category arts: participation rated highest). However, it is important to add that this is not necessarily to be equated with the actual amount of creativity in young people's leisure pursuits and work/school activities. There is a distinct possibility that young people misrecognise their own creativity.

(iii)   Closed item for 17 selected art forms

♦ For leisure time, the top five most frequently mentioned activities (i.e. those recording the highest percentages of 'a great deal' and 'some' degrees of participation) were dance (36 per cent), drawing/sketching (36 per cent), photography (32 per cent), music-making (23 per cent) and writing (23 per cent). Some of these activities, however, were often construed in 'recreational' rather than 'artistic' terms: e.g. social disco dancing, doodling and taking holiday snaps.

♦ At school, the five most cited activities (with the same degrees of participation) were writing (82 per cent), drawing (66 per cent), painting (49 per cent), drama (41 per cent) and computer graphics (34 per cent). Each of these art forms ranked a much higher participation rate in school time than as a leisure pursuit. In contrast, participation in music was only marginally higher in school than in leisure time. Levels of participation in art forms such as dance and photography were significantly lower in day-time activities compared with leisure-time pursuits.

♦ With respect to 'consumption' of the arts, English was, by considerable margins, the subject most likely to be mentioned by school students as the forum for engaging in the arts in an 'audience' or consumer role – though less so by ethnic minority respondents. In leisure time, the main forms of 'consumed' art were reading literature, listening to music and going to the cinema.

Put together, a strong emphasis on experiencing literary arts in school, both as participants and consumer is very evident, while music shows a particular significance in leisure-time.

Young People's Definitions of 'The Arts'

The schedule explored young people's understanding and interpretation of the term 'the arts' because it was felt that how young people define and construct the arts may have an important bearing on their level of involvement in them. The main findings are highlighted below.

♦ About one in eight interviewees (13 per cent) could give no meaning to the term, 'the arts'.

♦ One in three (33 per cent) had a single perspective view of the arts (i.e. mentioned only one art form) and 22 per cent of the total sample equated the 'arts' with only visual 'art'.

♦ Just over one in five (22 per cent) gave a double or dual perspective definition of the arts (nearly half of these mentioning performance arts e.g. dance/drama and visual arts). Additionally, 22 per cent had a multi-perspective view (i.e. their definition included at least three different art forms).

♦ Almost half (46 per cent) of those at school were unable to give an answer, or equated 'the arts' with visual 'art'.

It was found that appreciating the breadth of activities covered by the term 'arts' was part of a cluster of attitudes which denoted a positive predisposition towards them. It was evident that young people from higher social classes and those who had high educational attainment were more likely to offer a multiple perspective, noting that the arts involved creativity and expression. Equally, those older, in post-16 education, and females were likely to view the arts from a broad perspective and include creativity and expression in their definitions.

Beyond that, young people were asked how important the various traditional or 'high' art forms were to them, and also for their views on 'low' or alternative art forms. The main findings are summarised below.

♦ One in three (33 per cent) considered the 'high' arts not at all important; one in five (20 per cent) felt these arts were very important; while 47 per cent thought they were quite or sometimes important.

♦ The importance of the 'high' arts was acknowledged most often by those in full-time post-16 education. Registering the arts as personally significant generally increased with age, class and high educational attainment.

♦ While 58 per cent approved of the 'alternative' arts, 18 per cent approved for others and 24 per cent either disapproved or had personal reservations about them.

♦ Approval of the or 'alternative' arts was marginally most likely from those in post-16 education, in training schemes, over-21, in Social Class I and II and with more than four GCSEs.

The statistical evidence would seem to suggest that believing traditional arts are important and approving highly of alternative arts went hand in hand. The less important that arts were considered to be by respondents, the narrower their perspective of what the arts might entail. Those with a broader perspective were more likely to think highly of alternative arts; those disapproving of alternative arts were most likely not to know the meaning of the term 'the arts'.

Significantly, very few young people mentioned aesthetics or beauty in their definitions of arts. Arts were seen to offer a means of coming to terms with yourself, developing and discovering ideas and feelings, communication, imagination and entertainment. The opportunity for expression was seen as an especially important feature of, and rationale for, alternative arts.

Main Variables in Arts Participation Rates

All statistical data were investigated (or cross-tabulated) by key independent and demographic variables (e.g. current status, gender, class, age, ethnicity, educational attainment and urban or rural residency). The main variations in leisure participation (and particularly arts participation) are outlined below.

♦ **Leisure activity in rural and urban locations** It was felt that proximity and accessibility of facilities were not overriding factors in explaining arts participation. Generally, the greater availability of amenities did not appear to attract a higher share of young people in urban locales. However, rural young people had sport as most popular, while those from urban locations mentioned 'media-arts: audience' activities most.

♦ **Leisure activity by gender** While 27 per cent of females mentioned at least one 'arts: participation' activity, only 19 per cent of male respondents did so. 'Media-arts: audience' was the leading leisure category for females (64 per cent mentioned at least one), while sport was the highest ranking leisure activity for males (63 per cent mentioned at least one).

♦ **Leisure activity by social class** Participation in the arts was shown to be less than one in four (23 per cent) for the total sample, but this increased to one in three (34 per cent) for young people in Social Class I and II. (By way of example, musical instrument playing varied from 15 per cent in Social Class I and II to 1 per cent in Social Class IV and V). Similarly, interviewees from professional backgrounds were also more likely to refer to such 'media-arts: audience' activities as reading, cinema, listening to music and going to the theatre as leisure interests.

◆ **Leisure activity by ethnicity** It was found that white Europeans had a greater involvement in 'arts: participation': one in four (24 per cent) mentioned at least one activity, as opposed to about one in eight (13 per cent) of ethnic minority respondents. Ethnic minorities showed more involvement with 'media-arts: audience' activities, especially those from Asian communities.

◆ **Leisure activity by age** The rate of arts participation was particularly low for 17-20 year olds. Involvement in 'media-arts: audience' activities increased steadily through the three age bands, except for watching television and videos which showed a decline.

◆ **Leisure activity by current status** Young people in post-16 full-time education ranked highest in arts participation (34 per cent mentioning at least one activity), followed by students in schools (29 per cent). The lowest ranking was from trainees who recorded an approximate one in eight (13 per cent) arts involvement.

◆ **Leisure activity by educational attainment** It was particularly noticeable that painting/drawing and playing a musical instrument as leisure arts activities ranked highly with interviewees who had four or more GCSEs.

Put together, these findings suggest an inexorable trend that females and young people of higher social class and high educational attainment are more likely to be arts participants.

Arts and School

Interviewees were asked to describe and comment on their primary and secondary school arts experiences. The key findings relating to the primary phase of schooling are outlined below.

◆ One quarter (27 per cent) of the sample were negative about their primary school arts opportunities, but almost three quarters (73 per cent) were able to recall arts activities which they enjoyed or valued at primary school.

◆ The most likely candidates for non-enjoyment of the arts at primary school were males from partly/unskilled backgrounds (over a third responded in this way). In comparison, only one in six females from Social Class I and II registered negative responses to primary school arts.

◆ The highest educational achievers indicated the most positive recall of primary school arts.

◆ According to the recollections of this sample, acting in plays and drama were the most popular primary arts activities, followed by painting and drawing. Writing was rarely associated with the arts.

- On the issue of what young people felt they had learnt from primary arts, non-specific 'enjoyment' ranked the highest response, while less than one in ten saw primary school arts as producing any significant skill acquisition. One in a hundred felt it had been an occasion for realising talent.

- Statistics showed a tendency for females to more readily discern that their primary school arts were an opportunity to acquire social skills. Young people from professional backgrounds were more likely to recall primary school arts as enjoyable. (One in four as opposed to one in six from Social Classes III, IV and V.)

In response to identical questions on secondary school arts, the following trends emerged.

- A quarter (25 per cent) of interviewees had negative recall of their secondary school arts experiences (i.e. did not feel they had particularly enjoyed or valued any aspect of it); three-quarters had a positive recall.

- Negative recall was more evident among ethnic minorities, the over-21s, males, and interviewees from Social Class IV and V. Respondents with low educational attainment more consistently registered negative recall.

- Drama again was most often recalled as particularly enjoyable. Music increased its ranking compared to primary school and males' enjoyment of the music curriculum in secondary school was markedly higher than that in primary school.

- Specifically on the perceived learning outcomes of secondary school arts, most often mentioned again was non-specific enjoyment or excitement. Relative to the frequencies for the primary sector, there was a higher percentage of respondents who suggested that the delivery of specific arts skills, knowledge and understanding was also evident.

- More females than males nominated 'a sense of achievement', 'overcoming shyness' and 'acquiring arts techniques' as the major effects of secondary school arts involvement. The outcome 'how to make things' was the only category where boys outnumbered girls. Again, it suggests females were more likely to discern the arts as opportunities to acquire artistic and social skills.

- 'Sense of achievement' and 'self-expression' (i.e. those areas relating to personal development) were cited more by the over-21s; equally, Social Class I and II interviewees were more likely to offer social and personal development advantages.

- Just over half (55 per cent) of the sample affirmed they continued with their study of at least one arts subject as a separate or specialised discipline in Years 10 and 11.

♦ Specialism most usually meant taking only one arts subject: only 12 per cent of respondents studied two or more arts subjects. Females were more likely to study one or more arts subjects.

♦ An equivalent proportion of males and females took music but art and dance were studied by a higher percentage of females. None of the five arts subjects were studied by a higher proportion of males than females.

These findings continue to pinpoint the greater likelihood of positive attitudes to school arts emerging from females; and young people from higher social classes. Positive recall of the benefits of school arts was also more likely from Social Class I and II respondents.

Post-school Involvement

Questions were put to all those who had left school on whether their arts involvement had decreased, increased or stayed the same after the termination of their school career. Approximately one-third of the sample responded in each of these three categories of post-school involvement in the arts. Other main findings included the following.

♦ With respect to location of residency, 23 per cent of rural respondents and 36 per cent of urban respondents indicated that their involvement had increased. This was felt to be due to increased interest in and consumption of 'media-arts: audience' activities in urban areas.

♦ The 17-20 age group had notably lower percentages of 'gone up' responses, and slightly higher than average 'gone down' and 'stayed the same'. The increased involvement by 21-24 year olds was seen as a significant finding, confirming the upturn of interest in the arts by this older age group.

♦ Some 43 per cent of Social Class I and II nominated an increase in arts participation since leaving school, compared to 21 per cent of those in Social Class IV and V. Equally, only 26 per cent of young people from the professional class suggested their arts involvement had decreased after their school career, compared to 36 per cent of Social Class IV and V.

Overall, the results – particularly the significant age-related variations – are consistent with the hypothesis that in the immediate post-school years many young people, especially those who do not continue in full-time education, experience a decline in their level of arts participation. For some, this is followed by an increase in their late teens and early twenties.

Youth Clubs

In view of the contribution that the youth clubs movement has made to the advocation of youth arts, and the potential of the youth service for widening young people's access to the arts, it was considered important for the research to collect evidence on respondents' levels of participation in youth clubs, particularly in the arts domain. The relevant key findings are summarised below.

◆ The constituency of young people currently attending youth clubs (i.e. at least once within the year prior to the interview) was found to be approximately one-third of the 14-24 sample and this group seemed heavily biased towards school-aged young people. Some 93 per cent of previous attenders had ceased to attend a youth club before the age of 17.

◆ Social class was found to have a definite and consistent association with current attendance at youth clubs. Whereas 15 per cent of young people from Social Class I and II were in the habit of going to youth clubs at least once a week, 25 per cent and 47 per cent of skilled and partly/unskilled respondents respectively were doing so.

◆ Disaggregation by educational attainment also suggests that youth clubs have the capacity to attract young people of low academic achievement.

◆ The figures on both present and past attendance patterns at youth clubs indicate a male bias. Sporting activities were the most prevalent activities referred to at youth clubs – perhaps not surprisingly given the finding on male bias.

◆ Only 11 per cent of respondents' main activities undertaken at youth clubs could be categorised as arts participation.

◆ Asked if their clubs provided opportunities in the arts, half (53 per cent) of those who felt able to reply (N = 478) felt their youth club offered arts experiences.

◆ The vast majority of young people who had experienced arts at youth clubs were positive about them, citing social benefits, autonomy and enhanced access to materials and equipment among the distinctive features of engaging in youth club arts. However, overall the evidence suggested that, for most young people, involvement in the arts at youth clubs tended to be through sporadic 'one-off' experiences, with little sustained engagement.

The clientele of youth clubs (and therefore youth club arts) is clearly a powerful counterbalance to the usual constituency of arts participants. The low numbers taking up arts participation opportunities in youth clubs may need to be reconsidered, especially as youth club arts were usually referred to very positively.

Influences, Effects and Opportunities

The report also relayed findings on young people's accounts of salient factors influencing their arts participation and appreciation (and conversely any causes of 'aversion'). Views on the effects of their involvement in the arts to date were also reported. The study then provided evidence of young people's perspectives on which art forms were felt to be a regretted omission in their arts education and the kinds of arts activities which might be welcomed in the future. Finally, views on the difficulties constraining this future arts involvement and types of support required were described.

♦ One-third of the total sample felt they could not nominate any direct positive influence upon their appreciation or participation in the arts.

♦ Most frequently mentioned influences were people with whom the respondents had first-hand and on-going contact, particularly family, secondary arts teachers and friends.

♦ Parents – especially mothers – were often evident as nominated influences by females, Social Class I and II respondents, the younger age bands and high achievers.

♦ Secondary arts teachers, artistic role models and youth workers were relatively high nominations for males, lower social classes and younger age bands.

♦ The over-21s most often mentioned friends and peers as significant influences.

♦ Drama participation and theatre consumption ranked highest as significant 'arts-event' experiences in 'turning' young people on to the arts.

In this way, arts as a contagious phenomenon became evident, with a strong tendency for involvement to be a family inheritance.

When young people were asked to account for any factors which had 'turned them off' the arts, it was found that:

♦ over half (56 per cent) of the total sample did not experience any such arts aversion, and Social Class I and II respondents were more likely to accept the notion of something or someone turning them off the arts;

♦ friends (mentioned more by males) and secondary arts teachers (nominated most by Social Class I and II respondents) ranked highest as sources of arts turn-off, while family influences were rarely mentioned; and

♦ actual experiences of arts encounters or consumption were very rarely viewed as specific demotivating encounters.

In this way, being dramatically 'turned off' the arts is not a recognisable phenomenon for many young people, and certainly rarely perceived to be caused by actual encounters with arts. Peer influence and inappropriate teaching appear to be more significant.

On the effects of arts involvement, some notable results were:

◆ almost two-thirds (64 per cent) of the total sample affirmed that arts had had effects on them in some way, citing such aspects as increase in self-confidence, sociability, arts skill acquisition, motivation and general intellectual enhancement;

◆ overall, some four-fifths (83 per cent) of Social Class I and II acknowledged arts involvement had effects on them, but only three-fifths (59 per cent) of those from other social classes acknowledged this.

Thus, in almost all categories of effects of arts involvement, the predictable pattern again emerged: respondents who were female, older, from the highest social class and most successful in educational attainment recorded the highest percentages. The high level of responses affirming that the arts provide personal and social developments is perhaps particularly worth noting.

Interesting findings also emerged in connection with interviewees' perceptions of missed and future opportunities in the arts.

◆ Two-thirds (66 per cent) of the total sample said they would have welcomed more arts involvement in their past. Drama was the highest nomination, followed by opportunities to learn to play a musical instrument, paint or draw. Males were more likely to mention visual art forms, painting, drawing, design, sculpture and modelling; females more of ten mentioned such expressive arts as drama and dance.

◆ Two-thirds (66 per cent) of the total sample would also welcome arts involvement in the future, with the over-21s, Social Class I and II and high educational achievers having higher percentages of references to opportunities for art forms and activities that they would appreciate.

◆ Drawing and painting, drama, music and design with computer graphics were the top four rankings of types of art forms which would be welcomed.

Overall, these findings may suggest fairly traditional art forms and predictable gender differences. The prominence of drama as an art form that would have been welcomed by young people in their earlier school and leisure pursuits is noteworthy.

◆ Three distinct categories of perceived obstacles to participation in future activities emerged:

   – constraints of competing commitments or alternative interests;

   – deficit of funds, resources, opportunities or facilities for arts involvement; and

   – personal deficiency in attitude or aptitude.

♦ Alternative interests or competing commitments were consistently mentioned more by female, urban, Social Class I and II and high achieving respondents.

♦ The three highest ranked responses to the question of type of support wanted by young people to enable them to develop their artistic endeavours were tuition, venues (e.g. a place to practice etc.) and financial resources.

Many of these responses appeared to suggest a considerable advocation of the need for continued supervision and support, whether formal or informal. This may have significant youth arts funding and policy implications.

The Typology

A classification of attitudes towards the arts is attempted, citing both positive and negative attitudes (see Chapter 11). This was based on qualitative analysis of the sample's verbatim responses. The accompanying textual commentary tentatively offers a ranking of the most significant attitudes accompanying sustained commitment. Arts as self-expression, providing 'a buzz', or even a 'sense of identity' rate particularly highly.

The Cameos – A Summary

The report also set out a number of individual case-biographies or cameos of 'arts careers'. Key factors associated with an on-going 'successful' arts involvement which emerged from the cameos included:

♦ the importance of family, home and cultural background for facilitating an overt identification with the arts or, at least, ensuring support and encouragement to the young person's self-motivated arts involvement;

♦ the significance of 'others' – in effect, offering surrogate support not evident from family (e.g. a sense of a young people's arts engagement receiving personalised attention and support from a teacher, youth worker, friends and so on);

♦ the need for support and opportunities in arts engagement to be sustained;

♦ the prevalence of the view that the arts offer a unique feeling of excitement and exhilaration, '*the buzz*', and/or a sense of self-esteem which it is worth experiencing on an on-going basis;

♦ the awareness of the concept of 'the arts' as a forum for creativity;

♦ evidence of the capacity to learn about and invest in developing arts skills; and

♦ a commitment to the rigours and discipline of an art form.

These factors illustrate and corroborate the attitudes nominated in the typology.

Final Comment

Returning to the initial questions raised in Chapter 1 concerning the potential of the arts to engage and enrich the lives of young people, it has to be conceded that many of the project's findings might appear to make grim and disappointing reading. In terms of 'making' and 'doing' roles, the level of youth participation in the arts as a leisure activity (as perceived by the young people themselves) was limited, at least in comparison to involvement in sport. A sense of active participation in the arts was particularly low for certain groups: most notably, members of the ethnic minorities; males; 17-20 year olds; and those in training or employment. The constituencies which demonstrated higher levels of involvement included: young people from professional backgrounds; females; and students in further or higher education. Moreover, interpreting 'the arts' as more general and everyday 'imaginative or creative' activities did not greatly enlarge the sample's perception of being involved in artistic endavour. In terms of 'receiving' and 'perceiving' roles, most art forms received their highest support from middle class respondents. The exceptions were TV, videos and recorded pop music which, however, were often perceived to be unrelated to engagement in the arts. A wide range of negative attitudes were collected from a substantial sub-sample, who treated the arts with indifference and, sometimes, hostility. Approaching half of the sample were either unable to say what 'the arts' meant for them or equated it with a single art form, principally visual art. Arts experiences in primary and secondary schools though generally deemed enjoyable, often attracted some serious criticisms. The frequent predilection and high demand for more drama seemed to exceed the status given to this subject in the National Curriculum and the apparent popularity of music in young people's culture was not reflected in the number of respondents studying the subject or perceiving it to be an opportunity for imaginative and creative expression at school. Furthermore, only one in ten of respondents' main activities undertaken at youth clubs could be classified as arts-orientated.

Echoing one interviewee's remarks about the large amount of '*wasted talent*', the results suggest that unless young people are fortunate enough to inherit 'cultural capital' and/or experience the supportive and broadening influence of further and higher education, avenues through which young people can be encouraged to engage with the arts outside of formal education in a sustained way are somewhat inadequate.

Although these results are worrying and deserve the attention of arts educators and policy-makers, the overall picture emerging from the research is not as bleak as the findings summarised in the previous paragraphs suggest. The study also produced evidence of experiences and trends which offer grounds for optimism. By way of illustration, it was found that the sustained intervention of certain teachers, artists and youth workers were perceived to be highly instrumental in inspiring many respondents to participate in the arts. The illuminating experiences of some individuals clearly demonstrated the potential of arts facilitators to stimulate or re-awaken an enthusiasm for the arts – even among the most reluctant or hardened sceptics. Several analyses revealed an upturn of interest in the arts among the 21-24 year old group, not all of which was due to the horizon-widening effect of further and higher education. The research also garnered a wide and rich variety of positive attitudes and motivations towards the arts. The numerous accounts of the effects and benefits of arts participation were especially striking; with two-thirds of the total sample affirming arts had had an effect on them in some way. Particularly impressive were the testaments to the personal and social benefits of arts involvement, as well as the view that the arts were a humanising and civilising force. Finally, it can only be seen as encouraging that two-thirds of those interviewed wanted to have more involvement in the arts in the future.

14. Some Policy Implications

This short chapter offers a number of policy implications which have arisen directly from the study's findings and analysis. These concern arts in the school curriculum, some implications for arts provision in the new climate of school funding, funding for youth arts and those agencies and activities offering alternative provision within the field of youth arts. The chapter concludes by considering attitude formation in the arts. This has emerged as a particularly significant issue and one relevant to all agencies and providers in the arts.

It is hoped that a study of this length and substance will raise many issues for funders, policy-makers and practitioners within the field of youth arts, though it must again be stressed that the current report was not intended to offer specific recommendations. It is likely that the statistical evidence or accompanying commentary have highlighted certain issues and implications which have particular resonance for those with expertise and experience in the area, but which the researchers have not fully expanded. Such omissions are inevitable and desirable: the prime purpose of the research was to illuminate demographic trends and attitudes in order to inform policy rather than in any way focus on or appraise current praxis and provision within youth arts. Notwithstanding this caveat, there follows a set of 'data-driven' issues, presented as an interim inventory of policy implications which arose during the analysis and writing. These issues are grouped under the five policy-oriented themes outlined in Chapter 1.

1. ARTS IN THE SCHOOL CURRICULUM

♦ The reported young people's views would appear to offer considerable corroboration of the paucity of (pre-NC) arts education especially in the primary years, with an absence of rigour and progression in skill acquisition. This has in-service training implications, as well as raising issues of teacher deployment (specialist or generalist arts teaching).

♦ The secondary arts curriculum and its delivery was selected as a cause of arts aversion (or turn-off) by many young people. This may signal the issue of whether there was always sufficient differentiation in the arts curriculum to support and encourage those who perceive themselves as lacking arts ability. Equally, the report highlighted the idea of negotiation of arts curriculum activities.

♦ Lack of arts ability was often cited as a reason for non-involvement and negative attitudes. This suggests that attitude formation was predominantly through participatory activities. To counteract this, establishing positive attitudes to arts through consumption and appreciation may need further emphasis. Evidence of the sample's lack of association of arts with aesthetic enjoyment and discrimination may also point to a need to focus more on educating young people's 'receiving' faculties, (or what has been termed 'perceiving' and 'feeling' systems).

♦ Evidence of the prevalence of 'media-arts: audience' activities in the leisure life of young people would suggest the appropriateness and relevance of media education as a learning pursuit. The possible erosion of media education in the restructuring of the curriculum - and curriculum support services (see later) - may be a particular cause for concern.

2. DISCRETE OR INTEGRATED ARTS?

♦ A major finding of the research was the limited view of the term the 'arts', held by many young people, and the frequent correlation of single perspectives (e.g. the arts means or equals only 'visual art') with low levels of interest and non-positive attitudes. This may suggest that the full canon of art forms, and the affinities between the arts require greater emphasis for young people.

♦ Defining and describing arts participation as an exciting opportunity for self-expression through the act of imaginative creating was common to a large number of the committed arts enthusiasts interviewed. Opportunities for those less predisposed to arts engagement to be made aware of the possibility of this unique 'affective' experience seems an important aspect of arts education. This implies a need for developing a common vocabulary which describes creativity and creative outcomes, and encouraging its use with young people in their school arts education.

3. SUPPORT FOR ARTS PROVISION IN SCHOOLS

♦ The decline of a power-base for arts education in schools in the light of the erosion of LEA infrastructures (e.g. the demise of arts advisory roles and the decline of peripatetic services) may be a cause for concern given the findings that the most likely candidates for arts involvement were consistently among the most privileged in terms of social class. The possibility of equal provision and access to arts may indeed decrease as limited arts resources are increasingly associated with privatised market forces and philosophies. Equally, disseminating the good practice and opportunities available to schools in this new climate may also be a crucial issue.

♦ In the light of the point above, the likely unevenness of arts provision for young people may be a particular concern given the findings on young people's views on the benefits of arts involvement. Testaments to the arts as a powerful 'civilising' force are very evident: such benefits deserve careful perusal – perhaps not least by politicians as much as policy-makers or arts providers and educators.

4. ALTERNATIVE PERSPECTIVES ON THE 'ARTS' AND YOUNG PEOPLE

♦ There has been useful debate about the very meaning and substance of young people's artistic and cultural activities in the light of the work of Willis (1990). Quite rightly, it has enormous implications for both what activities can and should be funded, as well as how that funding is deployed to young people. It has to be said that Willis's cogent argument for the existence of a prolific and rich creative life inherent in youth culture does not emerge in most of the accounts of this sample of young people. The evidence from the research would suggest that many young people recognised their need for additional skill acquisition in the arts - through workshops, tuition etc., and indeed would welcome such support and structure. In doing so, it could be argued that they sensed how much creativity can be empowered and enriched by aptitude in the arts, both high and low, rather than just everyday, informal cultural activities.

♦ If skill acquisition re-enters the funding frame, it may also shift the policy issue to one which focuses on the type of support and opportunities that could be available and would be acceptable to young people. Given evidence of the constraints upon the arts curriculum in school and the unevenness of its success, it may be a particular challenge to develop, deliver and disseminate alternative pedagogues of arts which fit with young people's leisure life and local communities.

5. YOUTH ARTS ISSUES

♦ The erosion of LEA infrastructures particularly heightens the debate about other providers and funding sources within the field of youth arts. It may be important to stress that whatever type of alternative support is devised (such as artists in residence; community projects etc.), the evidence from the research suggests a key factor in successful involvement is sustained and on-going support and engagement. One-off events and experiences (without follow-up) may thus be rarely effective in developing self-sustained enthusiasm, and as such, their cost-effectiveness in terms of long-term outcomes and benefits must be questioned.

♦ Finally, all agencies may wish to consider the major issue of attitude formation. The research reveals a considerable amount of stereotypical – and indeed negative – thinking among young people about the arts and those who engage in it. This then in itself is perhaps a clear signal of the need to focus on equal opportunities and consciousness raising. Beyond that, the final challenge will be to consider an agency's role in the formation of positive attitudes, particularly to bring about the kinds of motivation most closely associated with sustained involvement.

Final Comment

This study has intended to offer demographic trends and attitudes in order to inform policy and practice in youth arts provision. Policy implications are suggested, only insofar as they arise from the data and analysis.

Five more over-arching issues have been suggested as useful concluding comments.

(a) Evidence from the cameos and from the quantitative data on influences firmly indicates that intervention can make a difference in young people's arts involvement. Encounters with significant others - on a sustained and/or individual basis particularly - can change attitudes and commitment to the arts.

(b) There is strong evidence to suggest that social class, gender and educational attainment remain closely linked to arts involvement and that, to those demographically favoured young people, arts opportunities appear to increase.

(c) One in four young people nominate an actual participation in arts. Whether this percentage is sufficient and acceptable may need careful consideration, especially when over half of the sample affirmed sports participation.

(d) Future arts opportunities would be welcomed by two-thirds of the sample, particularly in the form of tuition, workshops for skill acquisition, and direct participation. This raises a major challenge to policy-makers, funders and providers in the area of youth arts.

(e) From those young people who do show arts commitment, there is ample evidence to suggest there are very positive outcomes accruing from such involvement. Personal and social development opportunities are acknowledged: arts can be recognised as a powerful civilising aspect in their culture, adding quality to their daily lives.

While the study produced evidence that negative attitudes can constitute substantial impediments to young people's participation in the arts, it also provided many persuasive accounts of the benefits and effects which can be derived from sustained engagement in the arts (amply demonstrated by those young people displaying positive attitudes, or arts motivations). These effects were not only advantageous to the individuals involved, but they also offered enormous social gains to the community as a whole. Underlining the importance of both personal and social benefits, as well as the policies to widen youth participation in the arts, it seems fitting to conclude with an inspiring contribution from one of the respondents interviewed in the study.

The remarks were made by a young man in his early 20s, who had experienced considerable disaffection and alienation in his earlier teens, including problems with drugs. He now felt very strongly that he had 'found his identity' through the arts. In this way, he represents the late-arrival to arts commitment which was evident in the report's statistical evidence and also the cameos.

In particular, it seems appropriate to set the quotation against John Major's statements of his government's commitment 'to wage a battle against yob-culture' which were acknowledged in the introductory chapter of the report. This final comment by a young person may illustrate that the strategies to accompany the combative rhetoric of 'battle waging' could include taking account of the positive effects of arts which have been itemised in the report. Opening up arts opportunities to young people may thus be a valuable contribution to resolving disaffection among our young people.

> *... it's just that I feel as though ... because* [the arts are] *the most valuable thing in my life, I feel as though ... like in a way, we are, all of us ... are artists ... that's the first thing we did ... like in the caves and all that ... to draw what's around you and express what it is to be alive, and the more people that ... the larger it is, and the more people that do it, the more civilised we'll be, and these are the highest things in life ... that's it.*

References

ABBS, P. (1988). *Living Powers: The Arts in Education.* London: The Falmer Press.

ALEXANDER, R. (1991). *Primary Education in Leeds.* Leeds: University of Leeds.

ALLIED DUNBAR (1992). *National Fitness Survey: a Report on Activity Patterns and Fitness Levels.* London: The Sports Council and The Health Education Authority.

BEST, D. (1991). 'Art of the matter', *The Times Educational Supplement,* 8 March.

BYRNE, D. (1993). 'Dangerous places? A response', *North East Labour History Bulletin,* **27,** 75-81.

CALOUSTE GULBENKIAN FOUNDATION (1982; 2nd edition 1989). *The Arts in Schools: Principles, Practice and Provision.* London: Calouste Gulbenkian Foundation.

CHAMBERLAIN, D. (1991). *Intention to Reality: Developing Youth Arts Policy.* Leicester: Youth Clubs UK.

COOPERS and LYBRAND and MORI (1994). *Review of Instrumental Music Services.* London: Incorporated Society of Musicians.

CROALL, J. (1991). 'All together now?', *The Times Educational Supplement,* 11 January.

DEARING, R. (1994). *The National Curriculum and its Assessment, Final Report.* London: School Curriculum and Assessment Authority.

FELDBERG, R. (1991). *Youth Arts: Discussion Document.* London: Arts Council of Great Britain.

GARCIA, C and BECKET, P. (1993). *The GAP Pack.* London: Youth Clubs UK.

GARDNER, H. (1973). *The Arts and Human Development.* New York: John Wiley.

GREAT BRITAIN. DEPARTMENT OF EDUCATION AND SCIENCE (1978). *Primary Education in England.* London: HMSO.

GREAT BRITAIN. OFFICE OF POPULATION CENSUSES AND SURVEYS (1990). *Standard Occupational Classification, Volume 2.* London: HMSO.

GREAT BRITAIN: OFFICE OF POPULATION CENSUSES AND SURVEYS (1994). *General Household Survey 1992 - an Interdepartmental Survey carried out by OPCS between April 1992 and March 1993.* London: HMSO.

HARGREAVES, D. H. (1983). 'Dr. Brunel and Mr. Dunning: reflections on aesthetic knowing'. In ROSS, M. (Ed): *The Arts: a Way of Knowing.* Oxford: Pergamon Press.

HARGREAVES, D. J. (1989). *Children and the Arts.* Milton Keynes: Open University Press.

HARRIS RESEARCH CENTRE (1993). *Black and Asian Attitudes to the Arts in Birmingham.* London: The Arts Council of Great Britain.

HENDRY, L. B., SHUCHSMITH, J. and LOVE, J. G. (1989). *Young People's Leisure and Lifestyles: Summary Report of Phase I, 1985-1989.* Edinburgh: The Scottish Sports Council.

McGAW, S. (1987). 'Have an art? A personal account of the role of the performing arts in the school curriculum', *NUT Educational Review,* **1**, 2, 53-5.

NATIONAL COMMISSION ON EDUCATION (1993). *Learning to Succeed: a Radical Look at Education Today and a Strategy for the Future.* London: Heinemann.

NATIONAL CURRICULUM COUNCIL (1990). *The Arts 5-16: a Curriculum Framework.* Harlow: Oliver and Boyd.

RANDELL, N. and MYHILL, S. (1989). *Kaleidoscope - Arts Work That Works.* Leicester: Youth Clubs UK.

ROBINSON, K. (1991a). 'One for all and all for one', *The Times Educational Supplement,* 12 April.

ROBINSON, K. (1991b). 'Stop the arts breaker', *The Times Educational Supplement,* 29 November.

ROGERS, R. (1993a). *Looking over the Edge: the Survey; Local Education Authority Advisory and Inspection Services.* London: Arts Council of Great Britain.

ROGERS, R. (1993b). *Looking over the Edge: the Debate; Advisory Structures for the Arts in Education.* London: Arts Council of Great Britain.

ROWLEY, S. (1992). *The Training of Young Athletes Study (TOYA): Project Description.* London: The Sports Council.

RUST, J. and ALLEN, V. (1992). *Arts and Youth.* Dewsbury: Yorkshire and Humberside Arts.

SELLORS, B. and HULL, S. (1989). 'Arts in schools?', *Support for Learning*, **4**, 1, February, 32-4.

SERAFINE, M. L. (1979). 'Aesthetic creativity: thoughts on children's activities', *Journal of Creative Behaviour*, **13**, 257-62.

SHARP, C. (1991). *When Every Note Counts: The Schools' Instrumental Music Service in the 1990s*. Slough: National Foundation for Educational Research.

SPORTS COUNCIL (1994). *Trends in Sports Participation*. London: The Sports Council.

STEERS, J. (1990). 'The future of the arts in schools'. Paper given at the Bretton Hall Seminar, October.

STUBBS, K. (1990). 'Music in a balanced arts curriculum', *Brit. Journal of Music Education*, **7**, 3, 118-29.

SWANWICK, K. (1988). 'The National Curriculum implications for the arts', *Curriculum*. **9**, 1, 11-6.

TAYLOR, D. (1986). 'Integration in the arts', *Arts Initiatives I: Integration in the Arts*. London: National Association for Education in the Arts.

WHITFIELD, W. (1991). *Working with the Arts: Case Studies of Six Youth Arts Projects*. Leicester: Youth Work Press.

WILLIS, P. (1990). *Moving Culture*. London: Calouste Gulbenkian Foundation.

YOUTH CLUBS UK (1992). *Developing Youth Arts Policy: 1991 Conference Report*. Leicester: Youth Clubs UK.

APPENDIX 1

THE INTERVIEW SCHEDULE

YOUTH PARTICIPATION IN THE ARTS
INTERVIEW SCHEDULE

*Explain that the research is about young people between 14 and 24, particularly their views on the arts. Stress that it's okay not to have done any thing in the arts or not to like the arts. The views of **all** young people are important. Just be open and honest. The interview is confidential and anonymous.*

Card 1

SECTION A: YOUR CURRENT SITUATION

1. Name ....   ID No.   6–10

2. Gender (M or F)   11

3. How old are you?   Age   12–13

    (If at school, add year number)   Year   14–15

4. What do you do during the normal weekdays?

    at school in Years 9, 10 or 11   1   *go to Q. 17*

    (post-16) in full-time education   2   *go to Q. 5*

    training scheme   3   *go to Q. 8*

    full-time employment/self employed   4   *go to Q. 11*   16

    part-time employment/self employed   5   *go to Q. 11*

    unemployed (seeking work)   6   *go to Q. 14*

    not seeking work   7   *go to Q. 15*

    other *(please explain below)*   8

5. **For post-16 students in full-time education,** where are you studying?

    School   1   FE College   3   17

    Tertiary College   2   HE institution   4

    (If not sure) name of institution ....

6. What are the main subjects/courses you are taking?   18–19
    20–21

7. What qualifications do you hope to get through these courses?

    go to Q. 16   22–23

8. **For those on training schemes,** in which occupational area are you training?

    24–25

9. What qualification are you working towards (e.g. NVQ Level II in Secretarial Skills)?

    26–27

10. Is your training linked to employment ☐ or a work placement ☐ ?   28
    (If 'employed status' go to Q.11; if 'trainee status' go to Q.16)

284

For those in employment (full-time or part-time), what is your job?

29–30

In what type of organization do you work?

31

Have you had any other jobs since leaving school?   YES ☐   NO ☐

If YES, what jobs?

32
33
34

go to Q. 16

For those unemployed, what kind of job are you seeking?

35–36

go to Q. 16

For those not seeking work, any particular reason why you are not seeking work?

37

go to Q. 16

For all post-16 interviewees, what qualifications have you got?

Qualifications (grades/levels where appropriate)	Subjects	
Number of GCE passes, GCSE above `C', CSE Grade 1s: ☐		38–39 40–48
Number of A levels: ☐		49 50–53
Degree: ☐		54 55–56
Others (e.g. NVQ, HND, BTEC) below:		57–58 59–60

CTION B: YOUR CURRENT INTERESTS

(a)   What do you count as your main interests/most enjoyable activities at the weekends/in the evenings?

61–62
63–64
65–66
67–68
69–70

(b)   What else do you do then?

18. Do you currently do anything for or at *[INSERT: **school/college/training scheme/work** as appropriate]*
     which you would call imaginative or creative?   YES ☐   NO ☐
     If YES, what?

19. Do you currently do anything in the evenings or weekends which you would call imaginative or creative?
     If YES, what?   YES ☐   NO ☐

20. The term `the arts' can mean different things to different people.  What does the term `the arts'' mean
     for you?

21. (a) For some people, `the arts' include music, dance, drama/theatre, film, literature (novels, poems
          etc), painting, sculpture and so on. How important are those kinds of arts to you? *(Briefly probe
          reasons/different art forms)*

     (b) Some young people make up their own arts activities (e.g. scratching/mixing, devising their own
          fashion clothes, computer graphics, graffiti art). What do you think about those kinds of arts?

22. (a) Within the last year, as part of your school work/training/courses/job *(insert as appropriate)* have
          you read/listened to/watched **any** arts?   YES ☐   NO ☐

     (b) If YES, briefly what were they?

(a) Within the last year, outside of your school work/training/courses/job, have you read/listened to/watched **any** arts in the evenings or weekends?   YES ☐   NO ☐

(b) If yes, briefly what were they?

. Recently *(i.e. within the last year)*, have you taken part in any of the following activities:

	School/college/work-related				Own time and non-school/college/ work-related					
	A great deal	Some	A little	None	A great deal	Some	A little	None		
Painting	1	2	3	4	1	2	3	4	41	42
Drawing/ sketching	1	2	3	4	1	2	3	4	43	44
Computer graphics	1	2	3	4	1	2	3	4	45	46
Printing	1	2	3	4	1	2	3	4	47	48
Photography	1	2	3	4	1	2	3	4	49	50
Sculpture/ making	1	2	3	4	1	2	3	4	51	52
Drama/theatre	1	2	3	4	1	2	3	4	53	54
Dance	1	2	3	4	1	2	3	4	55	56
Writing stories/ poetry	1	2	3	4	1	2	3	4	57	58
. Video-making	1	2	3	4	1	2	3	4	59	60
. Music-making	1	2	3	4	1	2	3	4	61	62
. Scratching/ dubbing	1	2	3	4	1	2	3	4	63	64
. Fashion	1	2	3	4	1	2	3	4	65	66
. Textiles-making	1	2	3	4	1	2	3	4	67	68
. Jewellery- making	1	2	3	4	1	2	3	4	69	70
. Graffiti art	1	2	3	4	1	2	3	4	71	72
. Arts events	1	2	3	4	1	2	3	4	73	74
. ...	1	2	3	4	1	2	3	4	75,76,77	
. ...	1	2	3	4	1	2	3	4	78,79,80	

25. *[Ask about one (maximum) of the previous positive responses; if none leave blank]*

Card
1D6-1

ACTIVITY Number [＿＿＿] 11-12

    a. *[Question for **level of involvement**]*

Probe:
What you did/do?

13
14
15

How got involved?

16
17
18

    (b). *[Question **quality of experience and effects**]*

Why do/did
you enjoy it?

19
20

What do you get
out of it?

21,22

    c. *[Question **organization/independent**]*

24,25

Was it set up by
organization/adults
or just by you alone
and/or friends?

SECTION C: YOUR PRIMARY SCHOOL EXPERIENCE

26. Up until the age of 11 (i.e. primary school age), what were your main interests and hobbies outside of school time (i.e. in the evenings, weekends or holidays)?

26-27
28-29
30-31

27. (a) At that age, did you do any/any other arts activities out of school which you can remember?

32-33
34-35
36-37

(b) At that age, did you read/watch/listen to any sorts of arts activities out of school which you can remember?

38–39
40–41
42–43

. (a) Can you remember any arts activities (including drama, visual arts, music, literature etc.) which you particularly enjoyed or valued at primary school?　　　　YES ☐　　　　NO ☐

44

(b) If NO, was there any particular reason why not?

45,46

(c) If YES, what were they and why did you enjoy them?

47–48
49–50
51–52

(d) If YES to (a), can you say what you learnt or got out of these activities?

53–54
55–56
57–58

(e) Looking back, what did you think of the arts at primary school?

59
60
61

ECTION D: YOUR SECONDARY SCHOOL EXPERIENCE

. *For those who have left school,* what age were you when you left school? ☐☐

62–63

30. Between the ages of 11 and ☐ *(insert as appropriate)*, what were your main interests and hobbies outside of school time (i.e. in the evenings, weekends or holidays)?

64–65
66–67
68–69

31. (a) At that age, did you do any/any other arts activities out of school which you can remember?

70–71
72–73
74–75

   (b) At that age. did you read/watch/listen to any sorts of arts activities out of school which you can remember?

76–77
78–79
Card
1D6–1
11–12

32. (a) Can you remember any arts activities (including drama, visual, music, literature etc.) which you particularly enjoyed or valued at secondary school?   YES ☐   NO ☐   13

   (b) If NO, was there any particular reason why not?

14
15

   (c) If YES, what were they and why did you enjoy them?

16–17
18–19
20–21

(d)   Can you say what you learnt or got out of these activities?

22–23
24–25
26–27

(e)   Looking back, what did you think of the arts at secondary school?

28
29
30

(a)   Did you/are you doing/are going to do any of the following subjects in the 4/5th year or Years 10/11?

	1. Separate Subject	2. As part of ...	3. Not at all	
Art				31–32
Music				33–34
Drama				35–36
Dance				37–38
Media				39–40

(b)   *(For those ticked in colum 1)* what are/were your reasons for taking these particular arts subjects?

41
42
43

(c)   Why did you drop/not take arts subjects?
(Probe for any regrets)

44
45
46

(a)   Do you currently (ie within the last year) go to a Youth Club/Centre?

More than once a week	Once a week	About once/ twice a month	Less than once a month	Not at all
1	2	3	4	5

47

Type of centre ....

48

(b)   Did you used to go to a Youth Club/Centre?

Frequently ☐   Now and then ☐   Not at all ☐

49

(c) **For non-attenders only**, can you tell me why you don't/didn't/go or stopped going?

Approximate age stopped going ☐

(d) **For attenders** (d-i), what kind of things do you (did you used to) do there?

(e) Were there opportunities to do any arts activities there?   YES ☐   NO ☐

(f) Did you join in any of the arts activities there?   YES ☐   NO ☐

(g) *If NO*, can you tell me why you didn't do any of the arts activities?

(h) *If YES*, did you enjoy doing the arts activities there?

(i) *If YES*, do you feel that you got anything out of these activities?

SECTION E: YOUR OVERALL INVOLVEMENT IN THE ARTS

35. **For those who have left school**
    (a) In the period between leaving school and your current situation (*see Section B*), would you say that your involvement in the arts has: gone up ☐ gone down ☐ stayed the same ☐

    (b) Please could you say how and why it has

36. (a) Some people say that they got interested in the arts because somebody or some event turned them on to the arts. Looking back over your life, can you remember anything or anybody **turning you on** to any of the arts? *(Probe influential factors)*

(b) Similarly, can you remember anything or anybody **turning you off** any of the arts? *(Probe influential factors)*

13–14
15–16
17–18

Do you think that what you do now in the arts or what you've done in the past has had any effects on you? *If YES*, what are the effects?   YES ☐   NO ☐

19

20–21
22–23

(Personal development)

24–25
26–27

(Social development)

28–29
30–31

(Skills)

32–33
34–35

(Motivation/further interest in the arts)

36–37
38–39

(a) Looking back, would you have liked more opportunities to have been involved in the arts?
YES ☐   NO ☐

40

(b) *If YES*, what kinds of arts/creative activities would you have welcomed?

(c) *If NO*, why not?

39. (a) Looking to the future, are there any arts activities that you'd like to take further and do more of in the future? YES ☐ NO ☐

(b) *If YES*, what are they?

(c) Is there anything which is making it difficult for you to take these activities further and develop them?

(d) Do you need any assistance, support or opportunities to help you develop these activities? If so, what help do you need?

(e) *(Probe need for institutional or independent support)*

(f) *(Probe needs for skills development)*

Finally, some questions about yourself and your family

Are you   Single ☐   Married ☐   Separated/Divorced ☐   71

(a)   Name of village/town/city you live in ....

(b)   *(Ask only if necessary)* Is the place you live in   urban? ☐   rural? ☐   72

Please could you tell us about your parents' jobs.
(If either of them is not working at the moment, please tell us about the **last job** he or she had.)

	Father	**Mother**	
a. What is the name of the job?			73–74; 75–76
b. What kind of work do they do?			77–78 79–80
c. What sort of place or organisation do they work for?			
d. Are they self-employed?	YES ☐ NO ☐	YES ☐ NO ☐	**Card 6** 1D6–10

What job or career have **you** got in mind for the future?   11–12

(a)   Do you have any physical disabilities?   YES ☐   NO ☐   13

(b)   *If YES*, what are they?   14
15

(c)   *If YES*, have they affected your experience of the arts?   YES ☐   NO ☐   16

(d)   *If YES to c.*, how?   17–18
19–20

45. (a) Do you see yourself as belonging to one of these ethnic groups?

1 Black/Afro-Caribbean origin ☐
2 Indian/Pakistani/Bangladeshi origin ☐   21
3 White ☐
4 Other, please say what ☐

(b) Has the fact that you belong to *[insert appropriate group]* ethnic group affected your experiences of the arts?   YES ☐   NO ☐   22

(c) Please could you explain your answer.   23–24
     25–26

46. (a) Has the fact that you are male/female affected your experiences of the arts?
    YES ☐   NO ☐   27

(b) Please could you explain your answer.   28–29
     30–31

47. Finally, is there anything else you want to say about the arts you do or enjoy/or just what you think about the arts?   32–33
     34–35
     36–37

THANK YOU VERY MUCH FOR HELPING US WITH THIS RESEARCH